Linguistic Approaches in English for Academic Purposes

New Perspectives for English for Academic Purposes

Series editors: Alex Ding, Ian Bruce and Melinda Whong

This series sets the agenda for studies in English for Academic Purposes (EAP) by opening up research and scholarship to new domains, ideas and perspectives as well as giving a platform to emerging and established practitioners and researchers in the field.

The volumes in this series are innovative in that they broaden the scope of theoretical and practical interests in EAP by focusing on neglected or new areas of interest, to provide the EAP community with a deeper understanding of some of the key issues in teaching EAP across the world and in diverse contexts.

Advisory Board:

Jigang Cai, Fudan University, China
Nigel Caplan, University of Delaware, USA
Greg Hadley, Niigata University, Japan
Nigel Harwood, University of Sheffield, UK
Azirah Hashim, University of Malaya, Malaysia
Carole Macdiarmid, University of Glasgow, UK
Jennifer MacDonald, Dalhousie University, Canada
Geoffrey Nsanja, University of Malawi, The Polytechnic, Malawi
Brian Paltridge, The University of Sydney, Australia
Diane Pecorari, The City University of Hong Kong, Hong Kong
Nadezda Silaski, University of Belgrade, Serbia
Christine Tardy, University of Arizona, USA
Jackie Tuck, Open University, UK

Also available in this series

What Is Good Academic Writing?: Insights into Discipline-Specific Student Writing, edited by Melinda Whong and Jeanne Godfrey
Pedagogies in English for Academic Purposes, edited by Carole MacDiarmid and Jennifer J. MacDonald
Social Theory for English for Academic Purposes, edited by Alex Ding and Michelle Evans
Contextualizing English for Academic Purposes in Higher Education, edited by Ian Bruce and Bee Bond

Forthcoming in the series

Practitioner Agency and Identity in English for Academic Purposes, edited by Alex Ding and Laetitia Monbec

Linguistic Approaches in English for Academic Purposes

Expanding the Discourse

Edited by
Milada Walková

BLOOMSBURY ACADEMIC
LONDON • NEW YORK • OXFORD • NEW DELHI • SYDNEY

BLOOMSBURY ACADEMIC

Bloomsbury Publishing Plc, 50 Bedford Square, London, WC1B 3DP, UK
Bloomsbury Publishing Inc, 1385 Broadway, New York, NY 10018, USA
Bloomsbury Publishing Ireland, 29 Earlsfort Terrace, Dublin 2, D02 AY28, Ireland

BLOOMSBURY, BLOOMSBURY ACADEMIC and the Diana logo are trademarks of
Bloomsbury Publishing Plc

First published in Great Britain 2024
This paperback edition published in 2025

Copyright © Milada Walková and Contributors, 2024

Milada Walková and Contributors have asserted their right under the Copyright,
Designs and Patents Act, 1988, to be identified as Authors of this work.

For legal purposes the Acknowledgements on p. xvii and p. 84 constitute an extension of
this copyright page.

Series design by Charlotte James
Cover image © Tuomas Lehtinen / Getty Images

All rights reserved. No part of this publication may be: i) reproduced or transmitted in
any form, electronic or mechanical, including photocopying, recording or by means of any
information storage or retrieval system without prior permission in writing from the publishers;
or ii) used or reproduced in any way for the training, development or operation of artificial
intelligence (AI) technologies, including generative AI technologies. The rights holders expressly
reserve this publication from the text and data mining exception as per Article 4(3) of the
Digital Single Market Directive (EU) 2019/790.

Bloomsbury Publishing Plc does not have any control over, or responsibility for, any
third-party websites referred to or in this book. All internet addresses given in this
book were correct at the time of going to press. The author and publisher regret any
inconvenience caused if addresses have changed or sites have ceased to exist,
but can accept no responsibility for any such changes.

A catalogue record for this book is available from the British Library.

A catalog record for this book is available from the Library of Congress.

ISBN: HB: 978-1-3503-0030-9
PB: 978-1-3503-0034-7
ePDF: 978-1-3503-0031-6
eBook: 978-1-3503-0032-3

Series: New Perspectives for English for Academic Purposes

Typeset by Deanta Global Publishing Services, Chennai, India

For product safety related questions contact productsafety@bloomsbury.com.

To find out more about our authors and books visit www.bloomsbury.com and
sign up for our newsletters.

Dedicated to all EAP practitioners and researchers facing hardship and in particular to Tatyana Yakhontova who contributed to this volume under extremely difficult circumstances.

Contents

List of Figures	ix
List of Tables	x
List of Contributors	xii
Series Editors' Foreword	xv
Acknowledgements	xvii

1 Introduction *Milada Walková* — 1

Part I Fluency and Range of Expression

2 Formulaic Language in University Seminars: A Comparison of EAP Textbook Coverage and Authentic Language Use in ELF Settings *Ying Wang and Nok Chin Lydia Chan* — 11

3 Moves Away from Congruence: Interpersonal, Logical and Grammatical Metaphor in EAP *Jennifer Walsh Marr* — 34

Part II Complexity and Accuracy

4 The Role of Morphological Knowledge in EAP Writing: Evidence-Based Study *Elizaveta Tarasova and Natalia Beliaeva* — 63

5 Non-Finite Clause Use in Novice and Expert Academic Writing: A Corpus-Driven Analysis for EAP Writing Instruction *J. Elliott Casal and Xixin Qiu* — 89

6 Applying Complex Dynamic Systems Theory in EAP Curriculum Design and Teaching Practice: Challenges and Possibilities *Rosmawati* — 117

Part III Appropriateness to Academic Rhetorical Conventions

7 How Does Academic Writing Produced for the Abstracts of Articles in More and Less Prestigious Journals Reflect Grice's Maxims? *Mark Wyatt* — 145

8 Evaluative Genres of Research Communication: Article Comments and Peer Reviews from Linguistic and Pedagogical Perspectives *Tatyana Yakhontova* 168
9 Conceptual Metaphors as a Resource to Build a Coherent Text: A Socio-Cognitive Approach to EAP *Tomoko Sawaki* 193

Index 219

Figures

4.1	Conditional tree analysis of the relationship between the students' grade, text type, NZCEL level, the total number of morphologically complex words and the number of morphologically complex words assigned to specific levels	76
6.1	Non-linear development of syntactic complexity	129
6.2	Non-linear development of the use of nominalization, lexical diversity, the use of academic words and accuracy	131
9.1	Hjelmslev's biplanar perspective to generic structure components	199
9.2	Basic Semiotic Square	200
9.3	Verdicts on the Semiotic Square	200
9.4	Academic writing generic structure components on the Semiotic Square	205
9.5	*Lack* on the Semiotic Square	207
9.6	*Lack*-ICM within 'the rest'	208

Tables

2.1	EAP textbooks examined	13
2.2	ELFA seminar data breakdown	14
2.3	Speech functions and linguistic realizations drawn from the textbooks	18
2.4	Distribution of speech functions in the textbooks	19
2.5	Keywords and clusters characterizing seminar discussion in ELFA	20
2.6	Main speech functions fulfilled by the clusters characterizing seminar discussion in ELFA	23
3.1	Example clauses nominalized through experiential grammatical metaphor	35
3.2	Congruent to metaphoric shifts	44
3.3	Congruent clauses condensed through logical grammatical metaphor	46
3.4	A continuum of congruent to metaphoric	52
3.5	Interpersonal metaphor options	55
4.1	Data set summary	72
4.2	Average number of morphologically complex words in student essays across NZCEL levels	73
4.3	Output of a multiple logistic regression model predicting the students' grade, simple effects only	74
4.4	Output of a multiple logistic regression model predicting the students' grade, interaction terms included	75
5.1	Basic description of the CASAP	93
5.2	Search items of non-finite clause in CASAP	95
5.3	Proposed syntactic taxonomy of non-finite clauses	97
5.4	Type and token frequency of expert and student non-finite clauses	99
5.5	Top ten verb types and frequency for experts and students	100
5.6	Token frequency of expert and student non-finite adverbial clause	103
5.7	Token frequency of expert and student non-finite complement clause	106
5.8	Token frequency of expert and student non-finite post-modifiers	108
6.1	Constructs measured in this study	128
8.1	Moves and their quantitative distribution in the texts of article comments	173

8.2	Moves and their quantitative distribution in the texts of peer reviews	178
8.3	Quantitative distribution of evaluative words in the texts of article comments and peer reviews	181
8.4	Quantitative distribution of the types of evaluative acts in the texts of article comments and peer reviews	182

Contributors

Natalia Beliaeva specializes in word formation (in particular, lexical innovation such as blending and complex shortening) and morphological productivity, her most recent works being on the sentiment value of name-based blends (in an edited volume *Grammar of Hate*, 2022) and on factors that influence morphological productivity (a coauthored article in *Zeitschrift für Wortbildung/ Journal of Word Formation*). Natalia is also interested in second language acquisition, conducting research on the role of morphological awareness in second language acquisition and developing and delivering ESOL classes for learners with refugee background.

J. Elliott Casal is Assistant Professor of Applied Linguistics at the University of Memphis Department of English. His research interests include corpus linguistics and corpus-based writing pedagogies, English for Academic Purposes and second language writing. His recent work appears in the *Journal of Second Language Writing, Journal of English for Academic Purposes, English for Specific Purposes, Language Learning and Technology* and *System*.

Nok Chin Lydia Chan is a PhD student at Victoria University of Wellington. She obtained her M.A. in English (Language Science with a Specialisation in English Linguistics) at Stockholm University and her B.A. in English at The Chinese University of Hong Kong. Her research interests include Construction Grammar, Corpus Linguistics, Formulaic Language, Language Processing, Psycholinguistics, and Verbal Irony.

Xixin Qiu is a doctoral candidate in Applied Linguistics at the Pennsylvania State University. His research concerns corpus-based investigations into the linguistic characteristics of disciplinary discourse. His dissertation will examine recurrent lexicogrammatical patterns of different structural types of subordinate clause in Mechanical Engineering academic writing and assess the teachability to student writers recruited from an existing Academic Engineering Writing course. Currently, he is interested in exploring sub-disciplinary variation in professional academic discourse and analysing syntactic or metadiscoursal features across different modes of academic discourse. His recent work appears in *Lingua* and *Journal of English for Academic Purposes*.

Rosmawati is Assistant Professor in the Centre for Communication Skills at Singapore Institute of Technology. Her research interests include the application of Complex Dynamic Systems Theory (CDST) in Second Language Acquisition and Development, Academic Writing in English and Teaching English to Speakers of Other Languages (TESOL). She publishes on the development of syntactic constructs in academic writing in English as a second language from the perspective of CDST. More recently, her research has expanded to include fractal linguistics.

Tomoko Sawaki is an independent researcher. Her research interests include English for Academic Purposes, genre analysis and semiotics. Her work focuses specifically on the text structuring functions of interpersonal elements in academic writing. Her research has been published in such journals as *Journal of English for Academic Purposes*, *Functions of Language*, *English Text Construction* and *English for Specific Purposes*. She is the author of a book entitled *Analysing Structure in Academic Writing* (2016).

Elizaveta Tarasova is a TESOL and Linguistics Lecturer, and she also coordinates the work of Trinity TESOL programmes in IPU New Zealand. Her main research areas include derivational morphology, morphopragmatics and cognitive linguistics. Her most recent publications are focused on the issue of iconicity in morphology, which is explored through the lens of cognitive and constructionist approaches. Her second major research area lies in TESOL and the role of professional ESL/EFL teacher development on teachers' competence and performance in the language classroom.

Milada Walková is Lecturer in EAP at the University of Leeds, UK. Her research interests include various aspects of academic writing (such as metadiscourse, argument, intercultural rhetoric and writing for publication) and scholarship of EAP. She has published in a number of international journals, including *Journal of English for Academic Purposes*, *English for Specific Purposes* and *ESP Today*. She is currently working on a book for EAP practitioners *Teaching Academic Writing for EAP: Language Foundations for Practitioners* to be published by Bloomsbury.

Jennifer Walsh Marr is an academic English Lecturer at the University of British Columbia, Canada. She has contributed another chapter on using Systemic

Functional Linguistics (SFL) for EAP to this Bloomsbury series, as well as to the *Journal of English for Academic Purposes, TESOL Quarterly* and *College Composition and Communication*. Her research work has looked at intersections of power, identity and language in the academy, particularly with regard to Indigenous and settler histories in Canada. She draws on critical pedagogy, genre theory and SFL to help make implicit language patterns more explicit and accessible to both instructors and students.

Ying Wang is Associate Professor in English Linguistics at Karlstad University, Sweden. Her main research interests lie in areas of corpus linguistics and EAP. She has published on formulaic language use in spoken and written academic discourse in international journals including *English for Specific Purposes, Journal of English for Academic Purposes* and *International Journal of Corpus Linguistics*. Her most recent book is *Idiom Principle and L1 Influence* (2016).

Mark Wyatt is Associate Professor of English at Khalifa University in the United Arab Emirates. His research interests include academic writing, English as a medium of instruction, mentoring, practitioner research, reflective practice and the self-efficacy beliefs of language learners and teachers. His research articles have appeared in journals such as *Educational Action Research, ELT Journal, International Journal of Mentoring and Coaching in Education, Journal of Teaching English for Specific and Academic Purposes, Language Learning Journal, Language Teaching Research, Reading Psychology, Reflective Practice, System* and *TESOL Quarterly*. He recently coedited *International Perspectives on Mentoring in English Language Education* (2022).

Tatyana Yakhontova is Professor of English for Specific Purposes and Linguistics at the Ivan Franko National University of Lviv, Ukraine. Her research interests include genre theory and analysis, genre-based pedagogy, discourse theory and analysis, contrastive rhetoric and writing instruction. She has published articles and book chapters in international journals and volumes, two textbooks and a research monograph (in Ukrainian).

Series Editors' Foreword

As with the other volumes of this series, the contributions of this book remain true to the series theme, that of bringing new perspectives to the field of English for Academic Purposes (EAP). Focusing on the area of linguistic knowledge in EAP, the chapters of this volume explore this area of the knowledge base from a number of different directions and using different theoretical approaches, some of which are less familiar to EAP practitioners but all of which have been made accessible and relevant by the different contributors to the volume.

When there is an attempt to influence a way of thinking within an existing body of academic thought, such as through the current emphases in EAP on discourse and genre knowledge, it can be the case that existing understandings are too readily dismissed. The unintended consequence of such emphases can be a kind of intellectual throwing the baby out with the bathwater. It is a pleasure, therefore, to see the publication of this volume oriented at the core of the remit of all language educators, including those working within EAP: the close interrogation of language itself. But the focus on linguistics is not any retrograde 'back to basics' approach of the past. Instead, truly within the spirit of the 'New Perspectives' series, it broadens the linguistic knowledge base of EAP by applying theories that are marginalized and underexplored within mainstream EAP. It is inspiring to see how the practitioners who have contributed to this volume have been able to take well-researched theoretical areas from mainstream branches of linguistics and extend them to exploration within the EAP context.

In exploring academic English from the point of view of linguistics, this volume leads to more questions than it answers in two broad directions. First, the exploration of a different aspect of linguistics in each chapter immediately inspires thoughts of pedagogy, raising the obvious question for practitioners of the implications of these findings in linguistics for the teaching of EAP. But questions arise in another direction as well, that of subsequent scholarly inquiry. As shown in this volume, there is a wealth of inquiry within EAP to be explored further both within and beyond the well-researched genre studies which (rightly) continue to be examined. Within genre-framing as an important analytical approach in EAP, this volume illustrates the potential for better understanding language at the clausal, phrasal and lexical levels. Also, beyond genre there are large areas for further exploration from the use of formulaic sequences to metaphor, and in a way that takes full advantage of the wide range of theoretical lenses that exist within linguistics. Taken together, the chapters of this volume inspire us to recognize how much there is to gain when, as a discipline, we look beyond a single theory or approach in our scholarly inquiry.

As with the other volumes in the series, it is our wish that the different chapter contributions here are seen as works in progress, parts of conversations that will be ongoing, and that their varied approaches and explorations will inspire and lead to further contributions to EAP pedagogy and scholarship that focus on linguistic knowledge.

Melinda Whong and Ian Bruce, on behalf of the Series Editors
January 2023

Acknowledgements

As the volume editor I would like to thank, first of all, Alex Ding as Series Editor for encouraging me to put this volume together and for being supportive all the way. My thanks also go to all the contributors for joining the project, to Series Editors Ian Bruce and Melinda Whong as well as to Bloomsbury editors Laura Gallon and Maria Brauzzi for support and advice.

The editor, contributors and publisher gratefully acknowledge the permission granted to reproduce the copyright material in this book. Every effort has been made to trace copyright holders and to obtain their permission for the use of copyright material. However, if any have been inadvertently overlooked, the publishers will be pleased, if notified of any omissions, to make the necessary arrangement at the first opportunity.

Other third-party copyrighted material displayed in the pages of this book is done so on the basis of 'fair dealing for the purposes of criticism and review' or 'fair use for the purposes of teaching, criticism, scholarship or research' only in accordance with international copyright laws and is not intended to infringe upon the ownership rights of the original owners.

1

Introduction

Milada Walková

This volume explores the language of academic discourse through a linguistic lens. As linguistic research has traditionally and increasingly been a substantial part of the knowledge base of English for Academic Purposes (EAP) (cf. Ding and Bruce 2017; Riazi, Ghanbar and Fazel 2020; Hyland and Jiang 2021), the reader might question what new perspectives a volume on linguistics in EAP might bring. What this volume aims for is to counter what Bruce (2021: 26–7) calls *research orthodoxies*, that is, 'streams of research that take on a life of their own and become somewhat disconnected from actual practice'. In his view, research orthodoxies result in EAP research becoming limited in its scope by overexploring certain topics at the expense of others, as well as in its applicability to teaching practice, as such studies are rarely motivated by students' needs. The aim of this volume is therefore to broaden the linguistic research in EAP by approaches that, to date, have been used to a limited extent or by offering new ways of using well-established approaches on previously underexplored language or texts, all the while providing strong pedagogical implications for teaching practice.

When thinking about linguistic approaches in general, what comes to mind is the diversity that characterizes the study of language. Linguistics can focus on the study of the language system through its subsystems – from sound (phonetics and phonology), words and their parts (inflectional and derivational morphology), sentence structure (syntax) and meaning of linguistic forms (semantics); it can focus on the study of how meaning is communicated through stretches of spoken and written discourse (stylistics, text linguistics, genre and discourse analysis), the context in which language is used and the relationships between language and its users (pragmatics and functional linguistic approaches), social factors contributing to variation in language (sociolinguistics) or how languages are acquired (first and second language acquisition), among others;

it can seek to apply theoretical findings to address a variety of practical issues (from language education to forensic linguistics) and use methods of inquiry par excellence (corpus linguistics) or research methods from other disciplines (psycholinguistics). This volume attempts to draw on some of this diversity of linguistic approaches to EAP, including morphology (Tarasova and Beliaeva), syntax (Casal and Qiu), genre analysis (Sawaki), discourse analysis (Wang and Chan, Yakhontova), pragmatics (Wyatt), a functional approach (Walsh Marr) and second language acquisition (Rosmawati). All the chapters, however, are written with a practical application in EAP pedagogy in mind. The volume is therefore intended not only for applied linguists and EAP practitioners with a background in linguistics but also for EAP practitioners with a language teaching or another background, wishing to enhance their teaching practice by insights from linguistics.

Diversity is also reflected in the contexts in which the volume contributors work. In fact, readers might have different conceptualizations of what constitutes EAP (cf. Kirk 2018) than is presented in some of the chapters in this volume; this diversity of EAP pedagogy, however, needs to be acknowledged and embraced when taking a global perspective. The diversity of pedagogical contexts translates into the diversity of data presented: the chapters in the volume analyse the language of a range of speakers/writers, including those using English as their first (L1) or second/additional (L2) language, students from pre-undergraduate to postgraduate levels as well as academics conducting and disseminating research. The contributors themselves represent an amalgamation of researchers and practitioners, and it is hoped that this amalgamation will prove fruitful, making research and practice mutually informative.

The volume is divided into three parts focusing on aspects of formal and discourse competence a learner of academic English needs to develop. The first part of the volume focuses on fluency and range of expression. Fluency in spoken language, understood as speaking at an appropriate pace without unnecessary hesitations and repairs, can be aided by the use of formulaic sequences (Nergis 2021). Range of expression is understood in this volume as a repertoire of linguistic devices that users of language draw upon to convey their intended meaning.

Learners of English wishing to enhance their fluency in spoken academic language might turn to EAP textbooks offering a range of formulaic expressions or stock phrases. A question arises as to whether the expressions promoted in textbooks are based on data from authentic academic speech or 'on the writer's experience and intuition rather than on systematic research', as Hyland (2006:

5) noted on EAP textbooks in general almost two decades ago. *Chapter 2 by Ying Wang and Nok Chin Lydia Chan* therefore analyses formulaic sequences in authentic, tutor-led student seminars and researcher seminars. The authors extract formulaic sequences from an English as a Lingua Franca corpus of academic discourse, examine their rhetorical functions and compare and contrast them to the formulaic sequences for seminars provided in published EAP textbooks. Their results show that speakers in authentic academic settings do not use syntactically complex phrases promoted in textbooks but instead they rely on simple everyday formulaic sequences. These results support the trade-off between fluency and complexity proposed in the literature (Skehan 1998; Robinson 2005) and question the usefulness of teaching learners complex phrases which might be detrimental rather than conducive to spoken fluency. While this issue remains to be solved, one implication for the field is a greater need for learning materials based on research into authentic academic discourse, as after all, authenticity is one of the basic tenets of EAP (Watson Todd 2003; Hyland and Hamp-Lyons 2004). This in turn calls for more research into spoken academic language, which seriously lags behind research into academic writing.

As different registers are characterized by different linguistic devices (Biber, Gray and Poonpon 2011), learners need to develop a wide range of expression to navigate across several registers. Helping students develop a repertoire of linguistic devices for meaning-making is the focus of *Chapter 3 by Jennifer Walsh Marr*, set within the framework of Systemic Functional Linguistics (SFL). The author shows three types of shift from language congruent with language users' expectations to language used metaphorically, which can be problematic to language learners: first, grammatical metaphor for shifts from experiential meaning towards more abstract meaning; second, logical metaphor for shifts from explicit causation, contrast, condition and so on towards logical relations embedded in lexically dense language; and third, interpersonal metaphor for shifts from direct expression of mood and modality towards more polite language or more nuanced expression of one's position on ideas presented in discourse. The chapter amply illustrates the three types of metaphor and, making a case for the use of metalanguage, suggests teaching activities to help students understand the meaning embedded in texts and build a range of expression for particular contexts and purposes. The chapter thus serves as a model of drawing on SFL in teaching for EAP practitioners. Future research could further investigate the frequency and types of language metaphors in spoken and written academic discourse.

The second part of the volume focuses on complexity and accuracy: language accuracy refers to the extent a learner's use of language conforms to the accepted usage of the target language; complexity is understood here as the degree of sophistication of language used, at the lexical or syntactic level. As so much academic vocabulary comes in word families, or groups of words derived from the same base with different affixes, learning word parts can help increase learner vocabulary (Nation 2013). How, then, can learners acquire new vocabulary efficiently through a word-formation toolkit rather than through tedious rote learning of individual words? The answer to this question can be found in *Chapter 4 by Elizaveta Tarasova and Natalia Beliaeva* addressing complexity at the level of vocabulary. The authors analyse morphologically complex words in student writing using a framework of developing morphological awareness. Their results show that vocabulary in student writing becomes more complex as student writers develop their language proficiency and academic literacy and also point to some issues with accuracy in forming morphologically complex words. The results thus suggest that EAP pedagogy should pay greater attention to lexical complexity. EAP practitioners can use the findings to diagnose their students' level of mastery of morphological complexity and to teach them vocabulary at the next level of complexity. Further research into morphological complexity can explore complex words in expert writing across disciplines that is used as input in EAP classes, with the aim of helping learners guess the meaning of unfamiliar words derived from familiar bases.

In contrast to morphological complexity, syntactic complexity in academic discourse has gained ample research attention. However, this attention has been directed mostly at the phrasal level, since available research suggests a developmental trajectory of learner language from syntactic coordination through clausal subordination to phrasal subordination (Biber, Gray and Poonpon 2011; Parkinson and Musgrave 2014). This emphasis on phrasal complexity, however, has arguably overlooked the needs of learners at lower levels of language proficiency at the stage of developing clausal complexity. This is the motivation for *Chapter 5 by J. Elliott Casal and Xixin Qiu* analysing subordinate non-finite clauses in academic writing. The authors propose a taxonomy of non-finite clauses and compare and contrast the use of non-finite clauses in novice and expert writing using methods of corpus linguistics. Their results show that novice writers use non-finite clauses with a narrower range and less frequently than expert writers, especially when non-finite clauses are embedded within other syntactic structures. Although some accuracy issues are present in novice writing, the results suggest that it is mostly various functional uses of non-finite clauses that EAP classes should focus on. EAP practitioners can thus use Casal and Qiu's proposed taxonomy to help learners increase their syntactic complexity, both formally and functionally. They are also invited by the chapter authors to use corpus-based inquiry to inform their pedagogical practice; to this end, the authors provide some starting points. Further research can focus on exploring disciplinary differences in the use of non-finite clauses.

When learners increase their linguistic accuracy and morphological and syntactic complexity, what improvements can be realistically expected over an often limited period of time dedicated to EAP provision? It is on this issue that *Chapter 6 by Rosmawati* sheds some light, from the perspective of Complex Dynamic Systems Theory (CDST). After giving an overview of existing CDST-based research in second language acquisition and applied linguistics, the chapter considers and addresses reasons for the limited application of CDST in EAP to date. Rosmawati argues that CDST can be usefully applied in EAP, which she illustrates on a case study of a learner's academic writing, focusing on the development of syntactic complexity, lexical diversity and accuracy. The data shows that language development does not progress linearly in stages but involves periods of stagnation and even relapses. The implications for pedagogical practice include considering the role of learning environment, creating learning-centred EAP classrooms and providing multiple opportunities for revision and feedback. The chapter also calls for further CDST-inspired research that will highlight, rather than disregard, variations within and among learners as well as the interaction between learners and their environment.

The third part of the volume turns to appropriateness to academic rhetorical conventions. These include genre conventions related to the purpose and audience of a particular genre as well as more general conventions related to the need for academic communication to be effective and precise. Since written academic communication conveys the writer's message to the reader who is remote in distance and time, writing needs to be carefully crafted to make the communication effective. As certain rules of communication between academic writers and readers are unwritten and typically untaught, learners may struggle to follow these hidden conventions and to write texts that are engaging and persuasive. *Chapter 7 by Mark Wyatt* offers a perspective of written academic discourse that uses Grice's (1975) framework assuming cooperation between the speaker(s)/writer(s) and the audience. By analysing and comparing research article abstracts in less prestigious, regional journals on the one hand and more prestigious and competitive journals on the other hand, the author shows that more prestigious writing is characterized by relevance, appropriate informativeness, objectivity and clarity, whereas less prestigious writing might want in these qualities. As these qualities of writing are naturally tied to genre conventions (e.g. Swales 1990) and metadiscourse (e.g. Hyland 2005), EAP practitioners can add Grice's framework to the repertoire of approaches to teaching academic writing. Further research could use Grice's principle to analyse student writing at different levels of proficiency.

A crucial attribute that EAP learners need to develop is criticality. Since criticality includes, among other things, evaluation (Lai 2011), one way of developing criticality is writing evaluative genres (see e.g. Hyland and Diani 2009). *Chapter 8 by Tatyana Yakhontova* focuses on two such evaluative genres: one public but to date underexplored – article comments, also known as rejoinders, and one occluded – peer reviews. The chapter analyses not only their move structure but also the evaluation that is the core of these genres. The results show similarities and differences between the two genres resulting from their communicative purposes. While both genres aim to evaluate an academic article, article comments are more elaborated and evaluation in them is more mitigated compared to peer reviews. Moreover, unlike peer reviews, article comments contribute to the given research community by presenting the writer's views. The analysis in this chapter can be used by EAP practitioners to teach students how to evaluate an academic text effectively and to train researchers how to interpret and respond to peer reviews and article comments. In fact, responding to peer reviews in the occluded genre of rebuttals submitted along with revisions and to article comments in the public genre of author responses can be the subject of future research.

The motivation for the final chapter of the volume is learners' need to master a range of academic genres. The concept of genre has received ample research attention in various genre approaches (see e.g. Bawarshi and Reiff 2010 for an overview) that employ social, structural, linguistic and cognitive perspectives to different degrees. One important characteristic of genres is prototypicality, or the fact that different instances of a particular genre will be more or less typical representatives of their genre. How, then, can EAP pedagogy teach learners to produce academic genres, without being prescriptive? *Chapter 9 by Tomoko Sawaki* attempts to explore this issue by presenting a new genre approach that has prototypicality at its core. Sawaki's model is a cognitive one, based on cognitive images and conceptual metaphors, with a great range of linguistic realization. This approach to the analysis of academic texts challenges the notion of academic communication as by rule highly objective and precise and points out figurative language used to achieve desired rhetorical effects. EAP practitioners can draw on the chapter to help students uncover how academic texts use figurative language and to use conceptual metaphors and cognitive images appropriately in their own writing. Further research can unveil additional cognitive images and conceptual metaphors across academic genres and disciplines.

Overall, this volume hopes to be a modest contribution to expanding how EAP is taught and researched in various contexts and it is an attempt to open up new scholarly and pedagogical avenues. The readers are called upon to follow this attempt by further research into the areas explored here on the one hand and on the other hand by translation of the research presented here into everyday pedagogical practice.

References

Bawarshi, A. S. and M. J. Reiff (2010), *Genre: An Introduction to History, Theory, Research, and Pedagogy*, West Lafayette: Parlor Press LLC.

Biber, D., B. Gray and K. Poonpon (2011), 'Should We Use Characteristics of Conversation to Measure Grammatical Complexity in L2 Writing Development?', *TESOL Quarterly*, 45 (1): 5–35.

Bruce, I. (2021), 'Towards an EAP Without Borders: Developing Knowledge, Practitioners, and Communities', *International Journal of English for Academic Purposes: Research and Practice*, 2021 (Spring): 23–37.

Ding, A. and I. Bruce (2017), *The English for Academic Purposes Practitioner: Operating on the Edge of Academia*, London: Palgrave Macmillan.

Grice, H. P. (1975), 'Logic and Conversation', in P. Cole and J. L. Morgan (eds), *Syntax and Semantics, Vol. 3: Speech Acts*, 41–58, New York: Academic Press.

Hyland, K. (2005), *Metadiscourse: Exploring Interaction in Writing*, London: Bloomsbury.

Hyland, K. (2006), *English for Academic Purposes: An Advanced Resource Book*, London: Routledge.

Hyland, K. and G. Diani, eds (2009), *Academic Evaluation: Review Genres in University Settings*, London: Palgrave Macmillan.

Hyland, K. and L. Hamp-Lyons (2004), 'English for Academic Purposes: Current Challenges and New Issues', in P. Davidson et al. (eds), *Proceedings of the 9th TESOL Arabia Conference*, 3–14, Dubai: TESOL Arabia.

Hyland, K. and F. K. Jiang (2021), 'A Bibliometric Study of EAP Research: Who Is Doing What, Where and When?', *Journal of English for Academic Purposes*, 49: 100929.

Kirk, S. (2018), 'Enacting the Curriculum in English for Academic Purposes: A Legitimation Code Theory Analysis', doctoral dissertation, Durham University.

Lai, E. R. (2011), 'Critical Thinking: A Literature Review', *Pearson's Research Reports*. Available online: http://images.pearsonassessments.com/images/tmrs/CriticalThinkingReviewFINAL.pdf (accessed 25 October 2022).

Nation, I. S. P. (2013), *Learning Vocabulary in Another Language*, 2nd edn, Cambridge: Cambridge University Press.

Nergis, A. (2021), 'Can Explicit Instruction of Formulaic Sequences Enhance L2 Oral Fluency?', *Lingua*, 255: 103072.

Parkinson, J. and J. Musgrave (2014), 'Development of Noun Phrase Complexity in the Writing of English for Academic Purposes Students', *Journal of English for Academic Purposes*, 14: 48–59.

Riazi, A. M., H. Ghanbar and I. Fazel (2020), 'The Contexts, Theoretical and Methodological Orientation of EAP Research: Evidence from Empirical Articles Published in the Journal of English for Academic Purposes', *Journal of English for Academic Purposes*, 48: 100925.

Robinson, P. (2005), 'Cognitive Complexity and Task Sequencing: Studies in a Componential Framework for Second Language Task Design', *International Review of Applied Linguistics in Language Teaching*, 43 (1): 1–32.

Skehan, P. (1998), *A Cognitive Approach to Language Learning*, Oxford: Oxford University Press.

Swales, J. (1990), *Genre Analysis: English in Academic and Research Settings*, Cambridge: Cambridge University Press.

Watson Todd, R. (2003), 'EAP or TEAP?', *Journal of English for Academic Purposes*, 2 (2): 147–56.

Part I

Fluency and Range of Expression

2

Formulaic Language in University Seminars
A Comparison of EAP Textbook Coverage and Authentic Language Use in ELF Settings

Ying Wang and Nok Chin Lydia Chan

Introduction

Formulaic language is seen as a major hurdle for second language (L2) learners to achieve native-like fluency (Pawley and Syder 1983). The term 'formulaic sequences' (FSs), that is, fixed or semi-fixed word combinations that have 'an especially strong relationship with each other in creating their meaning' (Wray 2008: 9), has been used in the literature to mean anything from idioms (e.g. *in a nutshell*), through collocations (e.g. *highly significant*), to clusters or multi-word units (e.g. *at the end of*). Despite their differences in terms of idiomaticity, formal variability and frequency of occurrence, most FSs seem to be 'stored and retrieved whole from memory at the time of use, rather than being subject to generation or analysis by the language grammar' (Wray 2002: 9), making them particularly difficult for L2 learners to grasp. Over the last decade, corpus studies have revealed that FSs are particularly prevalent in academic discourse, providing an important means for discourse building (e.g. *on the other hand, as a result, as can be seen*) and stance taking (e.g. *we argue that, to some extent*), among other things (e.g. Biber, Conrad and Cortes 2004; Cortes 2004). Important as they are, most attention has been paid to academic writing and the challenges L2 or novice writers face thereof, whereas research on spoken academic genres has lagged behind in general (Basturkmen 2016).

Despite the awareness of the challenging nature of dialogic speaking in academic contexts for university students, particularly those who speak English as an additional or second language (Kim 2006), this type of events has been explored to a lesser extent than some other spoken academic genres such as lectures and classroom teaching (Aguilar 2016; Basturkmen 2016).

University seminars are designed for the exchange of opinions and evaluation of knowledge through face-to-face discussions (O'Boyle 2014). As a means of developing in-depth understanding, seminar discussion plays a particularly important role in teaching and learning at the tertiary level (Aguilar 2016). However, our understanding of the linguistic and communicative demands that academic interaction imposes on university students still remains very limited.

Conventional approaches to teaching academic discussion skills often focus on certain speech functions, such as Agreeing and Disagreeing, with textbooks providing lists of typical linguistic realizations, which normally consist of FSs. However, empirical studies have shown a more complex picture of real language use (Basturkmen 2016). Bardovi-Harlig and Vellenga (2015), for instance, found that *I agree* and *I disagree*, two ubiquitous expressions featured in EAP textbooks, are not used as frequently as one would expect in authentic academic discussion. But like many other studies exploring formulaic language use in academic speech, Bardovi-Harlig and Vellenga's (2015) observations were based on a wide range of speech events (including lectures, classroom discussions, lab sections and seminars) in English-speaking universities, using data such as the Michigan Corpus of Academic Spoken English (MICASE) (e.g. Simpson et al. 2002). Given the rapid spread of English as a lingua franca (ELF) in the last decade and the fact that L2 English speakers have now greatly outnumbered L1 English speakers, it is time to look at the role of L2 speakers in shaping the language as a means of international communication (Seidlhofer 2005; Formentelli 2017). The present study is partly a response to such a call, extending the scope of the enquiry to academic ELF settings.

More specifically, the present study is motivated from two parallel interests. First, it intends to offer an up-to-date overview of EAP textbook coverage of speech functions and their linguistic realizations targeting university seminars to see what functions and realizations might be taught in EAP classes. Second, it aims to examine L2 speakers' authentic use of FSs (i.e. their forms and functions) in seminar discussion, using corpus data produced in ELF settings. Drawing together these two strands of investigation, it will allow us to evaluate EAP textbooks against authentic language use and consider potential implications for the teaching of EAP.

Data and Methods

In this study, ten EAP textbooks, as presented in Table 2.1, were used to address the first aim. Textbook 1 is currently used in an English-speaking course offered at the

Table 2.1 EAP textbooks examined

Textbook 1	Anderson, K., J. Maclean and T. Lynch (2004), *Study Speaking: A Course in Spoken English for Academic Purposes*, Cambridge: Cambridge University Press.
Textbook 2	Barrass, R. (2006), *Speaking for Yourself: A Guide for Students*, London: Routledge.
Textbook 3	Cox, K. and D. A. Hill (2011), *EAP Now! English for Academic Purposes: Students' Book*, London: Pearson Education.
Textbook 4	McCormack, J. and S. Watkins (2009), *English for Academic Study: Speaking*, Reading: Garnet Publishing Ltd.
Textbook 5	Thaine, C. (2012), *Cambridge Academic English B1+ Intermediate Student's Book: An Integrated Skills Course for EAP*, Cambridge: Cambridge University Press.
Textbook 6	Hewings, M. and M. McCarthy (2012), *Cambridge Academic English B2 Upper Intermediate Student's Book: An Integrated Skills Course for EAP* (Vol. 1), Cambridge: Cambridge University Press.
Textbook 7	Hewings, M., C. Thaine and M. McCarthy (2012), *Cambridge Academic English C1 Advanced Student's Book: An Integrated Skills Course for EAP*, Cambridge: Cambridge University Press.
Textbook 8	De Chazal, E. and L. Rogers (2013), *Oxford EAP: A Course in English for Academic Purposes Intermediate B1+ Student's Book*, Oxford: Oxford University Press.
Textbook 9	De Chazal, E. and S. McCarter (2012), *Oxford EAP: A Course in English for Academic Purpose. Upper Intermediate B2 Student's Book*, Oxford: Oxford University Press.
Textbook 10	De Chazal, E. and J. Hughes (2015), *Oxford English for Academic Purposes Advanced C1 Student's Book*, Oxford: Oxford University Press.

first author's institution, namely Karlstad University, Sweden. The rest of the books were selected based on the scope (academic English skills), publication year (most recent ones) and publisher. All the textbooks were published between 2004 and 2015 by leading publishers in the field that are renowned for their quality control and market share. Among them, three (1, 2 and 4) target academic speaking specifically, while the others are general EAP textbooks addressing various communication skills including writing, reading, speaking and listening. Only the sections related to seminar discussion in these textbooks were examined to collect speech functions and their linguistic realizations featuring this specific type of interaction.

The authentic seminar data were drawn from a one-million-word corpus, ELFA (English as a Lingua Franca in Academic Settings, Mauranen 2008), which contains naturally occurring spoken academic ELF, transcribed from approximately 131 hours of speech events, both monologic ones (33 per cent), such as lectures and presentations, and dialogic events (67 per cent), such as seminars, thesis defences and conference discussions, recorded in universities based in Finland. The corpus covers a number of disciplinary domains including social sciences, technology, humanities, natural sciences and medicine. The data were produced by approximately 650 speakers from fifty-one different L1 backgrounds (see Mauranen, Hynninen and Ranta 2010 for more information about the corpus). The present study was based on the seminar data only, with a total of 32 files and 353,643 words.

More information about the data used is presented in Table 2.2, which shows that the majority of the data is made up of tutor-led seminars. The content of discussion may vary, though. For instance, the discussions in the social sciences seminars typically follow student presentations; seminars in humanities and medicine tend to centre on reading or other course content. Unlike in tutor/student-led seminars, which involve largely undergraduate students, research seminars are attended by staff members (senior and junior) as well as research students and occasionally also invited speakers; the discussion is normally a follow-up on a research presentation just given. Most of the seminars involve around ten speakers. L1 English speakers occasionally appear (one or two in some of the events), but none of the seminars was dominated by them. In other words, the data analysed may contain contributions from L1 English speakers, but the amount is negligible. In what follows, we present the methods used for the corpus study (a keyword + cluster analysis) as well as the rationale behind the approach.

The predominant trend in formulaic language research is to take a frequency-based approach (e.g. lexical bundles, *n*-grams), meaning that FSs are defined

Table 2.2 ELFA seminar data breakdown

Domain	No. of Files	Type	No. of Speakers	No. of Words
Humanities	6	Research seminar (2) + tutor-led seminar (4)	51	63,874
Medicine	5	Research seminar (1) + tutor-led seminar (4)	40	49,102
Natural Sciences	6	Research seminar (3) + tutor-led seminar (2), student-led seminar (1)	65	87,290
Social Sciences	9	Tutor-led seminar (6) + thesis defence seminar (3)	96	99,255
Other	6	Research seminar (2) + tutor-led seminar (4)	70	54,122

on the basis of frequency of co-occurrence and automatic retrieval methods are used to identify frequently co-occurring word sequences in a given corpus. However, as discussed in Wang (2018a), such an approach can be problematic when dealing with L2 learner data, where many seemingly idiosyncratic choices that are overlooked by the computer, as they do not reach the frequency threshold, may actually reveal important functional and formulaic features characterizing the whole community if they are examined together (see also Biber 2009; Ädel and Erman 2012, for other inherent limitations of the approach). The problem is further compounded when spoken data are involved, where hesitations, false starts and repetitions can interfere with the identification of FSs by breaking up their component elements (Wang 2018b). Given the nature of ELF communication, which features a high degree of flexibility and adaptability (Cogo and House 2017: 171), meaning that speakers may make a conscious effort in adapting their language use according to the needs of the other speakers present who do not share the same L1, formal variations may be especially prevalent and unpredictable, making it even more difficult to retrieve FSs automatically. Manual identification can help identify less frequent and discontinuous FSs (Wang 2018a, 2018b), but the amount of time and effort needed for a manual approach makes it infeasible to be carried out on a large scale to see the whole picture.

To address the methodological limitations as outlined earlier, in this study, we still opted for automatic methods, but we took a more targeted approach by starting from identifying distinctive keywords in seminars, using a refined method for keyness analysis, and then moving towards clusters they occur in. Doing so allowed us to be more focused in our search for meaningful sequences, discontinuous or not, which are also representative of seminar discussion. In what follows, we introduce the two types of analysis in more detail.

Keywords refer to words which occur 'with unusual frequency in a given text' in comparison with some kind of norm based on a reference corpus (Scott 1997: 236). The idea is widely employed in corpus linguistics research, with the underlying assumption that unusually frequent words would be especially informative about the characteristics of the texts in the target corpus 'in terms of aboutness and style' (Baker 2004: 347; see also Gabrielatos 2018). Traditional methods for measuring keyness (such as chi-square and log-likelihood), however, rely purely on frequencies, and the result is often a list of hundreds or even thousands of keywords, many of which (e.g. high-frequency function words, words that occur frequently but are restricted to a single text or a handful of texts) are not truly representative of the corpus or discourse domain in question (Baker 2004; Egbert and Biber 2019). To address such limitations, Egbert and Biber (2019) proposed a new method, namely text dispersion keyness, which is based on word dispersion across the texts in a corpus, giving preference to content words that are distinctive and generalizable to the content of the entire corpus.

Text dispersion keyness, incorporated in AntConc (version 4.0.7) (Anthony 2022), was employed in the present study. The target corpus consists of the seminar data drawn from ELFA as shown in Table 2.1 (32 files; 353,643 words). The rest of the ELFA corpus (130 files; 721,418 words) makes an ideal reference corpus, given that all the texts belong to the same broad discourse domain (spoken ELF discourse in academic settings) but at the same time differ from seminar discussion in terms of genre. Such a comparison allows for the identification of words that are particularly characteristic of seminar discussion, in contrast to the other main types of spoken academic communication.

The keywords were generated with the measure of text dispersion keyness (four-term) and a threshold of $p < 0.05$ (3.84 with Bonferroni). They were then employed as search words to find sequences they occur in within the corpus, using the Clusters Tool in AntConc. We decided to set the length of clusters to three words in order to retrieve as many meaningful sequences as can be manually manageable. Some three-word clusters retrieved in the study turned out to be extensions of two-word sequences (e.g. *yeah but* in *yeah but er, yeah but it, yeah but but, mhm yeah but*), and in such cases, the two-word sequences were also included in the analysis. Note that contractions (such as *wasn't, didn't*) are treated as two words by AntConc.

Findings

In the EAP textbooks under investigation, altogether, there are 1,181 examples (or linguistic realizations) provided, covering more than twenty-five different speech functions. Some functions may be named slightly differently (e.g. Rephrasing, Reformulating, Elaborating, Explaining) in the textbooks but were counted as the same one in the present study (as 'Reformulating/ reinforcing' in Table 2.3). Additionally, to aid readability, a number of similar functions, which are also relatively less common, were merged into one; for instance, Initiating and Responding to answers were merged with Managing contributions. After sorting out the functions in this way, we ended up with seventeen main functions, which are presented in Table 2.3, together with a selection of examples.

Table 2.4 shows the distribution of these functions in the textbooks. As can be seen, the functions of Agreeing and Partly agreeing are featured in all the textbooks. After these two are Disagreeing (nine out of ten), Turn-taking (nine out of ten) and Providing information, ideas, opinions (eight out of ten). Quite a few are included in seven out of the ten textbooks: Inviting comments, Checking comprehension, Reformulating and Making suggestions. Three out of these four functions (apart from Making suggestions) are typical interactional strategies that help bring the conversation forward by asking questions, checking understanding and clarifying the meaning of a comment. In contrast, those that occur in six out of the ten textbooks (Structuring discourse, Reference, Providing example, evidence, condition) have more to do with the structure of discourse, which could be within a single turn or across the whole conversation, or information communicated. Even less commonly featured functions are Requesting elaboration (five out of ten), Expressing (un)certainty, Responding to (difficult) questions and Managing contributions (four out of ten). Among these functions, the relatively limited coverage of Managing contributions is perhaps understandable, given that the function is normally associated with the leader of the discussion only. Considering the highly challenging nature of seminar discussion, however, it may be surprising to see that Playing for time is covered in only one of the textbooks.

With regard to the authentic seminar data produced in ELF settings, Table 2.5 presents the keywords (altogether thirty-three) together with the main clusters these keywords occur in. Looking at the keywords first, seven out of thirty-one are hesitation devices or fillers (*uh, hm, huh, mhm, oh, wh, ev*). Hesitations, which signal spontaneous speech, tend to increase when the speaking task is demanding (Martin and Strange 1968). The prevalence of hesitation devices in the keyword list may thus indicate that seminar discussion is indeed highly demanding – more so than the other academic genres (e.g. lectures and presentations). Among the rest of the keywords, we see an equal number (six) of negative words or forms (*wasn, couldn, didn, nobody, never, isn*) and those related to cognition and mental activity (*sure, remember, guess, thinking, wanna, agree*).

The clusters listed in Table 2.5 belong roughly to seven main functional categories, which are presented in Table 2.6. Some of the sequences may be used in a non-prototypical way or have multiple functions, which will be examined more closely in the subsequent analysis. The cited examples in the following discussion were taken directly from ELFA with the original markup, among which, S codes refer to speakers and USEMD codes stand for files. Boldface was added in this paper to highlight the target sequences.

Table 2.3 Speech functions and linguistic realizations drawn from the textbooks

Function	Examples
Agreeing	Yes, that's right.
	Absolutely. I totally agree.
	I couldn't agree more.
	[NAME] makes a good point.
	Can I just say that I think you're quite right to . . .?
Partly agreeing	I (can) see what you mean, but (don't you think . . .?)
	Yes, but on the other hand . . .
	Well, I sort of agree with that.
	That's interesting, but have you considered . . .
Disagreeing	I don't (really) agree (with you/ that) . . .
	I don't follow your argument, wouldn't that mean . . .
	I'm not sure I agree with you there.
	I don't necessarily agree with that point.
Inviting comments	[NAME], did you want to make a point?
	What are your views on this issue?
	What do you think?
Requesting elaboration	Sorry, I didn't follow what you said about . . . Could you explain that again?
	I'm not sure what you mean by . . .?
	Could you say something more about this?
Checking comprehension	Do you understand what I mean?
	Does that answer your question?
	Am I right in thinking that . . .?
Turn-taking	Can I just say/ ask . . .?
	Can I just come in here?
	Can I just come back to what you said about . . .?
Managing contributions	Shall we begin?
	Thanks, [NAME], for your contribution.
	Thank you, that's helpful.
Playing for time	Er, let me see . . .
Reference	As I said a few minutes ago . . .
	Regarding what you (both) say about . . .
	If we look along the bottom of . . .
Providing information, ideas, opinions	It is my view that . . .
	It seems to me that . . .
	Overall, we thought that . . .
Reformulating/ reinforcing	Look, to put it another way, . . .
	What's meant by that is that . . .
	What I was trying to say was that . . .
Structuring discourse	Our first point is . . .
	So moving on to look at . . .
	So, to sum up . . .
Providing example, evidence, condition	For example, . . .
	Well, according to our results, . . .
	This action should only be taken if . . .
	Unless . . .

Table 2.3 (Continued)

Function	Examples
Making suggestions	*I would suggest . . .* *Maybe we could . . . ?* *How about . . .*
Expressing (un)certainty	*I'm certain . . .* *There's no doubt (in my mind) (that) . . .* *It could well be that . . .* *I suppose it could be that . . .*
Responding to (difficult) questions	*To be honest, I don't know. I'll need to check on that.* *I must confess, I really don't know what the answer is.*

Table 2.4 Distribution of speech functions in the textbooks

	Textbook									
	1	2	3	4	5	6	7	8	9	10
Agreeing	√	√	√	√	√	√	√	√	√	√
Partly agreeing	√	√	√	√	√	√	√	√	√	√
Disagreeing	√	√	√	√	√	√	√	√		
Turn-taking	√	√	√	√	√	√	√			√
Providing information, ideas, opinions	√	√	√	√	√	√		√	√	
Inviting comments	√	√		√	√	√		√	√	
Checking comprehension	√	√		√	√		√	√	√	√
Reformulating/reinforcing	√	√				√	√	√	√	√
Making suggestions	√		√	√		√	√		√	√
Structuring discourse		√		√	√	√		√	√	
Reference	√			√		√		√	√	√
Providing example, evidence, condition	√	√	√					√	√	√
Requesting elaboration	√			√			√	√	√	
Managing contributions	√			√					√	√
Expressing (un)certainty	√			√			√		√	
Responding to (difficult) questions	√					√	√		√	
Playing for time	√									

Before commenting on the results, it is necessary to point out again that the keyness measure used in the study focuses on the differences (rather than similarities) between the target corpus and the reference corpus. The keywords and clusters retrieved this way are those which are significant particularly in seminar discussion in comparison with other genres (e.g. lectures). Some FSs that have been subjected to close scrutiny as commonly used in spoken academic settings, such as *you know* (House 2009), *kind/sort of* (Poos and Simpson 2002),

Table 2.5 Keywords and clusters characterizing seminar discussion in ELFA

Type	Rank	Clusters (Raw Frequency in Brackets)
uh	1	uh huh yeah/and/okay (11), [uh huh (70)]
hm	2	mhm-hm yeah/yes (62), yeah/yes mhm hm (39), hm mhm hm (36), mhm mhm hm (24), [mhm-hm (1,316), hm-mhm (82)]
alright	3	[alright yeah/okay (11), yeah/okay alright (9)]
oh	4	oh okay yeah (7), [oh okay (49), oh yeah (40)]
wasn	5	wasn't it (8), but it wasn (7), wasn't so (7)
sure	6	'm not sure (66), i'm sure (21), to make sure (10), sure if I (8), are you sure (5), not quite sure (5)
somewhere	7	i/we read (that) somewhere (7), [somewhere in (10), somewhere else (7)]
couldn	8	couldn't find (8)
remember	9	don't remember (22), if i remember (10), have to remember (9), can't remember (8)
wh	10	wh what is/are (8), [wh-what (17), wh-where (7), wh-which (4), wh-when (4)]
yes	11	yes yes yes (26), yes that's (21), yes it's (16), mhm hm yes (14), yeah yeah yes (13), [yes but (44)]
guess	12	and i guess (10), but i guess (7), guess i'm (5) [i guess (80)]
huh	13	see 'uh'
ev	14	[ev every/everybody/everyone/everything/even/evaluation (10)]
thinking	15	i was thinking (41), i'm thinking (13), thinking about the (8), i'm just thinking (7), ve been thinking (7)
didn	16	didn't have (36), didn't know (16), didn't get (15), didn't want (12), didn't say (11), didn't understand (9), didn't mention (8), didn't really (7), didn't you (7)
article	17	read(ing) this/an/one/some article (14), in this/the article (8), [this article (31)]
wanna	18	don't wanna (8), if you wanna (5), do you wanna (3)
else	19	[something else (33), what else (21), anything else (18)]
thanks	20	[so/okay/er thanks (15)]
your	21	what is your (14), part of your (12), in your (10), it's your (10), you have your (5)
please	22	please can/maybe you (4), [so please (23), yes please (9)]
anything	23	don't have anything (8), don't know anything (7), don't/can't/couldn't do anything (6), [anything about (29), anything else (18), anything like (7)]

mhm	24	see hm
nobody	25	[nobody knows (5), nobody else (4)]
yeah	26	yeah it's (90), yeah i think (85), yeah yeah yeah (80), yeah that's (69), mhm hm yeah (48), yeah but i (30), yeah mhm hm (30), [yeah okay (88), okay yeah (67)]
agree	27	agree with you (8), [i agree (38)]
never	28	i've never (7)
depends	29	it depends on (17), it just/really/always depends (6), depends very much (5), [depends on (34)]
isn	30	isn't it (14), isn't that (10), isn't the (6)
weeks	31	after/for/within/in two weeks (6), N weeks' time (4)

I mean (Mauranen 2012), *I would say* (Wang and Kaatari 2021), *I think* (Wang 2017), may also be fairly frequent in seminar discussion, but it is likely that they are equally frequent across the genres involved and therefore cannot be taken as typical of seminar discussion alone.

A few general observations can be made from comparing Table 2.6 and Table 2.3. First, the clusters retrieved from the authentic seminar data represent a small number of functions (seven out of twenty-five) that are covered in the EAP textbooks examined. Those that are related to textual (e.g. Structuring discourse) or ideational metafunction (e.g. Providing example, evidence, condition) as found in the textbooks (see Table 2.3) are not represented in Table 2.6, probably due to the method used, which means that these functions may be equally, if not more, frequent across the broad discourse domain of spoken academic communication. Moreover, the function of Disagreeing is not featured in the authentic language use either, indicating that direct disagreement in authentic ELF academic interaction may not be as common as one would expect. Interestingly, clusters used to express certainty do not stand out in authentic interaction, either, which seems more likely to involve expressions conveying some sense of uncertainty instead. Likewise, Turn-taking and Playing for time are not represented in Table 2.6, but as we will see in the following in-depth analysis, many clusters were used with multiple functions including these two. Finally, in terms of linguistic realizations of all these functions, it is quite evident that the EAP textbooks offer a much wider diversity than what was found in the authentic data.

We now turn to look at some clusters used in context to offer further insight into authentic formulaic language use. Starting from the hesitation markers, filled pauses (*uh, huh, mhm, hm*) often occur in the form of repeats (*mhm mhm hm*) and/or together with an agreement marker (*yeah*) in the corpus data under investigation. Unlike in ELF lectures where filled pauses and repeats are often a means of gaining time for online planning, associated with the speaker's limited processing capacity and/or time in L2 communication (Wang 2017), in seminar discussion, they seem more likely to be prompted by a need to be interactive, as in the following example.

(1) <S9> yeah (xx) in my country there's a big difference some other tribes are patrilineal <S2> [**uh-huh yeah**] </S2> [the father's] side is very dominant in [everything] <S2> [yeah] yeah </S2> like my own tribe <S2> **yeah [yeah]** </S2> [but] in others it's <S2> yeah </S2> mother's side it's powerful <S2> yeah yeah </S2> they give the @names and everything@ </S9> (USEMD160)

Table 2.6 Main speech functions fulfilled by the clusters characterizing seminar discussion in ELFA

Function	Clusters	Examples in Context
Agreeing	mhm-hm yeah/yes, yes yes yes, okay alright, yeah yeah yeah, i agree, agree with you	<S4> **[yeah yeah yeah** that's right] </S4> (USEMD30B) <S3> mhm i can start <S2> **okay [alright]** </S2> [erm] i have to apologise for my voice 'cause i was sick and i just got it back yesterday so it may fade away but don't mind about that </S3> (USEMD110)
Partly agreeing	yes but, yeah but I wasn't it, didn't you, isn't it/that, are you sure, what is your (expected result/impression/interpretation/reasoning), do you wanna, anything else, so please, it's your (time/turn)	**yeah but** it's not necessarily so if i go by what i have here on this slide (USEMD26B) <S2> okay fine . **anything else** or should we move to the second paper . okay who wants to continue </S2> (USEMD110) **so please**, raise your points and criticisms comments (USEMD020) <S1> **so thanks** <NAME S2> so there's plenty of time for [questions] </S1> (USEMD270)
Reference	somewhere in, i/we read somewhere, in this/the article, part of your (thesis/question/study), in in your case/paper/plan, in two weeks	<S1> i ha- i have seen you used some some reference there adopted from <S6> mhm-hm </S6> from **somewhere in** in one of the slides </S1> (USEMD290)
Providing opinions	i guess, i was thinking, it depends on, yeah i think	well i agree that it would be needed or that information on wild populations would be needed so **i guess** that could be a good topic to study (USEMD210) yeah **i think** it was very good paper thank you (USEMD100)
Expressing uncertainty	wasn't it, 'm not sure, don't/can't remember, i guess, don't know anything, if i remember	but **i'm not sure** if that is this is a feasible option (USEMD04B, S9) this one is coconut shell yes so and and you can see there's no- this is like plantation there's no under under like vegetation and these are **i guess** approximately **i don't remember** how old they were maybe thirty years or so (USEMD230)
Requesting elaboration	didn't get, didn't understand	mhm but **i didn't get it** (USEMD210) sorry **i didn't** @**understand** you (USEMD070)

Example 1 illustrates a typical phenomenon in the seminar data, where two speakers sometimes speak simultaneously (square brackets in the example denote a point where overlapping talk occurs). But instead of interrupting S9, S2's utterances, consisting mostly of repeats (*uh-huh yeah, yeah yeah*), seem to be meant for showing agreement with what has been said. The occurrence of the hesitation markers *uh huh* suggests a quick processing of the information. At the same time, those repeats also serve to elicit more information from S9's ongoing turn. Note that there is no overlapping at the start of S2's third utterance, meaning that there is a short pause there and S2's first *yeah* may well be intended to encourage S9 to continue, which S9 does. This intention can be seen more clearly in Example 2, where S2's *yeah okay* and *yeah so* are obviously taken by S10 as a prompt to say more.

(2) <S10> i think er that one i shouldn't have put little bit i should have put none <S2> **yeah okay** </S2> yeah i think that is a mistake <S2> **yeah so** </S2> because i don't [see anything] </S10> (USEMD160)

How to express (dis)agreement is among the most common topics covered in textbooks on academic speaking. However, apart from *i agree* and those clusters involving *yeah* or *yes*, which are associated with agreement, at least on the surface, few other clusters seem to be directly related to these functions. Disagreement, in particular, is more often expressed in a less confrontational way with the use of *yeah/yes but*, for instance, as exemplified in Example 3.

(3) <S5> [how i'm going to do this] yeah so that is at least the risk is there you only have to <S2> [yeah alright yeah] </S2> [take precaution the risk] if you are exposed to that <S2> [mhm mhm] </S2> [risk so] i think it's very high </S5>

<S2> **yeah but** er but i think it's not as high if if you go you're not haven't been to different kind of workplaces [you're not trained for that then it's then it's] </S2> (USEMD160)

Formal variations were found in the data. As shown in Examples 4–6, *but* can be separated from the agreement marker (not just *yeah* or *yes*) by some distance. In all these examples, disagreement is not expressed directly but preceded by agreement or acknowledgement, probably resulting from a need to mitigate the impact of disagreement.

(4) <S2> **yeah yeah but** i think that's needed as well if if you generally think about like, because not well **yeah yeah yeah** no- not all women are feminist **but** , they can still, kind of a question their, er the place that

they're put the the control that's imposed on them so i i think that's she does that </S2> (USEMD03A)

(5) <S1> @yeah@ **yeah yeah i believe you** [**but** er] <S3> [yeah], no </S3> i don't know what happened but are <S3> [(xx)] </S3> [these reliable sources] ho- how would you [how would you define] </S1> (USEMD03B)

(6) it's **er i agree** everything is arbitrary **but** knowledge is something you can't see (USEMD130)

The following examples (Examples 7–9) illustrate functional variations. Example 7 shows that *yeah but* is not necessarily followed by a different point of view; it can be used simply to elicit more information to see the other side of the issue. In Example 8, *yeah but* could be a strategy employed to deal with difficult questions, namely asking for clarification. The same expression occurs twice in Example 9. Again, they seem to have nothing to do with disagreement, the first one introducing a clarification of the question raised in the speaker's previous turn and the second one indicating agreement rather than disagreement.

(7) <S11> . . . if you are not married the child always get the name from the mother, maybe you can you can tell them you want to have the name of the father but er for example my parents are not married and i have the name of my mother i don't know </S11>

<S4> **yeah but** if the if they are married [it's a] </S4>
<S11> [i- if] they are married then it's the name of the father, i think </S11> (USEMD050)

(8) <S5> yeah i want to find out er er you mentioned some people say imposition of er candidates in the constituencies imposition of candidates in the constituencies imposing candidates <S4> [uh-huh] </S4> [on the] local people </S5>

<S4> sorry **yeah but i** have to tell you @i don't understand this question@ </S4> (USEMD26A)

(9) <S1> i was not quite sure when i when i read this er when er when voyeuristic pleasure and visual pleasure are the same thing . <S2> [mhm] </S2> [because i] noticed that they kind of </S1>

<S2> maybe they are these . the visual pleasure is the er f- <S1> [mhm-hm] </S1> [first] first thing and they as are part of the visual

pleasure <S1> mhm-hm </S1> voyeurism and narcissism narcissism <S1> mhm-hm </S1> and then yeah that's what i think </S2>

<S1> **yeah but i** [i mean in your paper] </S1>

<S2> [**yeah but** it wasn't clear] yeah it wasn't clear [yeah that's right] </S2> (USEMD03A)

Overall, the prevalence of the word *yeah* and the related clusters gives a strong sense of cooperation (rather than competition) among the seminar participants. Indeed, direct challenge of initial opinions was rarely seen in the analysis of the keywords and their clusters. When there are different points of view, they are either preceded with an agreement marker or expressed with some degree of uncertainty and in so doing striking a note of compromise rather than confrontation or conflict. As shown in Table 2.6, Expressing uncertainty is one of the few main features characteristic of authentic seminar discussion, associated with the prevalence of negative words/forms. In Example 10, we can see that sequences such as *i don't know* and *i couldn't find* (*any sources to back up my thoughts*) are used to show the speaker's uncertainty in his/her view. In this instance, the turn starts with *but i would also say*, which suggests disagreement with what has been said in the preceding turn. Whether or not the following uncertainty is genuine, the highlighted expressions do help mitigate potentially negative effects of direct disagreement to some extent.

(10) **but** i would also say that at least in my thoughts people can still feel that they are people of the north and but **i i i really don't know i i couldn't find** any sources for well couple of sources that estonian can feel northern people but , nothing more and 'cause i don't know any estonians i didn't go deeper to that (USEMD110)

Another negative phrase expressing uncertainty that occurs frequently in the data (*I'm not sure*) is illustrated in Examples 11–14. While in some cases the uncertainty seems more likely to be a strategy to avoid loss of face between the parties involved when suggesting an idea, as in Example 11, or offering a criticism, as in Example 12, in Examples 13 and 14 the uncertainty seems genuine. The difference between Examples 11–12 on the one hand and 13–14 on the other hand can be seen in the accompanying uncertainty markers (*I don't know, if I remember right*) and repeats (*I think I think, I don't I don't*) in the latter two, which can be taken as additional signals for a genuine lack of conviction. In these cases, such FSs may also be used as fillers or devices used to play for time, filling the pauses needed to think and organize thoughts while maintaining the floor, which is a commonly seen strategy across various spoken genres in ELF academic discourse (e.g. Wang and Kataari 2021).

(11) <S9> mhm , mhm sounds very good i was just the the one point i thought i could maybe suggest was the er the initiatives on the inclusive information society that might be a good starting point **i'm not sure** if this is a good idea but just to look at those initiatives and what they say about inclusion and then look at look at those and analyse what types of things they're expecting. [thank you] </S9> (USEMD04A)

(12) so **i'm not sure** if that is the, biggest erm missing link so far er maybe there are other parties who could be . . . (USEMD04B)

(13) <S7> yes but what do you think er in france the problem er <COUGH> the there are many young people that are unemployed so @the@ politicians are trying to solve this problem <S6> mhm-hm </S6> with a new working contract <S6> yeah </S6> what do you think should the german do the same or consider the same even </S7>

<S6> <SIGH> **i'm not sure** i think in i think in france it was more the graduates erm who wants to go and they went on the street yeah they went on the street and fight against the government plans and **i'm not sure** if i can **i don't know** </S6> (USEMD170)

(14) <S8> mhm i was er thinking about her paper like **i don't i don't i'm not sure if i remember right** but <S2> mhm </S2> there was this scene that where bess was i- er in a public bus <S2> mhm </S2> and she was like fondling some man <S2> [yeah] </S2> [old man] or something </S8> (USEMD03A)

The sequence *I guess* is also interesting to be examined closely in connection with the multifunctional character of many FSs in the ELF data. Examples 15–17 were taken from the seminar corpus to illustrate the multifunctionality of this sequence. As shown in Example 15, *I guess* often occurs in the middle of a turn, retaining its core meaning and function (indicating a lack of conviction). In this example, it is accompanied by another expression with a similar function (*I don't remember*). The use of *I guess* in Example 16, following *yeah yeah but*, helps further mitigate the effects of disagreement by expressing uncertainty. It is worth remarking that, as shown in many of the examples earlier, FSs of similar functions (e.g. *I guess, I don't remember, I don't know*) tend to occur together – a phenomenon that looks similar to repeats, except that the items that are repeated are not necessarily of the same form, most likely resulting from the dual pressure of the highly demanding task (dialogue involving joint knowledge construction) and the language used (L2).

(15) <S5> we didn't make it there was something weird in everybody's food or so so that we slept a bit longer but anyhow we went there later and we saw that they'd been tapped and the latex is falling to the i i don't know if it's <S13> [coconut shell coconut shell yeah] </S13> [it's plastic it think it's coconut] this one is coconut shell yes so and and you can see there's no- this is like plantation there's no under under like vegetation and these are **i guess** approximately **i don't remember** how old they were maybe 30 years or so </S5> (USEMD230)

(16) <S6> **yeah yeah** <SU> [mhm] </SU> [but] , **but i guess i guess** this was, yeah no yeah but **i don't know** how how much this has kind of affected this controversy but a- at least i fo- felt that er they had kind of made a really good effort in you know <SIC> resoluting </SIC> it let's not anymore nag about this thing @@ let's concentrate on more important things </S6> (USEMD210)

Example 17 illustrates an additional function of *I guess* as a turn-taking device. It is not explicitly stated, but we can see from what follows *and i guess* that unlike in Example 16, S8 in this case actually agrees with what S7 has said and s/he takes the floor to provide a somewhat strengthening factor. This function is very similar to that of a common cluster of *yeah* (*yeah I think*) (see Table 2.5). An example is provided in Example 18, where *yeah I think* is used to take the floor by agreeing with the preceding propositions (*connectivity* and *edge-effects*). These examples also go to show that agreement can be realized in various ways in ELF communication rather than by the use of 'prototypical' FSs as provided in EAP textbooks (such as *I totally agree, I couldn't agree more*).

(17) <S7> i think this <S1> [yeah] </S1> [topic] is especially would be especially interesting doing it only in finland <S3> yeah </S3> doing just evaluating that because we seem to be so well <S3> mhm </S3> and er <S1> mhm </S1> therefore it would be er the reason for studying it because there is social exclusion in finland but as you say nobody sees it nobody really recognise</S7>
<S8> **and i guess** it's increasing all the time </S8>
<S7> yeah </S7> (USEMD04A)

(18) <S3> yeah and also the yeah the ecolog- ecological main-structure i think we can include that as well like how much do we want them to be connected </S3>
<SS> mhm-hm </SS>
<S8> **yeah i think** we have to say something about connectivity <S3> [yeah] </S3> [and] and about that they are really small and that's why they have edge-effects and </S8> (USEMD200)

The word *think*, as featured in Example 18, does not occur on the keyword list for authentic seminar discussion, but again, it does not mean it is infrequent. In fact, the expression *I think* occurs for a total of 1,590 times (45 per 10,000 words) in the target corpus. However, it must be equally frequent in the reference corpus and therefore does not stand out in comparison. The form *thinking*, however, does emerge out of the comparison, with clusters such as *I was thinking, I'm (just) thinking* occurring relatively frequently in the seminar data. In Example 19, the expression *I'm just thinking about* was likely to be used purely in its literal sense. Note that in this example, the speaker seems very fond of *I think*, which occurs six times in this short stretch of utterance. The same opinion initiated by *I think (it's very personal)* is repeated three times and in some cases, the expression is most likely used as a filler as the speaker is struggling to produce and convey a coherent idea (*i think if I couldn't have children I think I would affect somehow*). In comparison with *I think*, which may have become a fixed expression that some speakers tend to cling on to and overuse (to an extent that it is similar to fillers such as *you know, I mean*), the formal variations in terms of tense choice and additional modifiers as in *I'm just thinking about* suggest it is still very much treated as a syntactically and semantically 'regular' expression. It occurs unusually frequently in seminar discussion probably because this genre does allow time for the participants to *think* while listening.

(19) <S8> i think it might be very personal i think if i couldn't have children i think i would affect somehow , me and my and how i see myself as a woman, but i think it's very personal <S1> yeah </S1> you don't have to have children to feel like a woman but *i **i'm just thinking about*** my aunt who never married and never had children and er , and she's very old now and i've talked to her about it and she says that now she regrets it because she doesn't have anyone doesn't have a real family <S1> mhm </S1> so, but i think it's very personal but i don't think you have to have children to feel like a woman i think that's a very, a stigmatised way to think about a woman mhm </S8> (USEMD050)

However, the expression may also be on the way of becoming 'formulaic' in the sense that some additional function seems to have been attached to it. Half of the instances of *I was thinking* (twenty-one out of forty-one) occur at the beginning of a turn, as in Example 20. While it retains its literal meaning, it may also be used as a turn-taking device. The repeat (*I was*) and the filler (*er*) surrounding it give further indication that the speaker was using this phrase to organize the utterance/thought while trying to take the floor.

(20) <S7> [no i don't think] so , i'm not sure. however the cholesterol synthe- synthesis is decreased in cirrhosis <S6> yeah </S6>, so cholesterol is sy- synthesised from fatty acids. so the synthesis is decreased, not the breakdown of fatty acids </S7>
<S6> mhm-hm </S6>
<P:08>
<S5> i was **i was thinking** er in cirrhosis er is increasing the the production of protein or something of a of a </S5> (USEMD080)

In short, the earlier examples (Examples 1–20) are only a few of those showing some of the most significant characteristics of authentic formulaic language use in university seminars dominated by L2 English speakers (e.g. what sequences are preferred, how they are used, what they can say about formulaicity in this type of communication). The main findings will be summarized and commented further on in the following section.

Conclusion

To recapitulate, compared to what is covered in the EAP textbooks about seminar interaction, the participants in authentic semantic interaction as investigated in the present study use a far more limited range of FSs, most of which are simple, everyday expressions such as *yeah but, yeah I think, I guess, I'm not sure*. Given the specific settings of communication (ELF) involved, it may be a conscious choice made by the speaker to stick to simple and transparent expressions to facilitate processing by the other participants who do not share the same L1, a phenomenon that has been thoroughly documented in the literature on ELF communication (e.g. Cogo and House 2017; Mauranen 2009, 2012; Seidlhofer 2009). Meanwhile, such expressions may also be more easily accessible in the speaker's mental lexicon than those taught in EAP textbooks that are more idiomatic or syntactically complex (*I don't follow your argument, can I just come in here, it is my view that, I couldn't agree more*). Considering the highly challenging nature of the task involved (i.e. participating in academic discussion with little to no planning time using L2), the speakers' reliance on these readily available expressions may well be a trade-off effect between complexity and fluency.

The in-depth analysis of some FSs in authentic use demonstrates a degree of 'unconventionality' or 'creativity' in terms of their formal and functional variations. Indeed, formal and functional variability in ELF phraseology has been found to be more 'wide-reaching' than in L1, but by no means 'random', thereby suggesting 'ELF-specific developments' (Mauranen 2012: 160–1; see also Wang and Kataari 2021). The fact that they are used successfully in fulfilling various functions and facilitating communication raises the question whether it is meaningful to teach all those FSs for academic interaction as listed in EAP textbooks or if efforts could be better made on teaching interaction strategies in academic settings such as how to avoid interpersonal conflict, especially when sharing different ideas and views, and how to compose and organize thoughts on the spot. Integrating signals of uncertainty in utterances, for instance, could receive more attention in EAP textbooks and teaching as an effective strategy in reducing the negative impact of conflict.

Another related question is whether EAP textbooks should simply rely on writers' intuitions (see e.g. Harwood 2005: Section 2.1) in deciding what are considered useful expressions as well as interaction strategies to be focused on in the classroom intended for L2 speakers who are more likely to use ELF with other L2 speakers from various L1 backgrounds rather than to engage in communication with L1 English speakers solely. In this increasingly multilingual society, particularly so when it comes to academia, data on ELF speakers' use of English, such as those we have analysed in the present study, can and perhaps also should be considered as a legitimate source to be incorporated in teaching materials, which currently still very much focus on a single, set form of communication derived from L1 speaker standards. In so doing, as Matsumoto (2011: 110) suggests, it would allow us to 'project more pedagogically realistic and sociolinguistically relevant goals' for the teaching of English in general and of EAP in particular.

References

Ädel, A. and B. Erman (2012), 'Recurrent Word Combinations in Academic Writing by Native and Non-native Speakers of English: A Lexical Bundles Approach', *English for Specific Purposes*, 31 (2): 81–92.

Aguilar, M. (2016), 'Seminars', in K. Hyland and P. Shaw (eds), *The Routledge Handbook of English for Academic Purposes*, 335–47, London and New York: Routledge.

Anthony, L. (2022), *AntConc* (Version 4.0.7) [Computer Software], Tokyo: Waseda University. Available online: https://www.laurenceanthony.net/software (accessed 3 August 2022).

Baker, P. (2004), 'Querying Keywords: Questions in Difference, Frequency, and Sense in Keyword Analysis', *Journal of English Linguistics*, 32 (4): 346–59.

Bardovi-Harlig, K. and H. Vellenga (2015), 'Developing Corpus-based Materials to Teach Pragmatic Routines', *TESOL Journal*, 6 (3): 499–526.

Basturkmen, H. (2016), 'Dialogic Interaction', in K. Hyland and P. Shaw (eds), *The Routledge Handbook of English for Academic Purposes*, 152–64, London and New York: Routledge.

Biber, D. (2009), 'A Corpus-Driven Approach to Formulaic Language in English: Multi-word Patterns in Speech and Writing', *International Journal of Corpus Linguistics*, 14 (3): 275–311.

Biber, D., S. Conrad and V. Cortes (2004), 'If you look at. . .: Lexical Bundles in University Teaching and Textbooks', *Applied Linguistics*, 25 (3): 371–405.

Cogo, A. and J. House (2017). 'Intercultural Pragmatics', in A. Barron, Y. Gu and G. Steen (eds), *The Routledge Handbook of Pragmatics*, 168–83, London and New York: Routledge.

Cortes, V. (2004), 'Lexical Bundles in Published and Student Disciplinary Writing: Examples from History and Biology', *English for Specific Purposes*, 23 (4): 397–423.

Egbert, J. and D. Biber (2019), 'Incorporating Text Dispersion into Keyword Analyses', *Corpora*, 14 (1): 77–104.

Formentelli, M. (2017), *Taking Stance in English as a Lingua Franca: Managing Interpersonal Relations in Academic Lectures*, Newcastle upon Tyne: Cambridge Scholars Publishing.

Gabrielatos, C. (2018), 'Keyness Analysis: Nature, Metrics and Techniques', in C. Taylor and A. Marchi (eds), *Corpus Approaches to Discourse: A Critical Review*, 225–58, London and New York: Routledge.

Harwood, N. (2005), 'What do We Want EAP Teaching Materials for?', *Journal of English for Academic Purposes*, 4 (2): 149–61.

House, J. (2009), 'Subjectivity in English as Lingua Franca Discourse: The Case of *you know*', *Intercultural Pragmatics*, 6 (2): 171–93.

Kim, S. (2006), 'Academic Oral Communication Needs of East Asian International Graduate Students in Non-science and Non-engineering Fields', *English for Specific Purposes*, 25: 479–89.

Martin, J. G. and W. Strange (1968), 'The Perception of Hesitation in Spontaneous Speech', *Perception & Psychophysics*, 3 (6): 427–38.

Matsumoto, Y. (2011), 'Successful ELF Communications and Implications for ELT: Sequential Analysis of ELF Pronunciation Negotiation Strategies', *The Modern Language Journal*, 95 (1): 97–114.

Mauranen, A. (2008), 'The Transcriptions of the ELFA Corpus', Downloadable Version [text corpus], Keilipankki – The Language Bank of Finland. Available online: http://urn.fi/urn:nbn:fi:lb-2014052721 (accessed 3 August 2022).

Mauranen, A. (2009), 'Chunking in ELF: Expressions for Managing Interaction', *Intercultural Pragmatics*, 6 (2): 217–33.

Mauranen, A. (2012), *Exploring ELF: Academic English Shaped by Non-native Speakers*, Cambridge: Cambridge University Press.

Mauranen, A., N. Hynninen and E. Ranta (2010), 'English as an Academic Lingua Franca: The ELFA Project', *English for Specific Purposes*, 29 (3): 183–90.

O'Boyle, A. (2014), '*You* and *I* in University Seminars and Spoken Learner Discourse', *Journal of English for Academic Purposes*, 16: 40–56.

Pawley, A. and F. H. Syder (1983), 'Two Puzzles for Linguistic Theory: Nativelike Selection and Nativelike Fluency', in J. C. Richards and R. Schmidt (eds), *Language and Communication*, 191–226, London: Longman.

Poos, D. and R. Simpson (2002), 'Cross-disciplinary Comparisons of Hedging: Some Findings from the Michigan Corpus of Academic Spoken English', in R. Reppen, S. M. Fitzmaurice and D. Biber (eds), *Using Corpora to Explore Linguistic Variation*, 3–23, Amsterdam: John Benjamins.

Scott, M. (1997), 'PC Analysis of Key Words – And Key Key Words', *System*, 25 (2): 233–45.

Seidlhofer, B. (2005), 'English as a Lingua Franca', *ELT Journal*, 59 (4): 339–41.

Seidlhofer, B. (2009), 'Accommodation and the Idiom Principle in English as a Lingua Franca', *Intercultural Pragmatics*, 6 (2): 195–215.

Simpson, R. C., S.L. Briggs, J. Ovens and J. M. Swales (2002), *The Michigan Corpus of Academic Spoken English*, Ann Arbor: The Regents of the University of Michigan.

Wang, Y. (2017). 'Lexical Bundles in Spoken Academic ELF: Genre and Disciplinary Variation', *International Journal of Corpus Linguistics*, 22 (2): 187–211.

Wang, Y. (2018a), 'As Hill Seems to Suggest: Variability in Formulaic Sequences with Interpersonal Functions in L1 Novice and Expert Academic Writing', *Journal of English for Academic Purposes*, 33: 12–23.

Wang, Y. (2018b), 'Formulaic Sequences Signalling Discourse Organization in ELF Academic Lectures: A Disciplinary Perspective', *Journal for English as a Lingua Franca*, 7 (2): 355–76.

Wang, Y. and H. Kaatari (2021), 'Let's Say: Phraseological Patterns of say in Academic ELF Communication', *Journal of English for Academic Purposes*, 54: 101046.

Wray, A. (2002), *Formulaic Language and the Lexicon*, Cambridge: Cambridge University Press.

Wray, A. (2008), *Formulaic Language: Pushing the Boundaries*, Oxford: Oxford University Press.

3

Moves Away from Congruence

Interpersonal, Logical and Grammatical Metaphor in EAP

Jennifer Walsh Marr

Introduction

One of the key challenges novice readers and writers have with English academic texts is recognizing and reproducing the abstract concepts of academia. Where non-academic texts tend to describe actions with verb-centred description, academic texts typically shift towards abstracted noun groups to represent phenomena that can be studied and evaluated objectively (Liardét 2016). The shift to nouns is known as *nominalization* and is the most common type of *grammatical metaphor*: concepts moving across grammatical categories towards abstraction (Halliday 2009). Concepts that manifest as expected forms (actions as verbs; people, places and things as nouns) are considered *congruent* and are close to reality, whereas shifts away from the concrete to the abstract are *metaphoric*. Metaphoric forms are also used for logic (e.g. showing condition without *if* or causation without *because*) and being polite (e.g. giving instructions with a polite question). The underlying premise is the same: to make explicit the shifts between congruent reality and metaphoric representations that might otherwise remain opaque to novice scholars developing their academic English language skills. Academic English instruction that engages with the phenomenon of grammatical metaphor enables novice scholars to both recognize and manipulate linguistic forms to suit the communicative context.

Academic disciplines all have discourse patterns and specialist terminology, and grammatical metaphor is 'a linguistic resource that allows the grammar to be condensed into the technical, abstract lexis privileged in these discourse communities' (McGrath and Liardét 2022: 1). To illustrate, compare the following:

(1) We cannot avoid throwing out some food because we want to protect people's health and safety. However, because consumers want cosmetically perfect fruits and vegetables, too much food is thrown out.
(2) The protection of health and safety means some food loss is inevitable, although excessive waste results from market demands and standards.
  (Excerpts adapted from Nance et al. 2017)

These examples move from a more congruent description of what happens and why in Example 1 to a more abstract representation of the causes of a phenomenon in Example 2. There is the condensation of meaning through a reduction in the number of clauses and an increase in abstraction through removing people doing things. Specifically, we see the clauses become nominalized in Table 3.1.

This is a process of shifting meaning across different grammatical forms; here, clauses centred around verbs shift into nominal groups. This movement is metaphoric, as not only does the grammatical form change but the meaning also becomes less direct, that is, less *congruent*. These shifts from *congruence* to *metaphoricity* manifest not only in experiential components such as verbs and nouns but also in logical representations as well as interpersonal meanings. The shift from the congruent action in the 'here and now' to an abstract phenomenon that can be named, described, held still and studied is what academic discourse does best; nominalization in particular and grammatical metaphor as a concept are means of access.

The concept of grammatical metaphor is from Halliday's Systemic Functional Linguistics (SFL hereafter), which connects individual vocabulary items with grammatical structures into *lexicogrammar* as manifestation of their interdependency. A systemic approach highlights how changes in one variable

Table 3.1 Example clauses nominalized through experiential grammatical metaphor

Clause	Nominal Group
we want to protect people's health and safety	the protection of health and safety
consumers want cosmetically perfect fruits and vegetables	market demands and standards
too much food is thrown out	excessive waste

can have impact on another, and using linguistic terms allows for analysis and recognition of patterns.

This chapter draws upon concepts of SFL to identify a range of metaphoric and congruent forms of experiential, logical and interpersonal meaning, though it does not assume any SFL knowledge. The chapter begins with a brief discussion of the role of linguistics in EAP; then some key concepts of SFL are introduced to illuminate features of academic discourse: the three metafunctions and an SFL transitivity analysis to contrast congruent and metaphoric excerpts. It focuses on experiential grammatical metaphor, specifically nominalization, as it is the most common. The chapter then explains and gives examples of logical then interpersonal metaphor. It establishes the congruent forms of each type of meaning, contrasts these to metaphoric realizations in order to make them visible and discusses the implications for meaning-making and pedagogy.

Literature Review

SFL in EAP: The Interacting Roles of Linguistics, Context and Metalanguage

The premise of this entire volume is to highlight the role of applied linguistics in EAP, an underdeveloped aspect of TESOL training and practice (Valenzuela 2020: v). This is relevant to the field of EAP as many instructors begin their practice in more general ELT contexts, moving into EAP often without adequate professional development on the particularities of academic genres, disciplinary practices and the linguistic features that realize them (Bruce 2011). Further, the technical aspects of grammar, let alone SFL, can be intimidating to the uninitiated. Holistic conceptualizations of language, particularly when infused with a bias for 'native speaker' intuition about what is accurate and not (Monbec 2018: 92), can perpetuate the dismissal of technical language to describe what language does and how it does it. It seems akin to pointing to a complete building as a model for a student to build their own without guiding students through an analysis of its architecture and construction. Using the same metaphor of the architecture of language, Halliday and Matthiessen (2013: 5) argue that description and explanation of language should be 'coherent, comprehensive, and richly dimensioned . . . as rich as the grammar itself [for] if the account seems complex, this is because the grammar is complex – It has to be, to do all the things we make it do for us'. This may mean producing blueprints of major sections or features, deconstruction of components to see how they are built and how they function with other components as well as practising constructing smaller samples to foster familiarity and confidence in preparation for integrating them into larger structures. For EAP, this means drawing from authentic texts and explicitly articulating the relations between the larger context from which they are drawn as well as the discrete linguistic components used to achieve their purpose. This is facilitated through deconstructing and comparing excerpts, explaining *how* components work and examining the mechanics of effective, contextualized passages. Extending the architecture metaphor further, SFL recognizes several layers of blueprints for the co-occurring systems; metalanguage is used to consistently name the components to make them visible and highlight how those components *function* and *interact* with one another.

Situating passages and components within a larger context is important, particularly from a systemic perspective. Bruce (2011: 100) argues that 'the teaching of linguistic knowledge should . . . examine and present linguistic items as part of an integrated, functional whole rather than as atomized, decontextualized elements' as 'an atomistic approach [to lexicogrammar] does not assist students to understand that the meaning and use of a grammatical or syntactic item may depend entirely on the textual setting and the larger context in which it is located' (2011: 84). Making contextual factors visible is of benefit to students, and using a consistent metalanguage facilitates recognizing patterns of usage across contexts. Interviewing successful multilingual writers reflecting on how they learned technical aspects of language, former EAP students indicated that 'the mechanics of writing were neither boring nor power free' (Kalan 2021: 163) as when embedded in contextualized, relevant examples, such attention to detail enabled nuanced comprehension and production of academic texts. They claimed that 'mechanics of writing are not *at the service of* communication; they *are* communication. Grammar, punctuation, and other formalistic features are communicative vehicles and should be treated as such: they should be taught and learned embedded in authentic communication contexts' (Kalan 2021: 164). This means not just replicating model texts but also building linguistic repertoires to use for students' *own* purposes, to assert their own perspectives, voices and knowledges.

This chapter embraces the role of metalanguage not for the purpose of adding another layer of difficulty to language learning but for acknowledging and naming what happens to, with and through language. An enhanced knowledge about language (or KAL, see Dreyfus et al. 2016) is a mechanism to better recognize what happens within texts and to transfer that knowledge across various contexts (Monbec 2018).

Basic Concepts of SFL

SFL metalanguage can be built on more familiar formal grammar, situated within authentic text excerpts. There is no need to throw the baby out with the bathwater and negate knowledge students (and teachers) have worked hard to acquire. In many ways, SFL is the embodiment of *applied* linguistics: What do we *do* with linguistics? How do we apply and *use* it? The F in SFL is functional; this takes the labelling of forms so common in traditional grammar instruction and extends it to function, interrogating how the components work in authentic contexts, what other choices are available and how we can further manipulate them to articulate what we want to communicate.

At first glance, this sometimes looks like giving different names to things we already (think) we know. What SFL calls *processes* sure look like verbs, and participants in those processes are most often nouns. Until they are not. Or, more relevant to the context of EAP, until we look at real texts and aim for more ambitious meaning-making.

SFL views language through three metafunctions that operate as interacting systems: the ideational metafunction which represents the ideas, concepts, experiences and logic of a particular context; the interpersonal metafunction that recognizes the tenor of a situation and its relationships and perspectives; and the textual metafunction which identifies the organizational patterns of meaning-making in the context. These three metafunctions interact in all communicative contexts, and shifts in one aspect typically result in shifts in the others and become manifest in linguistic realizations we study. For example, different word choices and analogies (from the ideational metafunction) are appropriate for a first-year undergraduate student versus a postgraduate; these interpersonal variables might also have impact on how the discussion is structured with regards to turn-taking and whether we begin with a story or abstract concept first and how we connect ideas (the textual metafunction). The mode of communication, be it an impromptu conversation, an email, a practised presentation or a written summary, also impacts language choices; beyond the grammatical accuracy of utterances, SFL identifies and describes the functions of various choices as well as what alternatives exist to achieve the same goals. Having metalanguage to label the functions of language components enables for the tracking of choices across different contexts, and deconstructing texts 'helps students realize that language use is not as arbitrary as they may have been told but reflects their disciplinary context' (Monbec 2020: 6). From a descriptivist disposition, it is important to acknowledge that one mode is not necessarily superior to another; it is more relevant whether the language choices achieve the communicative goals and suit the context. This is important in the context of EAP so as to facilitate student agency beyond merely reproducing prestigious patterns; it is also about having a more critical awareness of how meaning not only *is* but also *can be* constructed for varying contexts.

To illustrate the ideational components, the following excerpts are parsed for their processes (what is happening), the participants in those processes (who or what is participating in the process) and the contextualizing circumstances around them all. In terms of form, processes are realized by verbs, participants are realized by noun groups (and some adjective groups) and circumstances are realized by prepositional phrases and adverb groups. While all three discuss the same topic (or field), the variations in word choices and clausal structures represent shifts in their tenor (all excerpts adapted from Bertogg et al. 2016):

(3)   Thousands of years ago, people changed how they lived and ate because they began growing their own food. Since then, most cultures have been eating more meat.

	Thousands of years ago,	people	changed	how they lived	and	ate
function	circumstance	participant	process	participant	logical connector	process
form	adverbial group	noun	verb	relative clause	conjunction	verb

	because	they	began growing	their own food.
function	logical connector	participant	process	participant
form	subordinating conjunction	pronoun	verbal group	noun group

	Since then,	most cultures	have been eating	more meat.
function	circumstance	participant	process	participant
form	prepositional phrase	noun group	verbal group	noun group

(4) Since agriculture became central to the food supply thousands of years ago, most cultures have embraced a meat-eating lifestyle.

	Since	agriculture	became	central to the food supply	thousands of years ago,
function	logical connector	participant	process	participant	circumstance
form	subordinating conjunction	noun	verb	adjective group	adverb group

	most cultures	have embraced	a meat-eating lifestyle.
function	participant	process	participant
form	noun group	verbal group	noun group

(5) The advent of agriculture has led to widespread increases in meat consumption across cultures.

	The advent of agriculture	has led to	widespread increases in meat consumption	across cultures.
function	participant	process	participant	circumstance
form	noun group	verbal group	noun group	prepositional phrase

There are discrete linguistic changes that occur in the different versions. The identification of components demonstrates what is happening in a clause and how it is organized: there is a process in every clause, made up of a single verb or verbal group, participants in that process and sometimes circumstances that illuminate the process. Moving through these three examples, they move from more grammatically complex (the first excerpt has four clauses across two sentences) to grammatically simpler (the third excerpt has one simple sentence made up of one clause). Example 3 not only uses more clauses, but it also has simpler vocabulary and explicit references to when and why food habits changed. It is realized most *congruently*, with more processes represented with material activities (*change, eat, grow*) requiring concrete participants (*people*). This version might be used for a rudimentary introduction of the topic to an uninitiated audience. Example 4 maintains the key meaning, but it is condensed into a complex sentence of two clauses. The causal logic (*because*) is now embedded into the dependent clause with the subordinating conjunction *since*, and this logic is now the starting point of the sentence. It has shifted from describing people doing activities such as growing and eating food to the impact of agriculture on cultures' lifestyles. The final version (Example 5) has the most salient information condensed into more lexically dense, abstract participants (*the advent of agriculture* and *widespread increases in meat consumption*), and the causal logic is now embedded in the process, *has led to*, as the nucleus of the clause. The tense shifts through the transformation from the simple past *began to grow* in Example 3 to present perfect *has led to* in Example 5. Some details, such as *thousands of years ago* and what *people* did (Example 3), are elided in Example 5 through the condensation of meaning. The logical markers of causation shift from between clauses to within processes and participants, and verbs representing activities such as *eating* and *growing their own food* (Example 3), become the nouns *consumption* and *agriculture* (Example 5). These shifts are considered *metaphoric*, as they move away from the congruent 'here and now' towards abstract concepts. This final version is most likely to be found written in an abstract or a topic sentence of an academic paper.

This parsing of features and comparison 'makes it possible to see abstract patterns of meaning that go beyond more transparent literal meaning. . . . these patterns of meaning can be restricted or expanded by factors such as a person's stage of language acquisition or learning . . . that affects their control of the language system' (Coffin, Donohue and North 2009: 331). This repackaging of meaning is an aspect of grammatical metaphor and particularly relevant in teaching and learning academic discourses.

Metaphors

Distinguishing Types

This section begins by differentiating literary or conceptual metaphors from grammatical metaphors, then delves into discussion of various types of grammatical metaphor, focusing on the ideational and interpersonal metafunctions. Within the ideational metafunction, distinctions are made between experiential and logical meaning. Experiential meaning is carried by nominalization and the less common yet related phenomena of verbification and adjectification. Logical meanings are just what one expects: the logic of causation, contrast, sequence, condition and so on. The subsection on interpersonal metaphor highlights how mood and modality impact meaning. Throughout, the underlying premise of contrasting congruence with metaphoricity is used to highlight the different forms and impact on meanings.

Many Metaphors and the Challenge of Academic Texts

Grammatical metaphor is distinct from more familiar literary metaphors that relate 'one entity in terms of another (apparently unrelated) entity, [where] two *domains* (or "semantic fields") are being brought together, explicitly by the author, or implicitly by the reader's inferences' (Littlemore and Low 2006: 269). These literary or conceptual metaphors can be made through manipulating word choices and concepts, drawing on parallel connotations or analogies that are often culturally bound. The analogy of architecture to grammar used previously is an example of a conceptual metaphor. An awareness of both conceptual and linguistic metaphor, beyond vocabulary development and rule-bound grammar, is important for English language students to decipher and produce authentic texts (Littlemore and Low 2006). Consider the following excerpt from an introductory history textbook:

(6) Far from democratic at its inception, the academic discipline of history nonetheless opened the way over time to the inclusion of new groups of historians and new kinds of history. What had once been an elite profession, writing about the pasts of elites for the sons of elites, gradually, albeit with considerable foot-dragging, began to admit women, minorities, and immigrants to the profession and to history's pages. (Hunt 2018: 33)

Its challenging vocabulary includes: *albeit, democratic, discipline, elite, foot-dragging, inception, inclusion and profession*. *Albeit* is a contrastive conjunction that, while uncommon, is from a limited list (or closed set) of words with specific functions. In addition to conjunctions, this closed set includes prepositions, determiners, modal and auxiliary verbs and pronouns (Dreyfus et al. 2016: 65). The rest of these words are from an expansive, open set of English vocabulary; here they are disciplinary terms and easily understood through glosses. Perhaps the most difficult term, at least conceptually in context, is *foot-dragging*. It is challenging not because it is difficult to visualize or mime for students but because of being conceptually metaphoric. Historians were not literally increasing the friction on their footwear. We can assume that the elites did not wear through their shoes avoiding *women, minorities and immigrants*. They were comfortable with their elitism and reluctant to give it up through increased exposure to others' points of view and their inevitable critique. This is a conceptual metaphor, using the imagery of *foot-dragging* to represent reluctance. Such imagery adds another layer of difficulty to academic texts with complex meanings and lexicogrammatical structures.

Grammatical Metaphor

Grammatical metaphor is similar trickery, but instead of meanings shape-shifting, it is the grammatical form that shifts. *Elite* is presented as both an adjective and a noun in Example 6. The adjectival usage is closest (or most *congruent*) to its original form. However, some adjectives are used as nouns, particularly as a distancing mechanism to distinguish groups of people as 'other' (as in 'eat the rich'); this is somewhat metaphoric, as the adjective *elite* carries its descriptive power to a noun form, conferring the idea of being of a higher status to an entire group (or class) of people: *elites*. Moving even further away from its typical adjectival form, note the reference in the preceding paragraph to *their elitism* – an abstract status that is now representative of a phenomenon. An '–ism' if you will – a belief, status or practice. However, it is important to note this phenomenon is more than word roots showing up across different parts of speech. Comparing *elites* as a group of people (concrete, count nouns) to the phenomenon of *elitism* (an abstract, non-count or mass noun), we need to recognize the movement away from the concrete to the abstract.

Nominalization

Nominalization is the most common form of grammatical metaphor. It is the phenomenon of abstracted, noun-centred representation of events, 'removed from our everyday experience' (Halliday and Matthiessen 2013: 718) and representative of experiential meaning (a subset of the ideational metafunction). A process of shifting away from verb-centred description of what happens, 'nominalizing is the single most powerful resource for creating grammatical metaphor' (Halliday and Matthiessen 2013: 729). It is also a feature of academic discourse (Halliday 2009; Liardét 2016) and a marker of the successful development of nascent academic literacies (Liardét 2016). It has easily been the greatest 'value-added' aspect of an SFL-informed approach to teaching EAP (Walsh Marr 2021) and acknowledges to students the opacity of so much academic English. When parts of speech are introduced to language learners in traditional grammar contexts, nouns are typically described as 'a person, place, thing or idea'. More often than not, those ideas are nominalizations.

The shift towards more abstraction through nominalization means actions become nouns, which allows them to be 'nailed to the page, and reorganised as static, stable phenomena that can be taxonomised, measured, categorised, evaluated, and defined' (McGrath and Liardét 2022: 2). This is advantageous in academic discourses as 'the immediate environment of the noun, the nominal group, possesses great elasticity: it can be stretched syntactically and packed semantically. Grammatical metaphor takes advantage of the elasticity of the nominal group to accumulate or pack in meanings which would otherwise need to be distributed over a series of clauses' (Cullip 2000: 85). We can see this in Example 6, partially repeated here as Example 7, where the head nouns of each participant are *discipline* and *inclusion* – essentially the discipline opened to inclusion.

(7) Far from democratic at its inception, *the academic **discipline** of history* nonetheless opened the way over time to *the **inclusion** of new groups of historians and new kinds of history*. (Hunt 2018: 33)

The *discipline* is pre-modified with the adjective *academic* and post-modified with the prepositional phrase *of history*. *Inclusion* has significant post-modification, with the prepositional phrases *of new groups of historians* and *of new kinds of history*. *Inclusion* is a nominalization of the verb *include*. When used as a verb, participants have to include other participants; as a nominalization, *inclusion* becomes a phenomenon, a *thing* that can be pointed to, studied and referenced. And it is the inclusion of learners who may not have had access and/or support to recognize and incorporate these shifts in form that underpins the rationale for making these features visible through explicit, linguistically informed, EAP instruction.

Table 3.2 shows how an idea moves across congruent to metaphoric through shifts in forms, most typically through affixation. As grammatical metaphor represents a shift towards incongruence, it occasionally occurs when a noun becomes an adjective through *adjectivization*. Note the example of *promot/ion/al*; He and Guo (2021: 8) argue that *promotional* is actually a *more* metaphoric form,

Table 3.2 Congruent to metaphoric shifts

	Process	Quality	Concrete Participant	Abstract Participant	
Congruent close to reality 'here and how'	cause	causal	cause	causation	**Metaphoric** away from reality
	include	inclusive		inclusion	
	profess		professor	profession	
		democratic		democracy	
	promote	promotional		promotion	
		presidential	president	presidency	
	protect	protective		protection	
		elite	elites	elitism	

an adjectivization that is a 'further metaphorization of the –ion nominalization'. Such forms can pre-modify a nominalized head noun within a nominal group. Sometimes shifts happen through synonyms; the clause *consumers* **want** *perfect fruits and vegetables* becomes the noun group *market* **demands** *for perfect produce*. Such synonyms are hypernyms, at a higher level of abstraction, following the same principle and application as nominalization.

Dead Metaphors

It is worth acknowledging that English has changed through history as well, including discrete meanings (and connotations). From Example 6, *inception* might even be considered a 'dead metaphor' (Dreyfus et al. 2016: 75), for while *incept* can still be found in the dictionary, that is where it is most likely to be found. The source of a nominalization is of little consequence to students (McGrath and Liardét 2022); instead, what is important is to give it a name, acknowledge its purpose and provide mechanisms to both decode and produce it as appropriate to the context.

Logical Metaphor: Building in Logic

In the same way that experiential grammatical metaphor is used to shift from 'here and now' actions to abstracted phenomena, logical metaphor is used to shift the representation of logical relations from explicit conjunctions *between* clauses to embedding them *within* the experiential components of processes, participants and circumstances. In formal grammar, this is commonly understood as coherence relations; SFL distinguishes between congruent and metaphoric forms in the same fashion as for experiential metaphor; congruently, logic manifests between clauses with conjunctions such as *and, because, but, if, nonetheless, next, so, unless* and so on. Metaphorically, these relations are realized in processes (X *following* Y; X *resulting in* Y, X *generates* Y, etc.), participants (*contributors* to something, *effects* of something, etc.) and circumstances (*similarly, in contrast, likewise, in the event of,* etc.) and the interaction of less stand-alone meanings that build meaning in context.

Specific to causal logic, we can think of this as 'cause *in* the clause' (Martin 2013: 31), as highlighted in the later examples that parallel the phenomenon of shifting meaning away from congruent realizations (Table 3.3). These represent a shift from causal logic manifest in the coordinating conjunctions between

Table 3.3 Congruent clauses condensed through logical grammatical metaphor

Explicit Conjunction	Logical Metaphor
There will be irreversible changes in the tropical forests **because** farmers produce livestock through unsustainable agriculture.	Unsustainable agriculture **will lead to** irreversible changes in the tropical rain forests.
The agriculture industry is among the largest capital giants **and therefore** yields a lot of legal power.	The agriculture industry is among the largest capital giants, yield**ing** a lot of legal power.

Source: Exemplar sentences adapted from Bertogg et al. (2016); tasks from Walsh Marr, Lynch and Tervit (2019).

clauses in the explicit/congruent examples to embedded logical metaphor. The first example becomes one clause with its causal logic embedded in the process (*will lead to*), and the second example embeds the causal logic in a reduced non-finite clause (*yielding*).

Logical metaphor allows writers 'to reorganize clause complexes into lexically dense, relationally oriented simple clauses' (Liardét 2018: 65). This lexical density is often from nominalization, which can embed logic within. Further, when causal logic is incongruently manifest in processes and participants, this 'opens up a wide range of causal relations' (Dreyfus et al. 2016: 118), which can be further modified within the verbal and nominal groups. Martin and Rose (2003: 149) explain it thus:

> One of the reasons that writers use logical metaphors for conjunctions is that they can grade their evaluation of relations between events or arguments. This is a crucial resource for reasoning in fields such as science or politics, in which it is important not to overstate causal relations until sufficient evidence has been accumulated. This function of logical metaphors is oriented to engagement of the reader.

Causal verbs include *allow, cause, create, facilitate, foster, generate, hinder, increase, interfere, invoke, lead to, prevent, provoke* and so on and can mean they cause something to happen or cause something *not* to happen. Some of these processes are more absolute than others (i.e. does interfering actually prevent something from happening?), and disciplines employ logic differently: particularly in the social sciences, it is rare that a single factor causes an entire phenomenon.

While causal language is fundamental to explanations and therefore academic reasoning, it is not the only form of logic used across the disciplines. Comparison and contrast, condition and contingency, addition and exclusion and synchronous and asynchronous sequencing all represent different logical relations that can be embedded within processes, participants and circumstances through logical metaphor. The following examples represent a range of realizations: Example 8 contrasts cultural beliefs with health impact using a circumstance. The comparison of the production and impact of emissions (Example 9) uses both a concessive dependent clause and an explicit contrastive conjunction. In Example 10, condition is realized by a nominalization (Walsh Marr and Mahmood 2021: 2).

(8) Cultures and education around the world teach that meat and dairy are necessary for good health and growth – *in reality*, consuming meat and dairy has been shown to cause a wide variety of health defects. (Adapted from Bertogg et al. 2016)

(9) *While the transportation industry is a large producer of carbon dioxide and nitrous oxides*, the quantity and potency of these gases are far less destructive to the environment than those of methane. Animal agriculture is responsible for 18% of all greenhouse gases, *whereas* industry is responsible for 13%. (Adapted from Bertogg et al. 2016)

(10) *The elimination of the smallest coalition partner*, party A, would reduce the coalition's parliamentary support from a majority of the seats, fifty-five, to a minority of only forty-seven. (Lijphart 2012: 92)

Revisiting the assertion that reasoning and building argument requires nuance and graduation in the logic (Dreyfus et al. 2016; Martin and Rose 2003), we can appreciate how logical metaphor facilitates this: processes and participants can be modified, while explicit conjunctions cannot. Participants can be modified through pre- and/or post-modification within the noun group. In the following causal example, *impacts* is the head noun of the resultant participant:

(11) These changes in land utilization create *impacts on the environment.* (Adapted from Bertogg et al. 2016)

This could be further pre-modified to *negative impacts, significant negative impacts, significant, long-lasting negative impacts* and so on. These might be *impacts on the environment and residents* or other qualifiers through post-modification. Through logical metaphor, a causal process can be further modified for tense or modality (Halliday and Matthiessen 2013: 714), which is also a feature of interpersonal positioning.

Interpersonal Metaphor: Polite Obfuscation

The interpersonal metafunction is where and how we position ourselves – in relation to our confidence, in relation to our audience and in relation to the topic. Interpersonal choices are somewhat less about *what* we are discussing and more about *how* we communicate. This is manifest in being more or less direct in our speech and by employing various forms of modality. Discussions with students regarding some of these choices require exploring values regarding subjectivity and objectivity, confident and cautious positions and how (in)directly we communicate. In addition to particular word choices, choices within interpersonal grammatical metaphor impact meaning-making as well, particularly through choices of mood and modality.

Mood

In its most congruent forms, English uses its three moods as follows: a statement, for example, *You need to revise this*, is the declarative mood; a question, for example, *Did you revise this?*, is the interrogative mood; and an order, for example, *Revise this!*, is the imperative mood. However, there is also an expanded range of incongruent functions that often remain opaque to literal interpretation, specifically polite requests and offers. These use the interrogative mood to gain someone's compliance, as in *Can you please check this?* or, more politely, *Could you please do this?* The lines between requests and commands here are blurred and need not be the focus here; our attention to interpersonal metaphor parallels shifts away from directness to be polite with shifts from congruence to metaphoric meaning. Interpersonal metaphor of mood also occurs with requests, again using the interrogative mood, for example, *Would you like some assistance?*. This form represents both metaphor of mood (using interrogatives for offers) and metaphor of modality, shifting from *Do you want . . . ?* to *Would you like . . . ?*. Modality is discussed below.

Modality

Modality is the means of articulating probability, usuality, obligation and/or inclination. It is either congruently realized within the verbal group with modal verbs (*may, might, could,* etc.) or adjacent with modal adverbs (*likely, generally, sometimes, possibly, never,* etc.). Interpersonal metaphor of modality moves modality from its congruent form close to the process to elsewhere within or beyond the clause (Taverniers 2018). This is particularly powerful in EAP where writers need to not only paraphrase others' research and writing but also align or disalign themselves with the statements of others, and in appropriate measure.

These examples show where and how *likelihood* manifests grammatically (and lexically) beginning with the congruent form close to the process (Example 12), then subsequent incongruent realizations (Examples 13–16) with likelihood moved away from the process, including adding an additional clause (Examples 14–16) (all examples adapted from Nance et al. 2017):

(12) Households *are much more likely to compost* if it's provided for them, since it is a user friendly process that does not require much time or responsibility.

(13) *In all likelihood*, households will compost if it's provided for them, since it is a user-friendly process that does not require much time or responsibility.

(14) *Nance et al. (2017) claim* that households will compost if it's provided for them, since it is a user-friendly process that does not require much time or responsibility.

(15) *I believe* households will compost if it's provided for them, since it is a user-friendly process that does not require much time or responsibility.

(16) *It is more likely that* households will compost if it's provided for them, since it is a user-friendly process that does not require much time or responsibility.

Example 12 is the congruent form, as likelihood is realized in an adverb adjacent to the process. In Example 13, likelihood is shifted to a fronted circumstance, still within the same clause but away from the process. In Example 14, likelihood is shifted to an additional projecting verbal (aka 'reporting clause'), in Example 15 to an additional projecting mental (aka 'thinking') clause and in Example 16 to an additional projecting relational (aka 'anticipatory *it*') clause.

In EAP, an additional clause that projects what an individual thinks about a concept, as in Example 15, is rarely valued in formal written assignments. However, in spoken contexts such as classroom discussions, stating what one *thinks, believes, knows* or *wonders* is an important repertoire to develop.

The distinct projecting verbal clause (also known as 'reported speech') offers considerable delicacy of meaning (Taverniers 2018: 176), ranging from *claim* to *prove*, *question* to *refute* and *suggest* to *recommend*. This is particularly useful for writers positioning themselves in relation to others' research claims and establishing their own stance and expands students' repertoires beyond the neutral and overused *state* (Liardét and Black 2019).

A somewhat separate application of interpersonal metaphor is in deciphering formative feedback on students' assignments. Many instructors and tutors have faced the frustration of students seemingly ignoring corrections, without a more nuanced appreciation of the role of interpersonal metaphor. There is considerable incongruence between students interpreting *You might soften this claim* as merely a *suggestion* they can disregard when an instructor expects compliant uptake. It is important to acknowledge that congruent statements are most direct, and the metaphoric forms of politeness can obscure meaning. Those that are less direct can still be effective, so long as interlocutors appreciate the implicit meaning behind incongruent forms and play along. But where texts bury meaning in incongruent forms, explicit instruction in the various types of grammatical metaphor can enable EAP students to recognize and surface the intended meaning.

Pedagogical Applications

EAP instructors need to plot a pedagogical course through authentic texts, exercising judgement with regards to student needs, existing schemata, course requirements and disciplinary values. This section takes the theoretical underpinnings of the various types of grammatical metaphor described earlier and situates them in decoding and recasting strategies with which to build student repertoires. It outlines strategies from authentic course examples of decoding main ideas, identifying components and facilitating more nuanced comprehension through analysing texts. The examples are drawn from materials developed for first-year multilingual university students with no assumed familiarity with SFL. The courses' materials are designed to help students 'see' the valued language features of specific disciplines. This recognition is enabled by principled use of SFL-informed metalanguage to identify the phenomenon of grammatical metaphor and decipher the meanings embedded within. Metalanguage is judiciously and gradually introduced as needed and in response to context: specific texts, assignment specifications and student goals. The technical linguistic description is underpinned with philosophies of description (rather than prescriptivism), repertoire building (rather than compliance) and critical attention to existing and potential texts. This is in alignment with SFL's tradition of accessibility to *all* learners so that academic literacy and participation do not remain a privilege to only those who already know their way around.

The task sequence is typically to identify simple, congruent realizations of meaning that are readily accessible, then interrogate texts for embedded, metaphoric realizations, building students' repertoires of patterns and resources. The pedagogy here acknowledges metalanguage and grammatical metaphor in order to trace movement and manipulate components for paraphrasing and discipline-specific representation.

Decoding

Decoding work begins with an SFL transitivity analysis, identifying the processes and participants' head nouns, interrogating *what happened?* and *who/what participated in this?* In the student-facing history excerpt (Example 6) discussed earlier, this reveals

(17) [the] discipline opened to inclusion.
(18) [the] profession began to admit women, minorities and immigrants.

Identifying the head of complex noun groups is central to comprehension and yet a challenge for students (Priven 2020); presenting essentialized meaning of messy, authentic texts makes them more accessible to students. This then serves as a springboard to discuss the pre- and post-modification that occurs within these complex noun groups through grammatical metaphor. The focus on meaning is to counter the temptation to merely increase nominalization in order to sound academic (Liardét 2016); grammatical metaphor is a complicated phenomenon *and process* that needs to not only make sense but also suit its contextual usage.

Sorting Meanings and Tracing Shifts

Subsequent to identifying essentialized meaning is to recognize the range of realizations; developing metalanguage facilitates students *seeing* and identifying the components with which meaning is built. Identifying components allows for students to trace meanings as they shift across congruent and metaphoric realizations in the service of paraphrasing (Walsh Marr 2019).

Practice tasks include arranging a series of examples from most to least congruent, such as the following:

(19) We cannot avoid throwing out some food because we want to protect people's health and safety. However, because consumers want cosmetically perfect fruits and vegetables, too much food is thrown out.

(20) Some food loss is unavoidable for health and safety reasons, however, the consumers' demand for cosmetically perfect fruits and vegetables has created an unnecessary amount of waste.

(21) The protection of health and safety means some food loss is inevitable, although excessive waste results from market demands and standards.

(Excerpts adapted from Nance et al. 2017; tasks from Walsh Marr, Lynch and Tervit 2018)

Students discuss which realization would be most appropriate where, reinforcing the important interrelationships between context, purpose, text type and lexicogrammar. They then identify the types of changes made and interrogate where details go, either across grammatical forms or elided altogether in the most abstract representations (see Walsh Marr 2019 for a list of common shifts). Filling in a chart such as the one in Table 3.4 sorts lexical items along a continuum of congruence and builds students' repertoires.

Comprehension Questions to Surface Embedded Meaning

Beyond decoding and sorting, asking a series of comprehension questions more deeply interrogates *how* meaning is constructed. The following task interrogates logic in an assigned reading (Example 22), beginning with explicit markers and moving on to logical metaphor:

(22) Although cyberspace is not completely unregulated or free from state interference, it is less regulated than other environments and is not bound to a give physical territory or owned by a particular ethnic group or state. For indigenous peoples, this is advantageous since it is their identification as indigenous that often hinders their ability to take part

Table 3.4 A continuum of congruent to metaphoric

		Circumstance	Process	Quality	Participant	
Congruent (close to reality, 'here and how')	**Conjunction:** then	after	Followed	subsequent	sequence	**Metaphoric** (away from reality)
	Conjunction: because	because of, as a result of	lead to	causal	cause	
	Process: consume				consumption	
	Quality: imperfect				imperfection	
	Circumstance: instead of		replaces	alternative	replacement	

Source: Walsh Marr, Lynch and Tervit (2018).

> fully in state political discourse as citizens. Cyberspace thus allows those who are marginalized to speak more easily in their own voices without having to go through approved representatives or channels. As a result, indigenous peoples may demand boycotts and strikes, alert the world of human rights violations, and share political tactics and ancestral stories without having to be a present, identified body. (Belton 2010: 197)

The task sequence is (1) ask students to determine logic [causal] and markers [*since, thus* and *as a result*] in the text, and then (2) interrogate logic embedded within clauses with comprehension questions such as:

(23) What hinders indigenous peoples' full participation in politics? [*their* **identification** *as indigenous* (which may preclude their citizenship in a state)]

(24) Why is the unregulated nature of cyberspace a benefit for indigenous communities? [it **allows** those who are marginalized to speak more easily in their own voices without having to go through approved representatives or channels]

This question-and-answer format guides students to meaning in the excerpt and then serves as a springboard to discuss how logic can move from explicit logical connectors to participants and processes through logical metaphor. This practice of looking for meaning first, then analysing its linguistic components is to acknowledge the congruent forms many students have mastered in their earlier proficiency preparations and then extend them to more authentic, yet grammatically incongruent, usage.

For comparative logic, students identify what is being compared and how. The task sequence is to (1) surface the elided language, (2) determine the basis of comparison and (3) represent this as an abstracted phenomenon (nominalization), as follows:

(25) Most of us know that the transportation industry is one of the leading contributors of greenhouse gases. However, most of us do not know that agriculture is actually an even bigger contributor *[than transportation (is)]*.

Basis of comparison: how much greenhouse gasses transportation and agriculture produce
Nominalization: greenhouse gas production

(26) meat and dairy-based foods require considerably more water to produce than plant-based foods *[require/consume]*.

Basis of comparison: how much water livestock and agriculture consume/require
Nominalization: water consumption/water requirements

(Excerpts adapted from Bertogg et al. 2016; tasks from Walsh Marr, Lynch and Tervit 2019)

Subsequent interrogation highlights how the participants and processes of logical metaphor can be modified: in Example 25, we note the importance of the pre-modification in **one of the leading** contributors as well as the difference between the head nouns *contributor* and *cause*. In the example *Unsustainable agriculture **will lead to** irreversible changes in the tropical rain forests* (adapted from Bertogg et al. 2016), another interpretation might be to modulate the process, claiming it *may lead to* changes, and offer alternatives. While the congruent logic of conjunctions is easier to see and teach, metaphoric forms allow for more critical reading and more sophisticated presentation of students' own work.

Building Repertoires of Patterns

A similar process of identifying then interrogating the various types of interpersonal metaphor and their implications allows for a more nuanced discussion of the range of options available, the purposes they can serve and any patterns to disciplinary usage. In the sample task in Table 3.5, students examine the discrete language changes *and* the impact on meaning through a series of questions.

The initial deconstruction task is to identify the form of interpersonal metaphor that has been used: the first three are examples of moving the modality beyond the original clause to projecting anticipatory *it* clauses; *Experts believe* is a projecting mental clause; *Interestingly* is a fronted adverbial circumstance; and the final *Nance et al. (2017) state* is a projecting verbal clause. Determining the type through examples builds a list with which to expand students' repertoires to deploy in their own writing.

Subsequent analytical questions facilitate discussing some of the implicit implications of particular reworkings (answers following):

- Which of these statements is the most cautious? [*It could be argued that*]
- Which of these statements is the most confident? [*It is clear that*]
- Is it 'clear' that human behaviour must change? [Not necessarily]
    - What is the risk in using this projecting clause? [It does not leave room for a reader who does not think something IS clear. This is called a 'contracting' clause, as it contracts the discursive space (does not leave

Table 3.5 Interpersonal metaphor options

Direct Speech/Quote →	Metaphoric
'If humans wish to continue consuming a variety of produce, steps must be taken to modify attitudes, behaviours, and agricultural processes' (Nance et al. 2017: n.p.).	**It is clear** that that humans need to change food production processes and consumption patterns in order to maintain the availability of food choices (Nance et al. 2016). **It could be argued** that that humans need to change food production processes and consumption patterns in order to maintain the availability of food choices (Nance et al. 2017). **It is likely** that humans need to change food production processes and consumption patterns in order to maintain the availability of food choices (Nance et al. 2017). **Experts believe** that humans need to change food production processes and consumption patterns in order to maintain the availability of food choices (Nance et al. 2017). **Interestingly,** humans need to change food production processes and consumption patterns in order to maintain the availability of food choices (Nance et al. 2017). **Nance et al. (2017) state** that humans need to change food production processes and consumption patterns in order to maintain the availability of food choices.

room for other positions or evidence) and is a marker of novice writing (Liardét 2018).]

- How is *Interestingly, . . .* different from the other examples? [It conveys an attitude/evaluation. The others merely indicate confidence.]
- How confident does *it is likely* sound? [Fairly confident]
  - How could a writer make this statement stronger (where necessary)? [*It is very/most likely that . . .*]

This last prompt opens up the discussion of when, where and how writers could or should strengthen or soften their positions. It is something of a Pandora's box, often without definitive answers. What is productive is exploring the contextual features, the type of evidence and the means of argumentation that inform language choices. Students can then refer to the list of interpersonal metaphor options to prompt changes and compare them to original source material to ensure they have either maintained a stance they agree with or distanced themselves from a stance with which they disagree. With an expanded repertoire of forms, students are better able to position themselves and their texts. Building a repertoire of projecting processes (reporting verbs) beyond the default *state* or *say* is an important development of critical academic literacy skills (Liardét and Black 2019). As a repertoire-building exercise, students sort projecting verbs on a Cartesian plane according to strength of claim on one axis and alignment on the other. A follow-up activity is a corpus search of assigned readings for examples of contextualized usage and discussion of relevant contextual features.

Interpersonal metaphor of mood is typically an issue when making polite requests of others. Where typical EAP instruction may focus on accuracy and clarity, polite discourse requires more metaphoric forms. Matching (in)congruent forms with their implicit meaning, such as within formal letters and emails, and interrogating *What do they **really** want?* are productive and non-threatening ways to shift from literal interpretations. This also purposefully shifts any misunderstandings away from blaming students who are merely following rules of mood logically onto the incongruent means by which English users tell others what they want. For requests, students plot statements along a continuum of direct (*Do this*) to indirect (*It would be helpful if you did this*) to quite roundabout (*I would appreciate it if you could please consider doing this*) and discuss the contexts and implications of each. This is particularly applicable to letters of advocacy, either on students' own behalf or outreach and application of their research work.

Acknowledging the *range* of options for meaning-making, as well as the implications of their use, is a central principle of comprehensive, inclusive pedagogy. Beginning with naming the phenomena of grammatical metaphor in contrast with congruence, then highlighting the specific changes that are made, requires metalanguage for students to *see*, understand and ultimately manipulate language choices in texts. Metalanguage facilitates seeing what information is added in congruence and lost through abstraction and is useful for not only unpacking and repacking meaning but for also facilitating paraphrasing (Walsh Marr 2019), as it makes visible linguistic moves and complexity (Keck 2010; Wette 2017). Patterns of (in)congruence vary across modes, registers and disciplines (He and Guo 2021), and so articulating the relationships between context, purpose, text type and lexicogrammatical features is a powerful tool for EAP pedagogy.

Conclusions

In Halliday's theoretical work, interpersonal metaphor is described before ideational grammatical metaphor because it develops in that order for children (Halliday and Matthiessen 2013); when learning English in their home culture, children are acculturated to different means of instructions and requests. Ideational grammatical metaphor, particularly nominalization, develops later for children as it represents abstraction and higher-order cognition. For the purposes of EAP, I would suggest the entry point is reversed; ours are typically university students, working with abstract concepts and theories. Nominalizations are relatively easy to identify within academic texts, and revealing their patterns and processes of unpacking their meaning is a big lever in navigating academic English. In the humanities, nominalizations are used for 'reflection, generalization and interpretation' and for classification and explanation within science (Cullip 2000: 90); highlighting and making such metaphoric mechanisms clear is an exercise in accessibility. Grammatical metaphor is 'probably the most important concern as far as academic discourse is concerned' (Dreyfus et al. 2016: 68), and metalanguage is an entry point to not only name this phenomenon but also interrogate how something has shifted away from a surface or literal meaning and what is embedded within.

The point of the labelling is not to apprentice applied linguists. Instead, 'the purpose of analyzing a text is to explain the impact that it makes: why it means what it does, and why it gives the particular impression that it does' (Halliday and Matthiessen 2013: 731); it is to recognize *how* meaning is constructed. Revealing the phenomena of grammatical, logical and interpersonal metaphors articulates *how* meanings can be buried and/or surfaced. If a text is not explicit, then linguistically informed instruction and strategies can help. Academic texts are not inherently superior specimens of language; discussing the affordances *and limitations* of features within texts should facilitate engaging with and deciphering complicated texts and manipulating language choices to not only participate in but also potentially remake discourse communities.

References

Belton, K. A. (2010), 'From Cyberspace to Offline Communities: Indigenous Peoples and Global Connectivity', *Alternatives*, 35 (3): 193–215.

Bertogg, P., J. Danfeng, S. Chen and T. Turner-Johnston (2016), 'The Environmental Impact of Meat Consumption', *UBC Open Case Studies*. Available online: http://cases.open.ubc.ca/environmental-impact-of-meat-consumption/ (accessed 24 May 2018).

Bruce, I. (2011), *Theory and Concepts of English for Academic Purposes*, Basingstoke: Palgrave Macmillan.
Coffin, C., J. Donohue and S. North (2009), *Exploring English Grammar: From Formal to Functional*, London: Routledge.
Cullip, P. F. (2000), 'Text Technology: The Power-Tool of Grammatical Metaphor', *RELC Journal*, 31 (2): 76–104.
Dreyfus, S. J., S. Humphrey, A. Mahboob and J. R. Martin (2016), *Genre Pedagogy in Higher Education: The SLATE Project*, Basingstoke: Palgrave Macmillan.
Halliday, M. A. K. (2009), *The Essential Halliday*, London: Bloomsbury Publishing.
Halliday, M. A. K. and C. M. Matthiessen (2013), *Halliday's Introduction to Functional Grammar*, London: Routledge.
He, Q. and M. Guo (2021), 'A Corpus-Based Study of Adjectivizations in English', *Lingua*, 260: 103100.
Hunt, L. (2018), *History: Why It Matters*, New York: John Wiley & Sons.
Kalan, A. (2021), *Sociocultural and Power-Relational Dimensions of Multilingual Writing*, Clevedon: Multilingual Matters.
Keck, C. (2010), 'How Do University Students Attempt to Avoid Plagiarism? A Grammatical Analysis of Undergraduate Paraphrasing Strategies', *Writing & Pedagogy*, 2 (2): 193–222.
Liardét, C. L. (2016), 'Grammatical Metaphor: Distinguishing Success', *Journal of English for Academic Purposes*, 22: 109–18.
Liardét, C. L. (2018), '"As We All Know": Examining Chinese EFL Learners' Use of Interpersonal Grammatical Metaphor in Academic Writing', *English for Specific Purposes*, 50: 64–80.
Liardét, C. L. and S. Black (2019), '"So and so" Says, States and Argues: A Corpus-Assisted Engagement Analysis of Reporting Verbs', *Journal of Second Language Writing*, 44: 37–50.
Lijphart, A. (2012), *Patterns of Democracy: Government Forms and Performance in Thirty-Six Countries*, New Haven: Yale University Press.
Littlemore, J. and G. Low (2006), 'Metaphoric Competence, Second Language Learning, and Communicative Language Ability', *Applied Linguistics*, 27 (2): 268–94.
Martin, J. R. (2013), 'Embedded Literacy: Knowledge as Meaning', *Linguistics and Education*, 24 (1): 23–37.
Martin, J. R. and D. Rose (2003), *Working with Discourse: Meaning beyond the Clause*, London: Bloomsbury Publishing.
McGrath, D. and C. Liardét (2022), 'A Corpus-Assisted Analysis of Grammatical Metaphors in Successful Student Writing', *Journal of English for Academic Purposes*, 56: 101090.
Monbec L. (2018), 'Designing an EAP Curriculum for Transfer: A Focus on Knowledge', *Journal of Academic Language and Learning*, 12 (2): A88–101.
Monbec, L. (2020), 'Systemic Functional Linguistics for the EGAP Module: Revisiting the Common Core', *Journal of English for Academic Purposes*, 43: 100794.

Nance, E., A. Vadnais, C. Hicks and T. Lawson (2017), 'Insistence on Cosmetically Perfect Fruits and Vegetables', *UBC Open Case Studies*. Available online: http://cases.open.ubc.ca/insistence-on-cosmetically-perfect-fruits-vegetables/ (accessed 24 May 2018).

Priven, D. (2020), '"All These Nouns Together Just Don't Make Sense!": An Investigation of EAP Students' Challenges with Complex Noun Phrases in First-Year College-Level Textbooks', *Canadian Journal of Applied Linguistics/Revue Canadienne de linguistique appliquée*, 23 (1): 93–116.

Taverniers, M. (2018), 'Grammatical Metaphor and Grammaticalization: The Case of Metaphors of Modality', *Functions of Language*, 25 (1): 164–204.

Valenzuela, H. (2020), *Linguistics for TESOL: Theory and Practice*, Basingstoke: Palgrave Macmillan.

Walsh Marr, J. (2019), 'Making the Mechanics of Paraphrasing More Explicit through Grammatical Metaphor', *Journal of English for Academic Purposes*, 42: 100783.

Walsh Marr, J. (2021), 'Moving from Form to Function: Leveraging SFL Metalanguage to Illuminate Features and Functions of Texts in First Year University EAP', in C. MacDiarmid and J. J. MacDonald (eds), *Pedagogies in English for Academic Purposes: Teaching and Learning in International Contexts*, 43–58, London: Bloomsbury.

Walsh Marr, J., S. Lynch and T. Tervit (2018), 'LLED 200 Arts: Week 4: Grammatical Metaphor for Paraphrasing', unpublished teaching materials, UBC Vantage College.

Walsh Marr, J., S. Lynch and T. Tervit (2019), 'LLED 200 Arts: Week 21: Weaving Logic', unpublished teaching resources, UBC Vantage College.

Walsh Marr, J. and F. Mahmood (2021), 'Looking past Limiting Conditions: Prioritizing Meaning in EAP', *Journal of English for Academic Purposes*, 51: 100979.

Wette, R. (2017), 'Source Text Use by Undergraduate Post-Novice L2 Writers in Disciplinary Assignments: Progress and Ongoing Challenges', *Journal of Second Language Writing*, 37: 46–58.

Part II

Complexity and Accuracy

4

The Role of Morphological Knowledge in EAP Writing

Evidence-Based Study

Elizaveta Tarasova and Natalia Beliaeva

Introduction

It has been proposed that the ultimate goal of English for Academic Purposes (EAP) is to develop students' discourse competence (Bruce 2021: 24), which is understood as an ability 'to integrate a wide range of different types of knowledge in order to create extended written discourse that is both linguistically accurate and socially appropriate' (Bruce 2008: 1). The necessity to develop an ability to communicate and participate in academic activities determines the skills-based nature of EAP programmes, which are typically designed with the main aim of developing the key language skills (i.e. reading, listening, speaking and writing) essential for the processing and creation of academic texts. While the learning outcomes for skills development and discourse competence are rather clearly determined by the academic study context, the place of systemic competence and specific requirements of structural aspects of language knowledge are not as explicit. This is not surprising, since unlike TESOL, which is focused on overall language proficiency, EAP is mostly concerned with literacy and academic (rather than social) use of language (Bruce 2021: 24). Hence precision of expression, coherence and cohesion, rules of structuring discourse, understanding of the genres and styles and so on take priority in teaching EAP writing.

In relation to the systemic aspects of language knowledge, academic vocabulary development by far takes the lead in EAP for obvious reasons. While students are encouraged to study academic vocabulary word lists, the mismatch between the knowledge of words and understanding of their inner structure by learners noted in some recent research (e.g. McLean 2018; Ward and Chuenjundaeng 2009) indicates that not enough attention is given to building derivational awareness in language instruction. At the same time, the knowledge of word-formation patterns makes the process of vocabulary learning more efficient (Nation 2001), and has a positive effect on one's vocabulary skills like using words appropriately in terms of grammar and meaning, on understanding how words are linked with other words in terms of their morphology and semantic relationships as well as on breadth/range of one's vocabulary (Agbayani 2021; Priskinanda et al. 2021). The use of morphologically complex words, for example, *inexplicit* < *in-* + *explicit*, *government* < *govern* + *-ment*, also contributes to complexity of writing thus making the text more academic (Coxhead and Byrd 2007).

The current research aims to investigate if the use of morphologically complex words coincides with the learner's written language proficiency development, and if so, whether it is connected with the markers' evaluations of their written work. In this study, we treat the learner's ability to use morphologically complex words as a probable evidence of their derivational awareness, which can be viewed by the marker as a positive contributor to the perception of the learner's vocabulary as being complex and hence suitable for academic purposes.

In what follows, we first review the literature to outline the importance of lexical complexity and its connection with derivational complexity. We then focus on the development of derivational awareness in learners and present the framework and the outline of the current study. The results of the statistical analysis of the collected data are further clarified in the qualitative analysis section. We conclude by providing some pedagogical implications of the study and directions for future research.

Lexical Complexity and Derivational Complexity

Complexity in the foreign language teaching context is reflected in a wide range of characteristics of a learner's language that include vocabulary, grammatical constructions as well as communicative functions and genres. Lexical complexity is often referred to as 'lexical richness' or 'lexical diversity', that is, 'the range and the variety of vocabulary deployed in a text by either a speaker or a writer' (McCarthy and Jarvis 2007: 459). The indicators that are commonly associated with lexical diversity are the range of vocabulary, the use of the so-called 'sophisticated' (or advanced) low-frequency words as well as type/token ratio (TTR) (Ellis and Barkhuizen 2005). High levels of lexical diversity contribute to the overall complexity of the produced language, and complexity is concomitantly connected to a learner's language proficiency, alongside accuracy and fluency. Hence it is not surprising that measures of lexical diversity (e.g. vocabulary size test scores) have proven to be strong predictors of the level of general language proficiency in relation to language production and comprehension (Qian 1999; Schmitt, Jiang and Grabe 2011; Staehr 2009).

Complexity of derivational patterns in second language research seems to fall into the more generalized area of lexical complexity/richness (Read 2000). A large variety of lexical richness measures have been proposed in the first and second language acquisition literature with many studies on second/foreign language development examining the extent to which these measures (along with measures of accuracy, fluency and grammatical complexity) can serve as reliable predictors of learners' proficiency (see e.g. Larsen-Freeman 1978; Wolfe-Quintero, Inagaki and Kim 1998; Zareva, Schwanenflugel and Nikolova 2005). The most basic computational approach to the analysis of lexical complexity looks at lexical specificity, that is, the correlation between the word length and the TTR (Grant and Ginther 2000). TTR is computed by dividing the number of types in a text sample by the number of tokens. Type refers to the unique form of the words, and token means the individual words in a corpus. TTR is dependent on the data samples.

The inclusion of word length and TTR as key measures of lexical complexity is intuitively appealing. A greater use of a variety of words within a text signifies a higher level of language proficiency, and studies have noted that advanced second/foreign writers display greater lexical diversity compared to lower-level participants (Grant and Ginther 2000; Jarvis et al. 2003). Also, as shown by Lewis and Frank (2016), languages tend to encode conceptually more complex meanings with longer linguistic forms in general. This is not surprising since morphologically complex words, that is, derivatives (e.g. *unconvincing < convince, disestablishment < establish*), are normally longer and hence should be characterized by a higher degree of conceptual complexity as compared to their derivational bases.[1] Yet, the studies on lexical complexity do not seem to single out derivational complexity and the use of word-formation patterns into a separate measure or an indicator of language proficiency.

While the amount of research that focuses on measuring lexical diversity and its relation to the complexity of a written text is considerable, the role of morphological complexity in contributing to complexity in academic writing seems underexplored. For example, Bulté and Housen (2012) note that only six out of forty analysed studies of language complexity included morphological complexity measures. Moreover, the exploration of morphological complexity is generally limited to inflectional morphology, that is, grammatical markers required by syntax. Morphological complexity is generally understood 'as the diversity of inflectional types of a given word class' (Brezina and Palotti 2019: 100), which means that derivational morphology, that is, formation of new words by means of adding derivational affixes, has been excluded from investigation of morphological complexity.

One of the main reasons for this lack of attention to derivational morphology and its contribution to lexical complexity may be caused by the difficulty in determining whether derivational complexity evidenced in a learner's language output is evidential of the access to morphological knowledge outside of lexicon or whether the use of morphologically complex words is the result of rote learning. In the latter case, there is no awareness of the connection between the derivational base and the derivative in the learner's mind (Jiang 2000). It is also obvious that without formal instruction, first language speakers do not necessarily possess explicit knowledge of the word-formation patterns either. It has been suggested that first language speaker knowledge of the word structure is intuitive rather than conscious, and derivational knowledge is believed to be part of the lexical entry, which is accessed during lexical retrieval (Friedline 2011: 20). Vocabulary size and development of one's vocabulary with age are important factors for building the subconscious understanding of connections between words and intuitive knowledge of word-formation patterns.

On the other hand, the results of studies by Tyler and Nagy (1989) and Nagy et al. (1989) indicate that first language speakers develop a rather clear understanding of the relations between words with similar bases by the age of ten to eleven years. The estimates of vocabulary size at this age vary, but even if we accept a moderate number of 6,400 word families by the age of ten (Coxhead, Nation and Sim 2015), it is evident that such a large vocabulary promotes the development of the intuitive relational knowledge, which allows for making relevant connections between the words that have similar derivational elements, that is, bases and affixes (Tyler and Nagy 1989). This implies that for foreign language learners to acquire similar implicit derivational awareness, their second language vocabulary needs to be quite extensive for the brain to make similar generalizations. It has also been shown that even though second language learners may be able to demonstrate knowledge of a word receptively, their derivational awareness is limited (see Brown et al. 2022 for an overview of empirical studies), which indicates insufficiency of formal instruction within this area. Yet, as justly noted by Sasao and Webb (2017), increasing affix knowledge has shown to have a positive effect on general language proficiency and vocabulary learning, suggesting that explicit instruction on derivational complexity might be beneficial for learners.

Developing Derivational Awareness

It has been suggested that using explicit instruction is beneficial for acquisition of grammatical knowledge. Ellis (2006) stipulates that functionally simple grammatical structures that can be described using rules formulated in non-technical language are easier to acquire as explicit knowledge. This can be applied to vocabulary teaching/learning as well as to developing explicit morphological knowledge. In this regard, the notion of a word family as a unit of lexicon is very useful. A word family 'consists of a base word and all its derived and inflected forms that can be understood by a learner without having to learn each word separately' (Bauer and Nation 1993: 253). The idea behind this approach is that a word family member (e.g. *unteachable* < *teach*) would require little (if any) additional learning as long as the learner is able to recognize the base and is familiar with the common word-building devices in English. Hence, derivational awareness, which is understood as a demonstration of 'students' abilities to manipulate derived words, to recognize connections between different morphological forms of a word, and to produce new derivations of known words' (Kieffer and Lesaux 2008: 784), can be viewed as a desirable outcome of explicit language instruction.

In relation to the development of derivational awareness in EFL/ESL learners, Bauer and Nation (1993) propose a system of levels for affixes in the English language, which is aimed to be used as a practical guide for teaching vocabulary through developing the systemic knowledge of English affixation. Bauer and Nation's (1993) system is based on the assumption that with the development of language proficiency, the learner's awareness of English derivation consequently expands. At the same time, the learner's control of affixation may also be indicative of their language proficiency.[2] The second language research on the acquisition of derivational knowledge (e.g. Friedline 2011; Mäntylä and Huhta 2013; Leontjev, Huhta and Mäntylä 2016; Mochizuki and Aizawa 2000) highlights positive correlations between the knowledge of derivational affixes, vocabulary size and overall language proficiency.

Bauer and Nation's (1993) system classifies affixes into seven levels depending on such criteria as frequency of the affix, its productivity, predictability of the meaning of the affix, regularity of the written and spoken forms of the base and the affix and regularity of the function of the affix. The levels are cumulative, and the approach follows a developmental paradigm where the learner is expected to progress from Level 1 to Level 7 as their language proficiency increases. These levels can also be used as recommendation for the order in which the affixes should be taught. A brief summary of the levels, as explained by Bauer and Nation (1993: 258–62), is presented later.

At Level 1, the learner is only able to recognize individual words with very limited understanding of inflections, which comes at Level 2 (from now on, we will refer to the levels of affixes as L2–L7). L2 affixes include affixes that mark inflectional categories: plurality and possession for nouns, markings for third-person singular present tense, past tense, past participle and -*ing* forms for verbs and expressions of degree for adjectives.

L3 includes frequent, productive and regular derivational affixes, such as -*able*, -*er*, -*ish*, -*less*, -*ly*, -*ness*, -*th*, -*y*, *non-*, *un-*. At this level, regularity of spelling and pronunciation of both the affix and the derivational base and regularity of the function and predictability of meaning are important and distinctions should be made between homonymous suffixes; cf. -*y* is a nominalizer in *decency* and an adjectivalizer in *fatty*, -*ly* is an adjectivalizer in *friendly* and an adverbalizer in *stupidly* (Bauer, Lieber and Plag 2013: 546). Hence, as Bauer and Nation (1993) note, the use of the affixes is rather restricted at L3.

At L4, the focus is on the frequency of the affix rather than its productivity and on the regularity of spelling of the affix rather than its spoken regularity. The affixes included in this level are -*al*, -*ation*, -*ess*, -*ful*, -*ism*, -*ist*, -*ity*, -*ize*, -*ment*, -*ous*, *in-*. While the affixes are generalizable due to their high frequency, the use of the affixes at this level is restricted, that is, allomorphs (*insufficient* vs. *irregular*), spelling variations (-*ation* in *conversation* vs. -*tion* in *revolution*) and unpredictable uses (*successful* vs. *mouthful*) are not included in this level.

L5 affixes are characterized by regular behaviour but are not very frequent and are hence not very generalizable, even though some of them may be productive. L5 affixes include: -*age*, -*al*, -*ally*, -*an*, -*ance*, -*ant*, -*atory*, -*ent*, -*ory*, *mis-*, *sub-* and so on. This level includes the largest number of affixes (fifty affixes).

L6 deals with frequent but irregular affixes like -*able*, -*ee*, -*ic*, -*ify*, -*ion*, -*ist*, -*ition*, -*ive*, -*th*, -*y*, *pre-*, *re-*. These affixes may cause (sometimes) unpredictable orthographic changes in the bases, which include truncations of the base (e.g. *quantity* – *quantify*), additions/insertion of elements (e.g. *represent* – *representative*) or a combination of the two (e.g. *persuade* – *persuasive*). The lack of derivational transparency in the formation of the derivatives at this level explains why some of the affixes (e.g. *-able* as in *permeable*) included here are also featured in previous levels.

Classical roots and affixes (e.g. *pro-ceed, con-duce*), combining forms (e.g. *agri-culture, chrono-logy*) and prefixes like *ab-, ad-, com-, de-, dis-, ex-* and *sub-*, belong to L7 as they are referred to as 'learned word-formation' (Bauer and Nation 2020: 160). This means that despite some regularities that can be found in the structure of derivatives formed at this level, both first and second language speakers need to be taught these forms explicitly (Bauer and Nation 1993: 262).

While Bauer and Nation's (1993) list of affixes is not exhaustive, the principles of assigning affixes to various levels depending on the criteria of frequency, productivity, predictability and regularity provide comprehensive guidelines for setting specific goals in vocabulary teaching. The authors also specify that the ranking of the affixes according to the levels of difficulty should not be viewed as a theoretical framework but is aimed 'to give easily identifiable steps along the cline' (Bauer and Nation 1993: 257). While the system follows the principles of the developmental approach, there is no empirical evidence that the proposed levels correspond to the order of acquisition of derivational affixes. In fact, the acquisitional order of the affixes is yet to be established, and the current study looks at whether the principles underlying Bauer and Nation's (1993) classification can be evidenced in the development of derivational complexity in learners' writing.

Another limitation of Bauer and Nation's (1993) system is that it does not account for explicit or incidental exposure to frequent words with higher-order level affixes, for example, *government, dangerous, independence, American, Japanese*, which learners seem to be able to use even at the lower levels of language proficiency without being aware of their internal structure (Mochizuki and Aizawa 2000).

In this study, we recognize the limitations of Bauer and Nation's (1993) developmental hierarchy of affixes. Since the current research does not aim to test the system but uses it as a tool for the analysis of the degree of derivational awareness as demonstrated in learners' writing, the division of the affixes into the levels of complexity is appropriate for the purposes of this study.

The Current Study

The current research is based on the analysis of a corpus of formal written assessments completed by ten students in the course of study at the English

Language Studies (ELS) programme at Institute of Pacific United (IPU) New Zealand, a private tertiary institution.

Background Information: IPU NZ ELS Programme

The ELS programme at IPU New Zealand is based on the New Zealand Qualifications Authority[3] (NZQA) framework. The language courses that are offered in IPU lead to the academic pathway, that is, they prepare the students for undergraduate tertiary study in New Zealand. To enrol on the programme, the students need to do a placement test if they cannot present evidence of their language proficiency, that is, the results of an internationally recognized English test score. The requirements, aka 'unit standards', for each of the levels of language proficiency correspond to the descriptors of New Zealand English Language qualifications outlined by the NZQA descriptors (NZQA 2019), and the completion of each level results in gaining a New Zealand Certificate in English Language (NZCEL Levels 1–4) at the corresponding level. Each level includes unit standards for individual skills, and in order pass the requirements, the learner is expected to complete the assessments in all skills at this level with a satisfactory result. NZCEL Levels 1 and 2 are General English only. NZCEL Level 3 is subdivided into general and academic sublevels. IPU students need to take NZCEL Level 3 courses in general and academic English consecutively if they want to pursue academic study because of the considerable gap in the outcomes for NZCEL Level 3 General and entry requirements for NZCEL Level 4 Academic courses.[4]

The ELS programme at IPU New Zealand is skills-based, and each skill is taught as an individual module within a course. For each module, the learners receive at least five hours of formal instruction per week for two blocks of six weeks each. Since this research is only concerned with writing, the other modules are not discussed here.

The types of written assessments that students have to complete at different NZCEL levels differ in terms of the purposes of communication, the length of the expected written text, the level of complexity of the discourse and the linguistic range. The assessments correspond to a specific NZCEL unit standard, with two to three unit standards covered in each level.

At Level 2, the assignments include writing short (150 words) texts on familiar topics (e.g. recount, report) and writing a text for a practical purpose (e.g. instruction, directions). Unit standards for Level 3 General English include writing a 250-word text on a familiar topic (e.g. recount), a text for a specific purpose (e.g. giving advice) and a text for a practical purpose (e.g. a cover letter).

Level 3 academic English assessments place a strong focus on developing the students' ability to write clear texts (300–400 words) in academic contexts with the expectation that students are able to demonstrate some research skills. The text types, as determined by the unit standards, include essays, reports as well as research-based descriptions/recounts of events.

NZCEL Level 4 has a strong focus on the development of writing skills required for academic study with a lot of attention being devoted to process writing and student research. The analysed assessments at this level include writing a crafted academic text (e.g. an essay) of at least 800 words in length for academic purposes using researched material and writing an evaluative text of at least 500 words in length for a specific academic purpose.[5] Both types of assessments are completed under conditions that are similar to writing a university assignment, that is, the students research the assigned topic and work on their assignments over the course of six weeks in and outside the class. The students receive general feedback on their writing; formal instruction in class focuses on developing academic writing subskills like creating topic sentences, the structure of the paragraph, using discourse markers, paraphrasing, referencing and so on.

The assignments are marked by the course tutor, whose marking is then moderated by another tutor to ensure the validity of the grade. The assignments are marked on the pass/fail basis.

Methodology

The research question this study aims to answer is whether the use of a variety of affixed derivatives in writing contributes to the perception of the learner's writing as more complex and their vocabulary as more sophisticated, thus being partly responsible for a positive evaluation by the rater. Following the principles of Bauer and Nation's (1993) developmental approach, we also hypothesize that the derivational complexity demonstrated in the use of higher-order affixes increases with the level of language proficiency.

The study is based on the analysis of the formal written assessments completed by ten IPU New Zealand students (104 assessments in total) over two years of their study (2018–19 academic years[6]) in the ELS programme. The scripts were anonymized and all personal data were deleted before the analysis.[7] The grade that the student received (pass/fail) for the assessment as well as the results of the moderation (where applicable) were made available for the purposes of the research.

The collected data for the analysis are comprised of the written assessments at NZCEL Levels 2–4. Level 1 assessments were excluded from the data because most of the students whose work was analysed started their studies at IPU at Level 2. Also, the analysis of the available Level 1 scripts demonstrated minimal to no use of morphologically complex words.

Each script was analysed manually to identify morphologically complex words in the written text and to decide if the word was used appropriately (in terms of grammar, spelling and context). The identified words were then checked against the assignment brief to exclude the repetition of the words from the task. The remaining words were coded for the level of difficulty of the affix (L2–L7) based on Bauer and Nation's (1993) framework. As noted earlier, Bauer and Nation (1993) did not include all the affixes in their description and did not always explicitly specify which level a less regular use of an affix should be assigned. In such cases, the affixes were accounted for following the key principles outlined earlier. For example, the prefix *ac-*, as in *accustomed*, was coded as an L5 affix (i.e. regular but infrequent) and *-ate*, as in *integrate*, as an L7 one (added to the Latin base).[8]

L2 *-ed* and *-ing* affixes were only included in the analysis if they were used derivationally (Example 1) rather than inflectionally (Example 2).

(1) The revised edition of the book includes a glossary.
(2) I revised my presentation slides.

The number of tokens of morphologically complex words for each level, the word count of each text, the type of text (e.g. report, recount, letter, essay), the NZCEL Level (2–4) and the grade (pass/fail) were also included in the data set. Out of 104 submissions, 59 achieved a passing grade, with the overall number of passes higher in Levels 2 and 3 compared to Level 4 (see Table 4.1 for the distribution of grades).

Table 4.1 Data set summary

NZCEL Level	Number of Texts	Total Number of Passes	Total Number of Fails	Total Word Count
2	35	23	12	5,585
3a	18	13	5	5,017
3b	20	15	5	7,036
4	31	8	23	18,270
Total	104	59	45	35,908

The number of different morphologically complex words used in a text, that is, 'lexical diversity', was recorded to account for the range of complex words used by a learner within a script. This was done to account for the repetition of the same word and also for the use of words with multiple affixes. For example, for words like *independently*, which contains the prefix *in-* and the suffixes *-ent* and *-ly*, each of the affixes needed to be entered separately.

Quantitative Analysis

The quantitative analysis of the data aimed at testing the overall hypothesis that the derivational complexity demonstrated in the use of higher-order affixes increases with the level of language proficiency and also detecting any significant effects of morphological complexity factors such as affix level. The average numbers of morphologically complex words assigned to different levels in scripts submitted to NZCEL Level 2, Level 3 General (3a), Level 3 Academic (3b) and Level 4 are provided in Table 4.2 (the mean values for those texts that achieved the required grade and those that did not were calculated separately).

As shown in Table 4.2, student submissions that passed NZCEL levels contain higher numbers of morphologically complex word types, which is especially evident for NZCEL Levels 3b and 4. If we look at the number of morphologically complex words in essays that achieved the passing grade at one level of language proficiency, we can see that it is lower than the number of such words used in texts that did not receive a passing grade at the next level (cf. an average of 5.5 words with L3 affixes per text that passed NZCEL Level 3a vs. 5.8 words per text

Table 4.2 Average number of morphologically complex words in student essays across NZCEL levels

NZCEL Level	Grade	Average Number of Morphologically Complex Words Per Text					
		L2	L3	L4	L5	L6	L7
2	pass	1.4	1	2.2	1	0.2	0
	fail	3.6	1.4	2.2	0.7	0.1	0
3a	pass	2.2	5.5	4.9	2.2	1.4	0.3
	fail	0.8	2.6	4	2.2	0.8	0
3b	pass	3.1	6.3	4.9	2.4	1.8	0
	fail	2.6	5.8	2.6	1.4	0.6	0
4	pass	6.5	13.3	14.5	6.4	8.8	1.3
	fail	4.9	7.6	10	4	7.4	0.3

that did not pass NZCEL Level 3b, respectively). This result suggested that the likelihood of a certain text achieving the passing grade could be predicted not only by NZCEL level and the presence of morphologically complex words but also by the interaction of the two factors, which was considered in regression analysis.

A multiple logistic regression analysis was carried out to investigate the significance of the observed differences, with the students' grade used as the output variable and the random effect of participant included. At the first stage of the regression analysis only simple effects of the independent predictors were accounted for. The logistic regression model showed a significant effect of NZCEL level, as shown in Table 4.3 (the table includes only significant effects). Specifically, the proportion of essays that achieved the passing grade at NZCEL Level 3a and NZCEL Level 4 is significantly different from NZCEL Level 2 (p = 0.049 for NZCEL Level 3a and p = 0.004 for NZCEL Level 4). No significant effect of NZCEL Level 3b was detected at this stage, despite the observed numeric differences displayed in Table 4.2.

Provisional qualitative analysis of the texts showed that at lower levels of language proficiency, that is, NZCEL Level 2, the use of morphologically complex words was limited. Furthermore, the observed distribution of marks, namely the fact that average numbers of morphologically complex words required for texts to achieve the passing grade were consistently increasing across NZCEL levels, indicated that a possible interaction between NZCEL level and the number of morphologically complex words needed to be taken into consideration. Further multiple logistic regression analysis was carried out; the model included the same variables as the simple model described earlier, the random effect of participant and the interaction between NZCEL level and the number of morphologically complex words.

The significant interaction effects of the regression model summarized in Table 4.4 indicate that the number of morphologically complex words assigned

Table 4.3 Output of a multiple logistic regression model predicting the students' grade, simple effects only

Model formula:
achieved ~ n_level2 + n_level3 + n_level4 + n_level5 + n_level6 + n_level7 + total_tokens + total_types + n_lexdiversity + text_size + NZCEL_level + text_type + (1 | participant)

	Estimate	Std. Error	z value	p value
Intercept	−22.100	373.913	−0.059	0.952
NZCEL_level3a	−2.833	1.439	−1.969	0.049 *
NZCEL_level4	−11.504	3.965	−2.901	0.004**

Intercept levels: n_level1, NZCEL_level2, text_typecompare

Table 4.4 Output of a multiple logistic regression model predicting the students' grade, interaction terms included

Model formula:
achieved ~ n_level2 * NZCEL_level + n_level3 * NZCEL_level + n_level4 * NZCEL_level + n_level5 * NZCEL_level + n_level6 * NZCEL_level + n_level7 * NZCEL_level + total_tokens + total_types + text_type + n_lexdiversity + text_size + (1 | participant)

	Estimate	Std. Error	z value	p value
Intercept	−64.110	1362	0.000	0.999
NZCEL_level3b	−12.280	5.915	−2.076	0.038*
NZCEL_level4	−44.860	2.225	−2.016	0.044*
n_level5	3.789	1.487	2.548	0.011*
text_size	0.025	0.014	1.702	0.089
NZCEL_level4:n_level3	1.159	0.655	1.768	0.077
NZCEL_level4:n_level5	−3.162	1.414	−2.236	0.0254*

Intercept levels: n_level1, NZCEL_level2, text_typecompare

to L3–L5 are significant predictors of the grades of essays submitted for NZCEL Level 4. In addition to this, simple effect of NZCEL level holds in this model (p = 0.038 for NZCEL Level 3b, p = 0.044 for NZCEL Level 4) and the number of morphologically complex words that contain L5 affixes turned out to be a significant predictor of the students' grade (p = 0.011). The model including the interaction term demonstrated a better fit to the data, as shown by an ANOVA test (χ^2 = 48.652, Df = 16, p < 0.001), and therefore better explains the observed distribution of the grades. The significance of the interaction between NZCEL level and the number of morphologically complex words suggests that the students' marks are more sensitive to the presence of morphologically complex words at higher NZCEL levels.

This result is substantiated by a conditional inference tree analysis (see Figure 4.1), which is based on splitting the data set repeatedly so that 'the split leads to the best increase in terms of classification accuracy or in terms of some other statistical criterion when it comes to predicting the dependent variable' (Gries 2019: 618). Tree-based methods are particularly useful for analysing corpus data because, as pointed out in Gries (2019), they better match the distribution of corpus-based data sets (see also Hothorn, Hornik and Zeileis 2006 for more in-depth discussion of the method).

The conditional tree displayed in Figure 4.1 shows that NZCEL level is a significant predictor of the final grade, with an overall lower number of passes at Level 4 (Node 3), compared to other levels. In addition to that, the total number of morphologically complex word tokens is a significant predictor of NZCEL

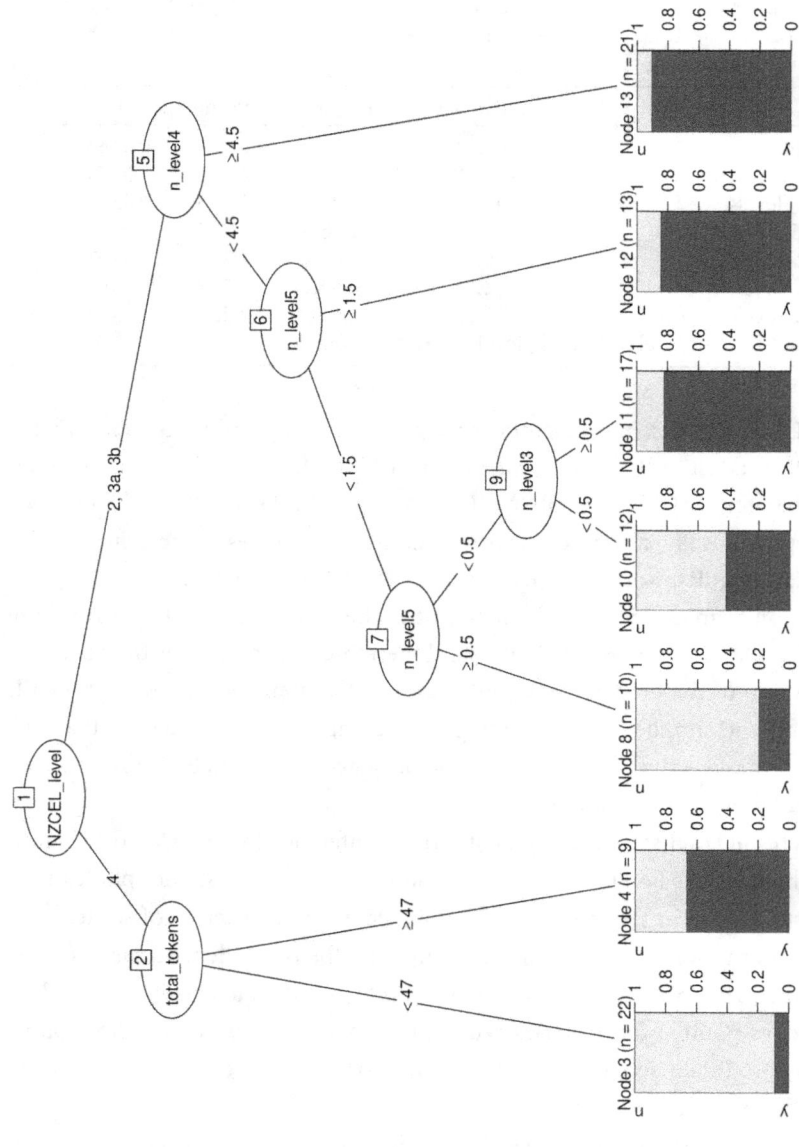

Figure 4.1 A conditional tree analysis of the relationship between the students' grade (passing grade achieved = y, not achieved = n), text type, NZCEL level, the total number of morphologically complex words and the number of morphologically complex words assigned to specific levels.

Level 4 grades, with higher number of passes observed among texts containing over forty-seven tokens of morphologically complex words (Node 4). For NZCEL Levels 2 and 3, the number of morphologically complex words can also be a valid predictor of the final grade. Moreover, the grade appears sensitive to the level of affix complexity as the essays that were granted a pass also tend to contain a higher number of L3 (Node 9), L4 (Node 5) and L5 (Nodes 6 and 7) affixes, compared to scripts that did not achieve pass in the required NZCEL level.

Thus, the key findings of the quantitative analysis indicate that (1) the demonstrated derivational complexity is a possible predictor for a passing grade, and (2) derivational complexity increases with the level of language proficiency, which is seen through the number of affixes used, their variety, the range of morphologically complex words and the use of higher-order affixes. This may also mean that for the learner to get the passing grade, they are expected to demonstrate higher levels of derivational awareness.

Qualitative Analysis

The following discussion is organized around the analysis of the scripts by level of language proficiency to provide qualitative insights into some of the trends identified in the quantitative analysis.

NZCEL Level 2

The statistical analysis described earlier indicated the lack of interaction between the passing grade and derivational complexity at lower levels of language proficiency, that is, NZCEL Level 2. This can be explained by the stronger focus on the clarity of the communicated messages and grammatical accuracy, which our study did not measure. Overall, the range of morphologically complex words used in Level 2 assessments is quite limited, and the learners tend to repeat one or two of such words several times within the assignment. For example, note the use of the word *famous* in Example 3 from a descriptive report.

(3) Taranaki is the famous mountain in New Zealand. . . . There are many famous animals in New Zealand. . . . Tuatara is the most famous reptile . . . Whales, dolphins, penguins and sea lions are also famous sea animals in New Zealand. (Level 2, Text 9)

Level 2 scripts demonstrate frequent use of the suffix *-ing* especially in deverbal nouns denoting activities (*skating, snowboarding*) as well as in adjectives (*interesting, exciting*), gerunds (*writing, studying*) and participles used adjectivally (*baking dish*). The use of the suffix *-ed* is limited to only three adjectives (*surprised, bored, excited*) and some adjectival uses of the past participle (*condensed/ sweetened milk, melted butter*). Most affixed forms included here are homonyms of the inflectional *-ing* and *-ed* suffixes. Such homonymy promotes their use with a variety of bases even at a lower level of language proficiency, which is consistent with Bauer and Nation's (1993) developmental approach.

L3 affixes used in NZCEL Level 2 writing include: *-ly* (*suddenly, easily*), *-er* (*player, teacher*), *-y* (*sleepy, funny*), *-able* (*comfortable*), *un-* (*unfortunately*). The lexical variety seems to be very limited, and the same affixed words seem to be repeated by different learners in different assignments.

Morphologically complex words that use Level 4 affixes demonstrate slightly more diversity of the derivational bases: *-al* (*national, international, normal*), *-ation* (*population, celebration, education*), *-ful* (*wonderful, beautiful*), *-ity* (*Christianity*), *-ment* (*equipment, commencement, government*), *-ous* (*famous, dangerous*), *in-* (*independence*). While the range of derivational bases is higher, the number of words formed with L4 affixes across NZCEL Level 2 scripts is limited to higher-frequency vocabulary.

The use of L5 affixes at NZCEL Level 2 is rather restricted and, though the number of tokens may be relatively high in some of the analysed scripts, the range of morphologically complex words is narrow. The list of affixed words is as follows: *-an* (*Indian, West Papuan*), *-ally* (*especially, eventually*), *-en* (*wooden*), *-ence* (*difference, independence*), *-ent* n. (*ingredient*), *-ent* adj. (*independent, different*), *-ese* (*Japanese*), *inter-* (*international*). The use of Level 6 affixes is limited to the suffix *-ive* (*native*), which was only used in the assignments where the students had to write a descriptive report about a country.

Overall, the use of morphologically complex words in Level 2 scripts is limited, and while some of the more complex affixes are used, these usually occur in frequent words and the learners may not be aware of their internal structure.

NZCEL Level 3

The assessments for NZCEL Level 3 General and NZCEL Level 3 Academic are analysed together. The qualitative analysis does not indicate a considerable difference in the demonstrated derivational awareness between general and academic scripts apart from the use of discourse markers, for example, for signposting, introducing an opinion and also for salutations (*firstly, secondly, thirdly, finally, in conclusion, in my opinion, in addition, faithfully, sincerely*). These are commonly observed in academic scripts and can be attributed to explicit instruction on structuring academic discourse that the learners receive in class. As these expressions are formulaic in nature and are learned via rote learning, they may not be understood as complex words by learners. Yet, their use in writing contributes to the positive evaluation of the student's work.

Overall, there is a considerable difference in the number of complex words used compared to NZCEL Level 2 assessments. The lexical diversity of the morphologically complex words is definitely higher, with the count of different morphologically complex words increasing from 3.68 to 9.6 per script on average. The overall growth of vocabulary is one of the most plausible explanations for the use of more complex words at this level of proficiency with more words formed with higher-level affixes used at this level, for example, L5 affixes *-al* (*arrival*), *-ally* (*enthusiastically*), *-ance* (*performance*), *-ant* (*assistant*), *-ship* (*relationship*), *ac-* (*accustomed*); some L6 affixes, for example, *-ive* (*positive, negative*), *-ion* (*conclusion, opinion*); and some L7 words, for example, *photograph, biography, psychology*.

A closer look at the students' writing at this level of proficiency provides evidence of growing derivational awareness and development of relational knowledge. This can be observed across several assessments completed by one learner (*responsible – responsibilities, known – unknown, comfortable – uncomfortable*) as well as on the level of one assessment, like in the Examples 4 and 5:

(4) (from a cover letter) I am always enthusiastic to meet new people. . . . I always work hard and enthusiastically. (Level 3, Text 4)

(5) (from the description of an artist) I think that Mariana Grande is so famous because she is very sincere. . . . Finally, her sincerity also makes her popular. (Level 3, Text 6)

L3 and L4 affixes that are used in NZCEL Level 3 scripts are largely the same as those noted in the analysis on NZCEL Level 2 assessments. There is a notable increase in the number of words containing L3 and L4 affixes, with the average number of words with L3 affixes increasing from 1 at NZCEL Level 2 to 5.5 at NZCEL Level 3a and 6.3 at NZCEL Level 3b. The average number of words with L4 affixes also increased from 2.2 at NZCEL Level 2 to 4.9 at NZCEL Levels 3a and 3b (as shown in Table 4.2). Furthermore, the variety of words that contain L3 and L4 affixes has increased, which may serve as evidence of the development of understanding how the words may be related to each other in terms of their morphological structure. For example, the suffix *-ly* is used with four bases at NZCEL Level 2 and with thirteen bases at NZCEL Level 3.

The use of more complex affixes is very limited at this level, and most of the examples of words with L6 and L7 affixes had to be excluded from the data due to their incorrect spelling (**qualifecation*, **representitive*) or use (*deduce* where *deduct* should be used, etc.).

NZCEL Level 4

The analysed scripts at this level demonstrate a considerable increase in the use of morphologically complex words and the use of affixes of all levels of complexity with the most notable changes in the number of higher-level affixes (L4–L7). As shown in the statistical analysis earlier (see Figure 4.1), the demonstrated derivational awareness is associated with the passing grade at this level of language proficiency in particular.

The number of morphologically complex words formed with the lower-level affixes (L2–L3) doubles compared to the average for the previous level (i.e. Level 3b). Moreover, the affixed words are characterized by a higher descriptive value and/or association with academic discourse. For example, we can observe an increase in expressions like *according (to)*, *discussed/analysed/evaluated (question/aspect)*, *trusted (source)*, *notwithstanding*, *similarly* and so on. Some of these are formulaic and were probably explicitly taught in class, so they may not serve as evidence of derivational awareness, yet it is obvious that their use is expected at this level.

Another notable trend is a considerable increase in the use of the suffix *-ly*, which occurs in evaluative/commenting adverbs that express degree (*slightly, totally, utterly, entirely*), certainty (*clearly, obviously, apparently, evidently*) and attitude (*interestingly, surprisingly*), all of which are typical of academic discourse.

All of the types of L4 affixes listed by Bauer and Nation (1993) are utilized in the analysed assignments, apart from the suffix *-ish*. The non-occurrence of this particular suffix does not necessarily mean that the students are not aware of it. Out of four main uses of this adjective-forming suffix listed in OED (n.d.), only the first sense, that is, forming nationality adjectives (*British, English*), seems to be suitable for academic writing, while the others (e.g. *boyish, brownish, earlyish*) do not seem to associate with formal discourse.

The lists of words containing L4 affixes are more extensive for the scripts that received a passing grade with the wide variety of bases to which the affixes are attached to. This becomes particularly noticeable when we look at the scripts cumulatively. For example, the adjectival suffix -*al* is used with seventeen bases (*environmental, mechanical, occupational, conversational, medical, professional, clinical, additional, physical, digital, natural, tropical, international, original, national, unusual, psychological*), which is a notable increase from NZCEL Level 3 assignments, where the affix was used with only four bases across the scripts.

The increase in the use of more complex affixes (L5–L7) is not surprising; however, words formed with L6 affixes occur more frequently than those formed with L5 affixes. Bauer and Nation (1993: 260–1) identify L5 affixes as 'regular but infrequent' and L6 as 'frequent but irregular', so the frequency of the affixes in English (and, possibly, learners' exposure to them) could be responsible for this disproportion.

The most frequently occurring L5 affixes of this level are -*ant/-ent* (*consultant, assistant, nutrient, pollutant*) and -*ance/-ence* (*difference, evidence, reference, significance*) with most of the frequently used words being repeated across the scripts. It is obvious that the lack of predictability in the spelling of these affixes causes confusion for the learners, and we had to exclude a number of tokens which were spelled incorrectly (e.g. **assistent, *defendent, *clearence*).

Most of the L6-affixed words that are used in the scripts are formed with the suffix -*ion* (*production, solution, attention, destruction, commission*, etc.). Another observable trend is the use of the suffix -*th* (*strength, length, wealth, growth*). While Bauer and Nation (1993) assigned these suffixes to L6 due to homography and allomorphy of the affixes and/or bases they attach to, both of which may cause issues with segmentation, their formal resemblance to lower-level affixes together with their general frequency and productivity may contribute to their availability for acquisition.

The extension of the range of words that employ the suffix -*ive*, both adjectives (*destructive, impressive, effective, ineffective, attractive, consecutive*) and nouns (*initiative, representative, incentive, explosives, perspective*), is also apparent, while at the lower levels of proficiency, the use of this affix is limited to only three high-frequency adjectives (*positive, negative* and *native*). The lower-frequency words used in NZCEL Level 4 assignments are characterized by specificity of meaning, thus contributing to clarity and precision of expression.

While the average number of L7 affixes per essay increases at NZCEL Level 4 compared to Level 3a (from 0.3 to 1.3), their overall use is very marginal, as shown in Table 4.1, which explains no significant effect of the number of L7 affixes in the statistical analysis. The more frequent occurrence of words formed with L7 affixes is probably best accounted for by the specificity and the complexity of the topics that the students discussed in their assignments, for example, environmental issues, technological advances and their influence on society, evaluation of an academic source and so on. The most common words are usually neoclassical compounds, that is, complex words that consist of combining forms of Greek and Latin origin, for example, *agriculture, methodology, sociology, photography, bibliography, geography*. While it is possible to suggest that learners may be familiar with frequent elements of neoclassical compounds like *-ology* and *-graphy*, it is hard to assert that the same is true for examples like *herbicide, pesticide*, which students may have been exposed to while researching the assigned topic. Also, there is no evidence that would suggest that the learners are aware of the internal structure of the words in which affixes attach to bound bases, even though these may be used in writing, for example, the use of the suffix *-ate* which occurs in words like *coagulate, disintegrate, separate, eradicate*, in one of the analysed scripts.

Another notable trend at this level of proficiency is the increase in the number of multi-affixed words, that is, words that are formed using several affixes, for example, *environmentally, unnoticeable* and so on. The statistical analysis showed a significant effect of lexical diversity (the use of different morphologically complex words) at NZCEL Levels 3 and 4, which suggests that the number of different morphologically complex words is a valid predictor for the passing grade. While the counts for lexical diversity are lower than the number of tokens in the NZCEL Level 4 scripts, the assignments that received a passing grade are characterized by the use of a variety of words derived from the same base, some of which may employ several affixes, for example, *occupied, occupational, unoccupied*.

Overall, a wider range of morphologically complex words on the level of an individual script and across the range is characteristic of NZCEL Level 4 writing and, as shown by the regression analysis (see Table 4.4), turns out to be a significant factor in the positive evaluation of students' writing. This, to a degree, correlates with the interaction between lexical diversity and language proficiency discussed earlier: the students seem to be expected to demonstrate the ability to use a variety of morphologically complex words and also a higher degree of complexity of these words through using higher-level complex affixes and multi-affixed derivatives.

The statistical analysis demonstrated a striking increase in morphological complexity of student writing at NZCEL Level 4 in particular. It is evident that since this level has a strong focus on the development of knowledge and skills required for academic study, introduction of research-based tasks that involve investigating complex topics, reading and analysing the information from academic sources and so on provides for incidental exposure to more complex and sophisticated vocabulary thus contributing, though indirectly, to the expansion of derivational knowledge.

Concluding Remarks

The presented analysis indicates that morphological complexity is an important predictor of writing quality, and that derivational awareness becomes more important at higher levels of language proficiency when learners are preparing for academic study. However, it is necessary to point out that it is certainly not the only factor determining the passing grade nor should it be the only one. While other factors like syntactic complexity, task achievement, clarity of communicated messages and so on are relevant, these are out of the scope of this analysis and were not accounted for.

The results of our analysis strongly resonate with Bauer and Nation's (1993) developmental approach and show that an increase in general language proficiency correlates with the growth of derivational awareness even in the absence of targeted morphological instruction. We observed a gradual increase in the types of affixes used, their levels of complexity and also the growth of relational knowledge as learners progress in their studies. The fact that derivational awareness seems to increase naturally with the expansion of one's vocabulary knowledge seems to raise a question if explicit instruction on morphological analysis is really necessary.

Nation's (2007) four strands principle, which stipulates the necessity of balancing meaning-focused input, meaning-focused output, fluency development and language-focused learning, accounts for incidental development of derivational knowledge. The first three of these strands are message-focused, and acquisition of systemic language knowledge is achieved through meaningful exposure to language through reading and listening, meaningful oral and written interaction and becoming fluent in the four skills through practice. While Bauer and Nation (2020) recommend that targeted language-focused instruction (teaching) should not take more than its fair share of the course time, they also point out that a large number of words in English 'are partly motivated, in that their structure reflects something of their meaning, and systematic exploitation of this motivation can ease the load of learning new vocabulary' (Bauer and Nation 2020: 1). Hence, developing understanding of word parts through giving deliberate attention to this aspect of language knowledge in class would allow for increasing the learners' ability to process vocabulary and enrich vocabulary knowledge (Bauer and Nation 2020: 10). Evidence from research on reading (Zhang 2015) also suggests that the ability to analyse word structure enhances building reading vocabulary. The results of the research presented here provide corroborative evidence of the positive effect of morphological awareness on production. Correspondingly, activities that focus on the analysis of complex words and their parts and learning about the meanings and functions of the most useful affixes will help raise awareness of word families hence contributing to the development of a more strategic approach of memorizing vocabulary as well as providing learners with a useful tool for autonomous learning. Bauer and Nation (2020: 10–17) provide ideas for useful activities aimed at raising derivational awareness that can be easily integrated in any teaching context.

It is worth pointing out, however, that focused teaching/learning of word parts should be appropriate for the level of language proficiency. The role of factors that Bauer and Nation (1993) set out as principles for assigning affixes to various levels (i.e. frequency of the affix, its productivity, predictability of the meaning of the affix, regularity of the written and spoken forms of the base and the affix and regularity of the function of the affix) cannot be underestimated. Our analysis clearly demonstrated that at each new level of language proficiency the morphological complexity increases in relation to those factors (even though some of the factors may have more influence than others). This indicates that development of derivational awareness by a learner is not haphazard and that these principles are applicable for investigation of the acquisitional order of the affixes in second/foreign language, which will be valuable for creation of targeted vocabulary teaching programmes to allow for more effective vocabulary teaching and learning.

Acknowledgements

We would like to thank Glenn Wickins for selecting, compiling and anonymizing the files for analysis as well as for his feedback on the early version of the parts of the chapter. We are also very grateful to the editor of the volume for constructive feedback and useful recommendations.

Notes

1 Derivatives formed by means of clipping (*exam* < *examination*), back formation (*edit* < *editor*) and blending (*infotainment* < *information* + *entertainment*) are excluded from our analysis since we only focus on affixed derivatives in this study.

2. Not surprisingly, some international language proficiency tests (e.g. Cambridge First Certificate in English, Certificate in Advanced English, Cambridge C2 Proficiency exam) include tasks that check the learner's ability to apply the knowledge of word-formation patterns.
3. NZQA is the New Zealand government organization that administers educational assessment and qualifications. NZQA framework is 'based on outcomes, described in terms of knowledge, skills and attributes, and their application' (NZQA 2019: 2).
4. The ELS programme in IPU only offers the courses that lead to the academic study, hence, for the reasons of space, we will not go into further detail on the division of the levels in NZQA framework.
5. The tasks for the assignments are based on NZQA Unit Standards #22750 and #3040 where the students '[W]rite a crafted text for a specified audience using researched material in English for an academic purpose' and '[W]rite an evaluation for a specific purpose in an academic context', respectively (NZQA 2019: 35). Hence the main difference is in the purpose of writing with the former being an expository text and the latter an evaluative one.
6. The academic year in New Zealand begins in late February or early March (end of summer) and finishes in November (spring). Even if an institution operates on a trimester rather than a semester system (as is the case with IPU New Zealand), the academic year still corresponds to the calendar year for consistency.
7. The research was granted a Human Ethics approval (#2021-06-09-16) by IPU New Zealand Research Committee.
8. In cases like these, judgements on the regularity and frequency of the affix were made based on the recommendations in Bauer, Lieber and Plag (2013) as well as OED online.

References

Agbayani, R. (2021), 'Redesigning Approach in Developing Vocabulary Skills among English Language (ESL) Learners: Efficacy of Direct Morphological Instruction', *International Journal of English Literature and Social Sciences*, 6 (1): 241–7.

Bauer, L., R. Lieber and I. Plag (2013), *The Oxford Reference Guide to English Morphology*, Oxford: Oxford University Press.

Bauer, L. and I. S. P. Nation (1993), 'Word Families', *International Journal of Lexicography*, 6 (4): 253–79.

Bauer, L. and I. S. P. Nation (2020), *English Morphology for the Language Teaching Profession*, New York: Routledge.

Brezina V. and G. Pallotti (2019), 'Morphological Complexity in Written L2 Texts', *Second Language Research*, 35 (1): 99–119.

Brown, D., T. Stoeckel, S. Mclean and J. Stewart (2022), 'The Most Appropriate Lexical Unit for L2 Vocabulary Research and Pedagogy: A Brief Review of the Evidence', *Applied Linguistics*, 43 (3): 596–602.

Bruce, I. (2008), *Academic Writing and Genre: A Systematic Analysis*, London: Continuum.

Bruce, I. (2021), 'Towards an EAP without Borders: Developing Knowledge, Practitioners, and Communities', *International Journal of English for Academic Purposes: Research and Practice*, 2021 (Spring): 23–37.

Bulté, B. and A. Housen (2012), 'Defining and Operationalising L2 Complexity', in A. Housen, F. Kuiken and I. Vedder (eds), *Dimensions of L2 Performance and Proficiency: Complexity Accuracy and Fluency in SLA*, 21–46, Amsterdam: Benjamins.

Coxhead, A. and P. Byrd (2007), 'Preparing Writing Teachers to Teach the Vocabulary and Grammar of Academic Prose', *Journal of Second Language Writing*, 16 (3): 129–47.

Coxhead, A., I. S. P. Nation and D. Sim (2015), 'Measuring the Vocabulary Size of Native Speakers of English in New Zealand Secondary Schools', *New Zealand Journal of Educational Studies*, 50 (1): 121–35.

Ellis, R. (2006), 'Current Issues in the Teaching of Grammar: An SLA Perspective', *TESOL Quarterly*, 40 (1): 83–107.

Ellis, R. and G. Barkhuizen (2005), *Analysing Learner Language*, Oxford: Oxford University Press.

Friedline, B. E. (2011), 'Challenges in the Second Language Acquisition of Derivational Morphology: From Theory to Practice', PhD diss., University of Pittsburgh, Pittsburgh.

Grant, L. and A. Ginther (2000), 'Using Computer-Tagged Linguistic Features to Describe L2 Writing Differences', *Journal of Second Language Writing*, 9 (2): 123–45.

Gries, S. (2019), 'On Classification Trees and Random Forests in Corpus Linguistics: Some Words of Caution and Suggestions for Improvement', *Corpus Linguistics and Linguistic Theory*, 16 (3): 616–47.

Hothorn, T., K. Hornik and A. Zeileis (2006), 'Unbiased Recursive Partitioning: A Conditional Inference Framework', *Journal of Computational and Graphical Statistics*, 15 (3): 651–74.

Jarvis, S., L. Grant, D. Bikowski and D. Ferris (2003), 'Exploring Multiple Profiles of Highly Rated Learner Compositions', *Journal of Second Language Writing*, 12 (4): 377–403.

Jiang, N. (2000), 'Lexical Representation and Development in a Second Language', *Applied Linguistics*, 21 (1): 47–77.

Kieffer, M. and N. Lesaux (2008), 'The Role of Morphology in the Reading Comprehension of Spanish-Speaking English Language Learners', *Reading and Writing*, 21 (8): 783–804.

Larsen-Freeman, D. (1978), 'An ESL Index of Development', *TESOL Quarterly*, 12 (4): 439–48.

Leontjev, D., A. Huhta and K. Mäntylä (2016), 'Word Derivational Knowledge and Writing Proficiency: How do They Link?', *System*, 59 (1): 73–89.

Lewis, M. and M. Frank (2016), 'The Length of Words Reflects their Conceptual Complexity', *Cognition*, 153: 182–95.

Mäntylä, K. and A. Huhta (2013), 'Knowledge of Word Parts', in J. Milton and T. Fitzpatrick (eds), *Dimensions of Vocabulary Knowledge*, 45–59, Basingstoke: Palgrave McMillan.

McCarthy, P. M. and S. Jarvis (2007), 'vocd: A Theoretical and Empirical Evaluation', *Language Testing*, 24 (4): 459–88.

McLean, S. (2018), 'Evidence for the Adoption of the Flemma as an Appropriate Word Counting Unit', *Applied Linguistics*, 39 (6): 823–45.

Mochizuki, M. and K. Aizawa (2000), 'An Affix Acquisition Order for EFL Learners: An Exploratory Study', *System*, 28 (2): 291–304.

Nagy, W., R. Anderson, M. Schommer, J. Scott and A. Stallman (1989), 'Morphological Families in the Internal Lexicon', *Reading Research Quarterly*, 24 (3): 262–82.

Nation, I. S. P. (2001), *Learning Vocabulary in another Language*, Cambridge: Cambridge University Press.

Nation, I. S. P. (2007). 'The Four Strands', *Innovation in Language Learning and Teaching*, 1 (1): 1–12.

NZQA (2019), 'New Zealand Certificates in English Language Levels 1–5'. Available online: https://www.nzqa.govt.nz/qualifications-standards/qualifications/english-language-qualifications/ (accessed 25 June 2022).

OED (n.d.), *Oxford English Dictionary Online*, 3rd edn, Oxford: Oxford University Press. Available online: http://www.oed.com (accessed 25 June 2022).

Priskinanda, A., Y. Nahak, T. Wea and B. Bram (2021), 'Morphological Awareness Instruction for ESL Students' Vocabulary Development and Reading Comprehension', *ELT Worldwide*, 8 (1): 40–51.

Qian, D. D. (1999), 'Assessing the Roles of Depth and Breadth of Knowledge in Reading Comprehension', *Canadian Modern Language Review*, 56 (2): 282–308.

Read, J. (2000), *Assessing Vocabulary*, Oxford: Oxford University Press.

Sasao, Y. and S. Webb (2017), 'The Word Part Levels Test', *Language Teaching Research*, 21 (1): 12–30.

Schmitt, N., X. Jiang and W. Grabe (2011), 'The Percentage of Words Known in a Text and Reading Comprehension', *The Modern Language Journal*, 95 (1): 26–43.

Staehr, L. (2009), 'Vocabulary Knowledge and Advanced Listening Comprehension in English as a Foreign Language', *Studies in Second Language Acquisition*, 31 (4): 577–607.

Tyler, A. and W. Nagy (1989), 'The Acquisition of English Derivational Morphology', *Journal of Memory and Language*, 28 (6): 649–67.

Ward, J. and J. Chuenjundaeng (2009), 'Suffix Knowledge: Acquisition and Applications', *System*, 37 (3): 461–69.

Wolfe-Quintero, K. S. Inagaki and H.-Y. Kim (1998), *Second Language Development in Writing: Measures of Fluency, Accuracy, and Complexity*, Honolulu: University of Hawai'i, Second Language Teaching and Curriculum Center.

Zareva, A., P. Schwanenflugel and Y. Nikolova (2005), 'Relationship between Lexical Competence and Language Proficiency—Variable Sensitivity', *Studies in Second Language Acquisition*, 27 (4): 567–95.

Zhang, H. (2015), 'Morphological Awareness in Vocabulary Acquisition among Chinese-Speaking Children: Testing Partial Mediation via Lexical Inference Ability', *Reading Research Quarterly*, 50 (1): 129–42.

5

Non-Finite Clause Use in Novice and Expert Academic Writing

A Corpus-Driven Analysis for EAP Writing Instruction

J. Elliott Casal and Xixin Qiu

Introduction

Complementing a rich history in English for Academic Purposes (EAP) research on phraseological and lexical conventions of community-specific genre practices, a growing number of studies are adopting syntactic lenses, emphasizing the use of complex structures. Particularly since Biber and Gray (2010) demonstrated that noun phrases are uniquely complex written academic discourse as compared to speech, researchers have carefully attended to the use of complex noun phrases in expert and learner academic writing (e.g. Ansarifar, Shahriari and Pishghadam 2018; Casal and Lee 2019; Li, Nikitina and Riget 2022; Parkinson and Musgrave 2014; Ziaeian and Golparvar 2022). The contributions of this research have been considerable, as such scholarship has highlighted important characteristics of the developmental trajectory of second language (L2) English academic writers' linguistic repertoires and the relationships between noun phrase elaboration and ratings of writing quality.

Clausal complexity perspectives have also long since factored prominently in research on proficiency development (particularly in writing), although non-finite clause (NFC) use has not been a major emphasis in EAP research. In part, the recent attention to complex noun phrases can be justified by the important differences in how noun phrases are used in academic domains of written discourse compared to other domains of discourse (Biber and Gray 2010; Biber, Gray and Poonpon 2011). However, NFCs are also strongly associated with written academic English (Biber et al. 1999). Much recent scholarship in EAP has more closely targeted the ways that writers vary their use of particular syntactic structures in the realization of functional or rhetorical goals (e.g. Lu, Casal and Liu 2020). Learners may benefit from instructional attention to the genre- and community-specific usage patterns of linguistic features, even when frequency-based patterns do not suggest observable differences in use. With a pedagogical aim in mind, the present study is an ongoing analysis of NFC use in expert and student research writing in agricultural sciences that is a continuation of the authors' interest in the development of second language academic literacy skills.

Non-Finite Clause Use in L2 Writing and Academic Discourse

As writing complexity research has proliferated in EAP over the past decade, it has become well established that many clausal subordination indices (e.g. finite dependent clauses) are more strongly associated with conversational communication, while phrasal indices (e.g. complex nominals) effectively distinguish advanced written academic discourse from other domains of English discourse (e.g. Biber and Gray 2010; Biber, Gray and Poonpon 2011; Biber et al. 1999; Staples, Laflair and Egbert 2017). However, NFCs, an index often operationalized under clausal subordination, also represent an important feature of academic written discourse. In particular Biber and colleagues (Biber and Gray 2010; Biber, Gray and Poonpon 2011) report that non-finite reduced relative clauses (e.g. *genes **involved** in different pathways*; *cultivars **showing** orange-to-red colour*) and non-finite noun complement clauses (e.g. *ability **to** flourish*; *effects of **adding** starches*) occur with greater abundance in academic writing than in conversation for the purpose of information compression. Such structural subtypes of NFCs form complex nominal phrases (Biber et al. 1999), thus increasing nominal complexity. Affirming the importance of non-finite structures within noun phrases, Shadloo, Ahmadi and Ghonsooly (2019) found that higher use of non-finite relative clauses is associated with increased quality of writing in academic essays, and Casal and Lee (2019) found significantly greater use of post-modifying participles in highly rated student writing in their analysis of student research papers written by L2 English writers.

Thus, while the importance of phrasal complexity in the analysis and teaching of academic English discourse practices is clear, there is also evidence that points towards the importance of at least some non-finite clausal structures from frequency-based perspectives. Attention to the role and function of non-finite elements in academic writing practices has also been fruitful, as recent research has reported differences in the use of NFCs in research articles across disciplines (e.g. Casal et al. 2021; Ziaeian and Golparvar 2022), across sections/part-genres (Casal et al. 2021) and across rhetorical stages within sections (e.g. Lu, Casal and Liu 2020). Turning to L2 writers, Atak and Saricaoglu (2021) found that first language (L1) Turkish learners of English at intermediate proficiency level progressed from reliance on finite relative clauses to non-finite relative clauses in argumentative writing. Similarly, in EAP writing complexity studies across various genres, the usage of NFCs has been found to be predictive of essay quality (Kyle and Crossley 2018) and to differentiate, together with finite subordinate clauses, emerging international publication writers from established writers (Yin, Gao and Lu 2021).

The Present Study

The present study presents a corpus-based linguistic analysis of expert and student English-language research writing in a specific academic discipline. Specifically, using a proposed syntactic taxonomy of NFCs, we examine the variability among the syntactic subtypes and their corresponding usage patterns in discursive contexts across expert- and student-produced texts. This study additionally discusses the pedagogical potential of incorporating corpus-assisted NFC instruction for awareness-raising activities in disciplinary-specific writing course design. The results of this study will further our understanding of disciplinary specificity in relation to the under-researched grammatical feature of NFCs. In particular, the study sets out to address the following two questions:

1. What are the distributional characteristics of NFCs in agricultural sciences academic writing between expert and student writers?
2. How do the two groups of writers differ in their use of common non-finite clausal patterns?

Methodology

Corpus Description

The corpus used in the study (hereafter referred to as CASAP, Corpus of Agricultural Sciences Academic Papers) is composed of research writing in agricultural sciences. It includes 225 published research articles by L1 English writers and 225 drafts of research writing for publication purposes by L1

Chinese graduate student writers, both balanced across five sub-disciplines of agricultural sciences (Animal Science, Food Science, Horticulture and Forestry, Life Science, Plant Science) with forty-five texts from each sub-discipline. A numerical overview of the corpus is presented in Table 5.1.

The texts in CASAP were sampled from HZAU CQPweb (Liu, Huang and Liu 2015) by using 'create/edit subcorpora' function afforded in its online query interface.[1] According to the compilers' report of corpus data collection (cf. Liu, Huang and Liu 2015), HZAU CQPweb, originally built for EAP instructors in Huazhong Agricultural University, is a useful tool for analysing disciplinary-specific usage patterns employed by expert and student writers because of its careful data selection and rigorous data preparation. For the collection of expert articles, the selection of the journals to be included in the HZAU CQPweb was primarily based on the university's then academic division of agriculture-related disciplines and Discipline Catalogue of Degree Accreditation and Talent Education released in 2011 by the Ministry of Education in China. The corpus team also consulted specialists in the Department of Agricultural Sciences on the basis that they are peer-reviewed journals with high impact factors and strong disciplinary reputation. The articles were randomly selected based on their length, textual organization and year of publication. For the student component, the compilers accessed the writing inventory of the university's writing workshop to collect revised manuscripts originally contributed by then-enrolled master's and doctoral students across nine sub-disciplines within the Department of Agricultural Sciences.

For the protection of copyright and student privacy, the HZAU CQPweb query interface permits no access to the original writing data yet allows for both CLAWS-tagged (Constituent-Likelihood Automatic Word-Tagging System, Garside 1987) and tag-free searches.

Extraction of Non-Finite Clauses in CASAP

To extract reliably instances of NFCs in a corpus, previous studies always employed an automated syntactic analysis tool. However, the operationalization of NFCs (i.e. how NFCs are defined and identified in a given text) in different tools has recently been found to be inconsistent, thus calling for developing and testing 'more fine-grained measures for the right writing genres, mediums and tasks' (Deng, Lei and Liu 2021: 1027). To clarify the operationalization in this study, we provide a brief structural description of NFCs. In this study, a NFC is marked by a non-finite verb in

Table 5.1 Basic description of the CASAP

	Animal Science	Life Science	Food Science	Horticulture and Forestry Science	Plant Science	Total
Expert						
Texts	45	45	45	45	45	225
Sentences	8,878	9,707	9,526	10,045	11,818	49,974
Tokens	265,851	284,382	270,898	306,554	324,754	1,452,439
Types	19,712	20,763	19,176	20,347	20,024	37,005
Student						
Texts	45	45	45	45	45	225
Sentences	6,427	6,538	6,432	8,963	8,336	36,696
Tokens	181,705	188,099	176,816	235,466	226,936	1,009,022
Types	13,156	13,401	12,256	14,385	14,181	24,031
Sub-Disc. Total						
Token	447,556	472,481	447,714	542,020	551,690	

three forms: *-ing*, *-ed* and *to-* infinitive irrespective of the composition of this clause (Greenbaum 1996: 328; Quirk et al. 1985: 992). A NFC could be as short as just the non-finite verb itself as in '[I keep [NFC moving]]', and coordinated predicates will be treated as two NFCs.

Once CASAP was created in HZAU CQPweb, potential NFC candidates were extracted. Although automated tools are available for identification or counting of NFCs (e.g. L2SCA, Lu 2010; TAASC, Kyle 2016), we rely only on part-of-speech (POS) tag-based queries to identify potential instances of NFCs; we manually filtered the resulting instances and categorized the data in accordance with our proposed syntactic taxonomy in order to provide a descriptive overview that captures a wide range of structures and maximizes implementability into an educational setting.

To extract NFCs, a search list was developed following the query syntax afforded in CQPweb (Table 5.2). While the search patterns are input using the built-in syntax (cf. section Insights for Implementation for more details), we present here the POS patterning and a corresponding example to illustrate the structural type of NFC being extracted. Importantly, readers should be alerted that many patternings do not exclusively return NFCs. Rather, the search list considerably narrows down the pool of possible NFCs, so further manual cleaning is an important part of the methodology used here. This follows with the aim of employing a methodology which is reproducible by EAP educators and students. At the same time, overproducing potential instances and manually filtering the returned items allow for a highly accurate, if somewhat inefficient, result. In Table 5.2, we note here that the 'mistagged' category is not shown in full because the list would be too long. However, it is available to interested readers upon request to the authors.

The framework for NFCs (outlined in Table 5.3) proposed in this chapter is based on previous research, which supports the division of NFCs into three syntactic categories: adverbial, complement (or nominal) and post-modifying (or relative) clauses (Biber et al. 1999; Greenbaum 1996; Huddleston and Pullum 2005; Leech et al. 1984; Quirk et al. 1985). These categories are further classified into structural subtypes as illustrated in Table 5.3, with additional reference to empirical studies of subordinate clauses (Biber 1988; Granger 1997; Malá 2010; Martínez 2012). The resulting NFC taxonomy is comprehensive, easy to use by researchers and educators and operationable in the query syntax afforded within CQPweb interface. Items such as sentence-initial participle form (Examples 1 and 2), *to*-headed infinitive (Example 3) and preposition- and conjunction-headed

Table 5.2 Search items of non-finite clause in CASAP

	Pattern	Examples from Data Set
-ing participle (VBG)	ADV + VBG	This had prevented scientists from **accurately mapping** nodulation across extant plant species.
	UNIT + VBG	OCT-embedded samples were sectioned at a thickness of 10 **mm using** a CryoStar NX70 cryostat and allowed to dry at room temperature.
	DET + VBG	Among peripheral CD3+ T cells, **those expressing** a TCR formed by the V9 and V2 variable regions (hereafter referred to as V2 cells) constitute up to 90% of T cells.
	NOUN + VBG	The **mechanism reducing** the diversity and evenness of AM fungal communities in summer may be similar.
	PREP + VBG	Cell death was determined **by staining** with trypan blue and determining the percentage of viable cells.
	PUNC + VBG	Individuals were classified as being red **(containing** visible anthocyanin in the inner pericarp) or non-red (no anthocyanin observed in the inner pericarp).
	SUB-CONJ + VBG	The rot indexes were angularly transformed **before calculating** mean value .3.
	TO + VBG	The ability of microbiomes to reproduce their effects on soil processes and host plant traits is critical **to advancing** the use of soil microbiomes in plant production systems.
	VBN + VBG	Product replacement and purchase intent of the breads were **rated using** five-point scales.
	VERB + VBG	To **begin addressing** this possibility, we included covariates for flowering time and height in our analyses.
-ed participle (VBN)	ADV + VBN	As **previously described**, all Ly6Chi monocytes from T. gondii-infected small intestine lamina propria expressed MHCII.
	ADJ + VBN	Only two cases were included as **aggressive based** solely on a high Gleason sum.
	DET + VBN	Some of these symptoms are similar to **those induced** by Ca.
	NOUN + VBN	Serotype 2 is the most common **serotype associated** with diseases in pigs and humans.
	PUNC + VBN	Among genotypes, **averaged** across node position, LRL ranged between 1.25cm and 2.44cm.
	SUB-CONJ + VBN	**When translated**, the insertion element in pillar results in a premature stop codon at amino acid position 102.

(*Continued*)

Table 5.2 (Continued)

	Pattern	Examples from Data Set
to- infinitive (VBI)	TO + VBI	In both studies, participants were requested ***to place*** the value markers (sticker dot or digital dot) onto KI map locations representing those values.
Mistagged	VBN + VBN	However, because the life cycle simulation model in which they were ***used averaged*** across the weevil population developing over 1–3 years, this smoothing would have little effect.
	PREP + ADJ	Single nucleotide polymorphism markers can be used ***for determining*** parentage and to provide unique molecular identifiers for tracing sheep products to their source.
	VERB + PREP	We have previously shown that the thymidine kinase reaction ***catalyzed by*** T7 gp1.7 is reversible.

Note: ADJ = Adjective; ADV = Adverb; DET = Determiner; PREP = Preposition; PUNC = Punctuation; SUB-CONJ = Subordinating conjunction; UNIT = Unit of measure; VBG = Present participle; VBI = Infinitive; VBN = Past participle

gerund form (Examples 4 and 5) were included because of their predominant (for some, exclusive) usage as a NFC.

(1) ***Compared*** *with previous reports*, we compared our result with four previous reports on pig CNVs. (26DWKXS;[2] CASAP-Student)
(2) ***Using*** *this polymorphism*, we mapped CUT1 to the top arm of chromosome 1, at 35.98 centimorgans. (41ZWKX; CASAP-Expert)
(3) None of these translated regions were found ***to be*** *without an internal stop codon*; therefore, the corresponding elements are likely to be inactive. (98YYLX; CASAP-Expert)
(4) Grittiness of fish bone powder can be minimized *by **decreasing*** *its particle size*. (56SPKXS; CASAP-Student)
(5) The cell suspensions were centrifuged as previously, *after **discarding*** *the supernatant*, the pellets were suspended into the drying carrier solutions. (22SPKX; CASAP-Expert)

In order to refine the search list, we subsampled ten texts from each group of writers and manually coded all NFCs. The output was then compared to what we had extracted using the search list we created at the first stage. By cross-checking the results, we added two new types of search items into our list: one is a mistagged grammatical relation between a word and a non-finite verb (e.g.

Table 5.3 Proposed syntactic taxonomy of non-finite clauses

Types	Subtypes	Examples
Adverbial	*to*-headed	On the other hand, *to **lower** the feed costs*, many cost effective feedstuffs as replacement for the conventional ones were exploded in poultry dietary.
	Subordinator-free	It indicated that structural adaptation for temperature stability exerts a greater effect of lowering the catalytic efficiency ***compared** with alkaline stability adaptation*.
	Conjunction-headed	Different tree species have different accuracy *when **using** different features*.
	Preposition-headed	With 1 g of eggs ***being** weighed and counted* under stereomicroscope, the volume of eggs from each adult cage was recorded daily during the egg production period.
Complement	Adjective-controlled	Thus, we conclude that cGAS is *essential for **inducing** IFNb and other ISGs in response to M*.
	Extraposed *to*-controlled	It was *important to **note** that* CsRNS2 and CsRNS3 showed stronger pistil specific with the basic characteristic of S-RNase genes.
	Verb-controlled	The next day, almost all female moths *started **calling** soon* after lights off and peaked on the third night.
	Noun-controlled	Our *protocol for **preparing** Trichoplax for immunofluorescence microscopy by freeze substitution* was adapted from a previous protocol.
	Other (control-free)	***Increasing** TG, TC and LDL levels and decreasing HDL levels* are normal phenomenon in the diabetic mice.
Post-modifying	Participle	Recent research ***based** on genomeCwide resequencing* identified three novel segmental duplications in Kit region.
	to-clause	One of the few studies *to **look** at this method* has been [citation].

mistagging a gerund verb as an adjective when preceded by preposition *for*) and the other is a frequent yet overlooked item (e.g. *including*, *regarding* and *considering* are treated as prepositions in CLAWS7 instead of gerund verb). This refinement resulted in Table 5.2, which was then piloted on a different testing data set of ten texts from each sub-corpus. Of the twenty texts, the data extracted by the search list was first manually checked for non-finiteness and then compared to the manually coded results so as to report on the overall

F-measure, which turned out to be satisfactory. The expert corpus precision was 100 per cent (1573/1573) and recall was 95.55 per cent (1573/1643), while the student corpus precision was 100 per cent (925/925) and recall was 93.3 per cent (927/987), resulting in an overall 0.98 for the expert corpus and 0.97 for the student corpus. The search list is not intended to be exhaustive, but it includes the most common and most frequent forms co-occurring with a non-finite verb and are designed to maximize the pedagogical importance and to facilitate pedagogical implementation. If given access to original data, researchers can devise a modified query syntax list (based on Table 5.2) compatible with the chosen concordance tool and POS tagger. Alternatively, they can undertake a different path to identifying NFC in a corpus such as parsing with Stanford PCFG Parser (Klein and Manning 2003), which breaks clausal elements into hierarchical positions corresponding to their syntactic roles (e.g. NP, DT, PP) and achieves overall F score of 0.86. The extraction could then be carried out using the Tregex tree-search tool (Levy and Andrew 2006), but these methods require knowledge of the related corpus tools.

The finalized search list was applied to the entire CASAP through HAZU CQPweb, followed by manual checking by the second author. The analysis of the resulting instances targeted the frequent NFC use as well as the range and frequency ranks of verbs utilized in the structure across sub-corpora. A follow-up analysis of frequently recurring patterns was conducted to compare usage across expert and student sub-corpora.

Results

The first point of comparison between the agricultural sciences expert and student research writing corpora is the frequency data of broad types of NFCs, non-finite verb forms and verb frequency lists (Tables 5.4 and 5.5). The narrower subcategories of NFCs are then discussed in more depth (Tables 5.6–5.8), with attention paid to common student errors and differences in the usage of frequent structures. Throughout this section, we note that examples of student errors are marked by an asterisk (*).

A comparison of the type and token frequency of NFC use overall and by adverbial, complement and post-modifying categories is presented in Table 5.4, with the types presented as raw frequency and the tokens presented as a value normalized to occurrences per 10,000 words. As can be seen, NFCs are more densely concentrated in the published texts by expert writers than they

Table 5.4 Type and token frequency of expert and student non-finite clauses

	Adverbial		Complement		Post-Modifier		Totals	
	Expert	Student	Expert	Student	Expert	Student	Expert	Student
NF -ing	56.3	49.9	13.6	10.5	25.6	16.2	95.6	76.6
NF -ed	21.5	22.8	0.0	0.1	46.6	34.4	68.1	57.3
NF - to - inf	34.6	31.9	35.0	21.2	2.9	2.2	73.8	55.9
All forms	112.4	104.6	48.6	31.8	75.2	52.8	237.5	189.8
Types	959	667	907	511	753	482	1392	918
Ty Overlap	60%		55%		62%		63%	
Tk Overlap	95%		87%		92%		96%	

Note: Overlap values are presented as percentages, types represent the raw counts and all other values are frequency counts normalized to occurrences per 10,000 words. Ty = Type; Tk = Token.

Table 5.5 Top ten verb types and frequency for experts and students

	Adverbial		Complement		Post-Modifying	
	Expert	Student	Expert	Student	Expert	Student
Verb 1	Use (2813)	Use (1780)	Be (894)	Be (552)	Contain (600)	Contain (427)
Verb 2	Include (782)	Compare (752)	Have (190)	Understand (72)	Use (425)	Use (234)
Verb 3	Compare (779)	Include (556)	Identify (124)	Use (67)	Associate (319)	Involve (167)
Verb 4	Describe (529)	Base (533)	Determine (123)	Identify (62)	Encode (248)	Induce (130)
Verb 5	Follow (503)	Follow (378)	Regulate (96)	Improve (54)	Involve (238)	Describe (124)
Verb 6	Base (428)	Show (238)	Use (88)	Investigate (53)	Derive (213)	Encode (121)
Verb 7	Suggest (415)	Indicate (210)	Increase (86)	Study (51)	Express (207)	Obtain (115)
Verb 8	Determine (400)	Describe (196)	Understand (80)	Develop (49)	Observe (186)	Cause (113)
Verb 9	Indicate (375)	Suggest (174)	Induce (73)	Regulate (48)	Describe (176)	Associate (106)
Verb 10	Identify (240)	Determine (173)	Reduce (72)	Control (46)	Identify (147)	Treat (97)

Note: Frequency of each verb occurring in the specified context listed in parenthesis.

are in the student texts by a wide margin (237.5 occurrences per 10,000 words to 189.8 occurrences per 10,000 words), they are more densely concentrated in expert texts in each structural category and they are more densely concentrated across the verb-form comparisons with two narrow exceptions in the NF *-ed* constructions. Thus, while advanced students demonstrate an ability to utilize all analysed non-finite structures that are abundant in expert texts, there appears to be a considerable gap in the usage of NFCs from a frequency perspective across nearly all these broad categories. From a clause-type perspective, the largest gaps in normalized frequency are evident in complement and post-modifying structures, with students producing roughly two-thirds as many instances as experts, while the disparity is much narrower in adverbial structures. The wider gaps in complement and post-modifying NFC production align with Biber, Gray and Poonpon's (2011) hypothesis that these patterns emerge later in developing L2 English academic writers. From a pedagogical perspective, these gaps suggest that even advanced students may benefit from targeted attention to the structural patterns of NFC use in academic writing, as will be discussed later. From a verb-form perspective, a gap in all three broad patterns is observable, with the largest gaps appearing in *-ing* and *to-* infinitive structures. The *-ing* form is the most abundant structure for NFCs in both corpora, but while the experts produce the *to-* infinitive NFC verb form second most frequently, students produce this structure even less than the *-ed* form, although the margin is slim.

A verb type and verb overlap perspective highlights that experts not only utilize nearly all structures of interest more frequently than students but that they also make use of a greater variety of verbs within the structures. As can be seen in Table 5.5, there is a notable overlap in each broad structure and overall regarding the most frequent verbs to occur in each structure, with the greatest differences between experts and students occurring in the post-modifying category, discussed later. Overall, these trends suggest that students have the linguistic knowledge to produce the patterns in focus and have access to more prototypical verbal patterns which account for the majority of their uses, but that they do not yet have sophisticated productive capacity in some cases. Thus, pedagogical focus can beneficially target the range of patterns that occur within each structural context and the functional purposes for which they are used, in addition to grammatical knowledge of how to produce the forms themselves.

Adverbial Non-Finite Clauses

Non-finite adverbial clauses function adverbially in a dependent manner to modify a verb, adjective or adverb within a larger clausal structure, as demonstrated in Examples 6–10. This is the category of NFCs which is used most abundantly by both populations of agricultural sciences writers, the category which demonstrates the greatest variability in terms of the verb-form patterns and verb types identified in both expert and student texts and also the category in which the students align most closely with the experts in frequency and usage patterns.

Nevertheless, when adverbial NFCs are broken down into the four subcategories listed in Table 5.6, some minor disparities in expert and student usage are detectable. Most notably, while subordinator-free adverbial NFCs are used less frequently by students than by experts overall, it is apparent that the verbal patterns themselves differ notably from a structural standpoint in that the students use non-finite *-ed* patterns more frequently and non-finite *-ing* patterns much less frequently than experts. This can be in part explained by disparities in the use of particular structures. For example, students rarely use the highly frequent sentence initial *-ing* adverbial of *to use* in order to explicate methodological procedures (Example 6), instead almost exclusively producing this structure in a mid-sentence position immediately following a verb (Example 7). While expert writers utilized both patterns abundantly (and utilized *use* in adverbials over 2,800 times), students utilized the second pattern almost exclusively (and utilized *use* in adverbials approximately 1,800 times).

(6) **Using** *a combination of electrophysiology and intracellular chloride photometry*, we demonstrated that visTRN dynamically controls visual thalamic gain through feedforward inhibition. (70SMKX; CASAP-Expert)

(7) Genomic DNA samples were extracted from whole blood of all pigs **using** *a standard phenol method*. (26DWKXS; CASAP-Student)

However, careful comparison of Examples 6 and 7 also reveals a wider disparity between the usage of non-finite adverbials with the verb *to use* across the expert and student corpora. The adverbial in the student sentence (7) functions to specify a methodological manner in a sentence entirely devoted to methodological description by modifying the preceding main verb *to extract*, which is a pattern the expert writers also employed frequently. In addition, the authors of the expert texts made use of an additional functional affordance of non-finite adverbials with the verb *to use*, as Example 6 displays an adverbial clause which foregrounds the specific method being used as well as establishes the experimental footing upon which the following proposition is based. This technique contributes to expert writers' ability to draw on a diverse range of structures to construct rhetorically sophisticated and propositionally dense

Table 5.6 Token frequency of expert and student non-finite adverbial clause

	Conj-Head		Sub-Free		Prep-Head		To-Clause	
	Expert	Student	Expert	Student	Expert	Student	Expert	Student
NF -*ing*	2.9	5.1	42.1	32.5	11.3	12.3	–	–
NF -*ed*	10.9	8.2	9.8	14.1	0.8	0.5	–	–
NF – *to* - inf	–	–	–	–	–	–	34.6	31.9
All forms	13.8	13.3	51.9	46.6	12.1	12.8	34.6	31.9
Types	317	215	369	181	502	288	582	401

Note: Types represent the raw counts, and all other values are frequency counts normalized to occurrences per 10,000 words. Conj-Head = Conjunction-headed; Sub-Free = Subordinator-free; Prep-Head = Preposition-headed; To = To-clause.

prose. In this case, it is evident that instructional attention on how to produce adverbial NFCs with this prototypical verb is unlikely to benefit advanced EAP students, yet attention to the functional affordances of this pattern may expand students' repertoires for making complex writing decisions – particularly when space constraints limit of many academic genres is taken into account.

The examination of common patterns in discursive context across the corpora also highlights the following rhetorically oriented differences in usage. While expert writers utilize non-finite adverbials headed by the *-ing* form of *to suggest* nearly twice per text on average at 402 times (as in Example 8), the students utilize this pattern less than half as frequently, mirroring their reduced use of the verb *to suggest* as a hedging device for cautiously advancing interpretive claims. In a more stylistic disparity, expert writers utilized non-finite adverbials headed by the *-ed* form of *to follow* to link methodological processes within a single sentence abundantly, with the overall pattern occurring 138 times (see Example 9). In contrast, students produced this pattern only fifty times, opting in many cases to produce shorter sentences or rely on the conjunctive *and* to link procedures.

(8) We also identified one OTU matching closest to rumen bacterium RC-2 that was affected in its abundance upon MNV-1 infection in both diet groups, **suggesting** *a specific correlation with viral infection.* (73DWKX; CASAP-Expert)

(9) Hybridization was done on a GeneChip Wheat Genome Array, **followed** *by scanning with the GeneChip Scanner 3000.* (71ZWKX; CASAP-Expert).

While student errors were somewhat infrequent for adverbials relative to the other two major categories, it was noted that students used non-finite adverbial clauses headed by the *-ed* form of *to base* over 530 times (roughly 2.3 times normalized frequency) and abundantly in sentence initial positions, often resulting in awkward prose such as Example 10, where the writer perhaps intends a meaning closer to *by means of*.

(10) **Based** *on the read depth methods*, we discovered copy number variations from 47 individuals of both Chinese and Western pig breeds. (45DWKXS; CASAP-Student)

When students do make errors in the production of NFCs which we can convincingly link to adverbials, they tend to involve producing the incorrect verb form in the NFC, with *to suggest* surfacing as one of the most problematic instances. In Example 11, a student produces the hedging pattern discussed in Example 8 but with the incorrect form of the verb *to suggest*, which is a commonly observed error. Without direct interaction with the student writers producing these structures, it is difficult to attribute this particular error to a definitive cause, but it is noteworthy that the errors surface in a pattern which involves careful articulation of the strength of a claim (see Example 11) rather than the more direct meaning as a reporting verb that is not associated with this pattern.

(11) Eight cis-elements response to MeJA were tested in promoter of CsRNS1, *strongly *suggested that CsRNS1 probably take part in the senescence process.* (54YYLXS; CASAP-Student)

Complement Non-Finite Clauses

A non-finite complement clause (also referred to as nominal clause) completes the meaning of an associated noun, verb or adjective and thus can occupy a (logical) subject, object or subject complement position. The overall profile of non-finite complement use across the expert and student texts in the agricultural sciences corpora indicates that students produce such structures considerably less frequently overall (31.8 to 48.6 occurrences per 10,000 words) and less frequently across the subcategories. As can be seen in Table 5.7, these differences are most prominent in verb-controlled and adjective-controlled complements, where students produce the structures roughly two-thirds as frequently as experts and utilize less than half the number of verb types.

One of the most striking differences in the verb frequency list is the relative frequency of the verb *to have* in this structure within the expert corpus (190 occurrences), as it occurs only once in the student corpus. *To have* is used in this structure as both a lexical and auxiliary verb, and by examining the co-occurring verb pattern in context, we found that expert writers predominantly favour verbs *to show* and *to appear*, using them much more frequently than students (*to show*, 348 vs. 47; *to appear*, 269 vs. 40). As can be seen in Examples 12 and 13, *to have* forms part of relatively complex multi-verb structures along with *to appear* and *to show* which are used by expert writers for reporting claims agentlessly. This pattern places the focus on the claim, rather than the researcher, as in the multi-verb pattern in Example 12. These also may have a hedging functionality, as in Example 13, where the author demonstrates much less confidence in their commitment to the claim regarding the properties attributed to the object in

Table 5.7 Token frequency of expert and student non-finite complement clause

	Extrp.		Verb-C		Adj-C		Noun-C	
	Expert	Student	Expert	Student	Expert	Student	Expert	Student
NF-*ing*	–	–	2.0	1.9	2.1	1.4	6.1	5.3
NF-*to*-inf	2.0	1.8	21.7	12.8	5.5	2.5	4.9	2.4
All forms	2.0	1.8	23.7	14.8	7.6	3.9	11.0	7.7
Types	119	84	587	279	375	181	464	245

Note: Types represent the raw counts, and all other values are frequency counts normalized to occurrences per 10,000 words. The infrequent 'control-free' subcategory is excluded; the infrequent NF-*ed* pattern also excluded. Extrp. = Extraposed to-clause; Verb-C = Verb-controlled; Adj-C = Adjective-controlled; Noun-C = Noun-Controlled.

focus. In these and similar cases, the structure places focus on the objects/concepts, rather than researcher agents, and all intertextual components are relegated to non-integral citation or generalization.

(12) First, paternal diet has been shown **to have** *marked effects on the metabolic physiology of offspring* conceived after the fathers diet had been manipulated. (85SMKX; CASAP-Expert)

(13) Here it is shown that OsMTP1 appears **to have** *some Fe transport activity* as it is able to reduce the Fe hypersensitivity of the yeast ccc1 mutant. (82ZWKX; CASAP-Expert)

Considering the verb frequency lists (see Table 5.5) and examining the most common patterns in context also reveal a functional difference in the use of complement clauses, as the verb *to understand* surfaces roughly 1.5 times as frequently in the student corpus as it does in the expert corpus when normalized per 10,000 words. While the experts do utilize this specific complement structure to introduce general phenomena towards which research is directed, as a student does in Example 14, they also utilize a variety of non-finite complement patterns with verbs such as *determine, identify* and *detect* which specify questions of inquiry (Example 15).

(14) Mutants are very important for us **to understand** *biological or ecological functions of organisms*; however, mutant may not reflect real aspects of these functions if it is not chosen properly. (04ZWKXS; CASAP-Student)

(15) It also should be noted that re-examination of the previously reported C or N response mutants is also important as it will help **to determine** *whether the genes represented by the mutants or transgenic plants are involved in signaling to the C balance or specifically to C alone or N alone.* (24SMKX; CASAP-Expert).

A frequent pattern in the expert corpus was *[adjective] to [verb]*, such as the frame-based formulaic sequence *it is [important, useful, helpful, surprising, interesting] to [consider, discuss, note]* which writers often utilize to orient readers' attention to discursive shifts or to introduce findings. This pattern is not only underused in this particular functional manner, but it is also the source of many verb-form errors in the student corpus similar to that in Example 16, where the student writer produces the *-ing* form of the verb instead of the infinitive. Many students exhibited difficulty in producing the correct form of the verb in non-finite complements, frequently producing the incorrect verb form in infinitive constructions (e.g. *tended to *disassociating; had been shown to *binding; might help us to *understanding*).

(16) **It is critical to *exploring** diapause regulation mechanism, insecticide resistance mechanism, and other mechanisms in the cabbage beetle. (28ZWKXS; CASAP-Student)

Noun Post-Modifying Non-Finite Clauses

The final category of non-finite verbal constructions examined in this chapter is those which are produced as post-modifiers for nouns in complex noun phrases. This category has received heightened attention in EAP research over the past decade due to the emphasis that many researchers now place on complex noun phrases. As has been discussed, complex noun phrases have been shown to perform an important role in the construction of compressed written academic discourse (Biber and Gray 2010), and the two non-finite clausal structures discussed in this section contribute to noun phrase complexity. In the present analysis, noun post-modifying present and past participle constructions (i.e. reduced relative clauses; see Examples 17–19) are examined alongside *[noun] + to [verb]* constructions (e.g. *an issue to investigate*). While all analysed noun post-modifying non-finite verbal elements are more frequent in the expert corpus than they are in the student corpus (see Table 5.8), the disparities in the participle category are observably large. Experts produced 46.6 non-finite noun post-modifying *-ed* participle constructions per 10,000 words and 25.6 non-finite noun post-modifying *-ing* constructions per 10,000 words, with students producing 34.4 and 16.2 per 10,000 words, respectively.

Non-finite participle constructions within noun phrases are strongly associated with methodological discussions in both corpora, and a number of

Table 5.8 Token frequency of expert and student non-finite post-modifiers

	Participle		N + *to*	
	Expert	Student	Expert	Student
NF -*ing*	25.6	16.2	–	–
NF -*ed*	46.6	34.4	–	–
NF – *to* - inf	–	–	2.9	2.2
All forms	72.3	50.6	2.9	2.2
Types	498	264	194	106

Note: Types represent the raw counts, and all other values are frequency counts normalized to occurrences per 10,000 words.

shared and highly common non-finite participle constructions are observed. The most salient is the pattern *[noun] + containing*, where general research object nouns (e.g. *medium, solution, buffer*) or more study-specific nouns were post-modified by *containing* in methodological description (Example 17).

(17) An enclosed **vial *containing*** BLG/PEO *fiber sample* was placed in a water bath at 80 for one hour. (02SPKX; CASAP-Expert)

Examining the most frequent verbs used in the non-finite post-modifying pattern (see Table 5.5), it is clear that while the most prototypical patterns may be similar across the corpora, there are a number of noticeable differences. While the experts make significantly more frequent use of *derive (deriving), express (expressed and expressing), observe (observing)* and *identify (identified)*, students make much greater use of *induce (induced), obtain (obtaining), cause (causing)* and *treat (treated)*. Of these, one of the most apparent differences was the production of the pattern *[noun] + expressing*, which was used considerably more frequently by experts than students, with a highly overlapping set of domain-specific nouns (*cells, mice, plants, roots* and *lines*) to introduce genetic traits or behaviours. The pattern is exemplified in Example 18.

(18) Again, mice ***expressing*** *b12* exhibited weight loss over a period of 2 weeks. (19DWKX; CASAP-Expert)

Experts also used the complex pattern *those/that + [verb]-ed* much more frequently than students, functioning as a comparison (Example 19), which can be intertextual in some cases. Students make use of this pattern infrequently.

(19) All of the MWP suspensions exhibited flow behavior similar to **that *shown*** *in Figure 4a*, with shear stress increasing with increasing shear rate in a fairly linear manner. (11SPKX; CASAP-Expert)

With regard to errors, students demonstrated a greater difficulty in forming full and reduced post-modifying clauses than they did with any of the other structures, at least as far as our search terms were able to properly identify instances. As can be seen in Examples 20 and 21, the most common error was mixing finite relative clause with a non-finite participle verb form (i.e. *which + [verb]-ed/-ing*).

(20) This gene *****which *catalyzing*** *the conversion of glycerate 3-phosphate to glyceraldehyde 3-phosphate* was important for the glycolysis. (44YYLXS; CASAP-Student)

(21) The PCR reactions were carried out with 300 ng male antennal cDNAs with two pairs primers, *****which *based on* the cloned full-length***. (27ZWKXS; CASAP-Student)

In summary, the frequency comparison demonstrated that expert writers make use of NFC structures more frequently overall, have a larger repertoire of NFC structures and employ a greater variety of non-finite verbs in these patterns than student writers do. Subsequent analysis of common patterns of each of the syntactic subtypes (adverbial clause, complement clause and post-modifying non-finite verbal elements) further revealed that expert writers utilize these structures in a more rhetorically sophisticated and strategic manner than the analysed student writers, who may benefit from pedagogical attention to the linguistic and rhetorical potential afforded in certain NF structures. Common errors and misuse patterns in student writing were also discussed.

Conclusion

In this chapter we have outlined an ongoing analytical endeavour to examine differences in frequency and structural and functional usage patterns of NFCs in expert and advanced student writing in agricultural sciences. The frequency-based analysis highlighted that expert writers within this discipline utilize a wide variety of NFC structures more frequently (normalized to text length) and with a greater variety of verbs than students. Follow-up analysis of more fine-grained forms of adverbial clause, complement clause and post-modifying non-finite verbal elements similarly revealed that expert writers utilize these structures with greater frequency and in more varied ways. Nevertheless, it is important to note that students demonstrate the ability to produce well-formed instances of all three major categories of NFCs examined here. The student writers demonstrate the greatest similarities in their production of adverbial NFCs, with complement NFCs and noun post-modifying NFCs representing progressively large divergences from expert usage as well as increasing numbers of detectable errors in formation. This strongly resonates with Biber, Gray and Poonpon's (2011) hypothesized developmental trajectory, as complements and post-modifying NFCs are theorized as structures students master later. Important differences were found in comparing the most frequent structures in the expert and student sub-corpora, highlighting differences in the particular verbal patterns that writers rely on and some functional affordances that are exploited variably across the two corpora. In general, students demonstrate a reliance on a narrower range of more prototypical patterns that are also frequent in expert writing, but experts demonstrate a greater command of NFCs in terms of the variety of verbs and verbal patterns employed and the variety of functional intentions. As English for Academic Purposes instructors and researchers, we note a number of important pedagogical implications of these findings and provide guidance for interested instructors.

Pedagogical Implications

While it is noteworthy that expert writers use considerably more NFCs in their research writing than students (237.5 to 189.8 per 10,000 words), it is significant that students still produce this structure at a high frequency. Pedagogically, this has the important implication that many advanced students of EAP writing may not need instructional support on *how to form NFC patterns broadly*. Of course, EAP students at lower levels of proficiency are likely to benefit considerably from attention on how to produce NFC patterns, and our analysis of advanced students did uncover issues through consideration of student errors (particularly for postmodifiers). However, we argue that the majority of instructional attention would be best directed towards *how NFCs are used*, that is, what functional affordances they provide to academic writers.

To this end, the portion of our ongoing analysis presented here underscores that students in our corpus make use of a reduced range of non-finite constructions in terms of the verbal patterns themselves and the discursive functions of the chunk overall. Across the considered structures, it is clear that students share an overlapping set of highly frequent and prototypical patterns (e.g. the NF adverbial *[research action verb] + using*) to articulate the means by which a methodological procedure was performed, but experts make use of additional patterns that students may benefit from (e.g. the non-finite complement *to determine/detect/identify* + specific phenomena). In addition, and perhaps closer to the core of EAP's aim of empowering students for agentive activity in target communities, experts often make use of patterns whose mastery students demonstrate developing in similar ways, but they also display more rhetorically complex uses of such structures (e.g. sentence initial non-finite adverbials *[Using]* to attach methodological details to other propositions). EAP students across proficiency levels are likely to benefit from any linguistic insights which connect formal elements to functional affordances, as they both empower students to think about writing in new ways and equip them with resources to accomplish – or at least attempt – their goals.

Insights for Implementation

More concretely, this type of EAP instruction is particularly suited to corpus-based genre-analytic approaches to writing pedagogy that integrate discourse analysis and corpus analysis as interfacing classroom activities (e.g. Casal 2020; Charles 2007). More technical details are provided later, but in concrete terms this means that EAP instructors can work with learners to (1) identify NFC elements via corpus-assisted analytical activities, (2) examine the functional affordances of NFC elements via discourse/text analytic activities and (3) provide opportunities to reflect on how the findings of both sets of activities resonate with each other. Corpus-assisted analysis can draw on strict data-driven learning (Johns 1986) approaches that place learners directly in control of corpus querying, more directed searchers where instructors or materials developers have carefully selected search terms and contexts or prepared corpus activities where instances have been extracted from texts and provided to students, thus rendering the technicalities of the corpus invisible while maintaining the broad lens of the approach.

In addition to arguing for the inclusion of NFCs in EAP writing instruction and profiling the usage patterns of NFCs in expert and student research writing in agricultural sciences, part of the aim of this chapter is to facilitate the implementation of NFC analysis into EAP pedagogies for instructors who do not have extensive background in corpus or computational techniques. To this end, two important issues are discussed in this section, the corpus resource used in this study and the search techniques outlined in Table 5.2. To the first of these points, the non-finite instances were extracted in the CQPweb online query platform (Xu and Wu 2014) built to serve disciplinary academic writing instruction in China. While the agricultural sciences database has not been released to the public, the platform offers a wide-ranging principled collection of published research articles in disciplines such as philosophy, engineering, medicine and biology. Importantly, the webpage provides instructions for accessing the corpora and a manual for querying through the interface.

Secondly, Table 5.2 outlines a subset of particular grammatical patterns that were used in our search, representing the most productive search patterns overall. While those who have not worked with POS-tagged corpora may find the tagging to be an initial obstacle, a complete list of the CLAWS tags is available, and our complete list of search terms is available upon request. To perform a search in any corpus listed in the platform, users will find the search window for word-based searches to identify specific patterns (e.g. *suggest; suggesting; by using*). Alternatively, they may query via specific CQP syntax using the template for syntax-based searches *[word='.*'&pos='input POS tag here']*, which will yield a list of words in the POS indicated in 'input POS tag here'. To retrieve patterning between a preposition and a *-ing* verb, users should first place side by side two templates and input the POS tag for preposition (e.g. 'I.*' captures all variants of prepositions) in the first template and tag for *-ing* verb ('V.G' captures all *-ing* verbs) in the second template. Importantly, the patterns will all overproduce, and manual examination of the hits will be required. Thus, while one of the advantages of this approach is accessibility and – after manual filtering – increased accuracy, other more computationally complex tools or approaches would potentially yield easier to manage results. Given the clear differences in frequency overall and by NFC subtype, as well as the fact that expert writers demonstrated a greater range of verbs used within and functional patterns of NFCs than the advanced L2 English student writers analysed here, we believe that there is considerable value in dedicating pedagogical attention to NFC use in EAP writing courses.

Notes

1 By taking advantage of the powerful technical foundation in CQPweb (Hardie 2012), HZAU CQPweb online corpus query interface was developed with the aim to offer disciplinary-specific linguistic analyses at EAP instructors' service and to respond to a broader call (Xu and Xu 2017: 65) for making accessible professional disciplinary writing data to all EAP instructors around major universities in China (if interested, please explore a list of disciplinary-specific corpora of expert research article writing freely accessible at http://114.251.154.212/cqp/).
2 This is the code used by HZAU corpus to sequence collected textual files. The first two to three digits stand for the numbering of the files in respective sub-corpus; the following four upper-cased letters stand for the sub-discipline; the last optional slot indicates if this file is from the student sub-corpus.

References

Ansarifar, A., H. Shahriari and R. Pishghadam (2018), 'Phrasal Complexity in Academic Writing: A Comparison of Abstracts Written by Graduate Students and Expert Writers in Applied Linguistics', *Journal of English for Academic Purposes*, 31: 58–71.

Atak, N. and A. Saricaoglu (2021), 'Syntactic Complexity in L2 Learners' Argumentative Writing: Developmental Stages and the Within-Genre Topic Effect', *Assessing Writing*, 47: 100506.

Biber, D. (1988), *Variation across Speech and Writing*, New York: Cambridge University Press.

Biber, D. and B. Gray (2010), 'Challenging Stereotypes about Academic Writing: Complexity, Elaboration, Explicitness', *Journal of English for Academic Purposes*, 9 (1): 2–20.

Biber, D., B. Gray and K. Poonpon (2011), 'Should We Use Characteristics of Conversation to Measure Grammatical Complexity in L2 Writing Development?', *TESOL Quarterly*, 45 (1): 5–35.

Biber, D., S. Johansson, G. Leech, S. Conrad and E. Finegan (1999), *Longman Grammar of Spoken and Written English*, London: Longman.

Casal, J. E. (2020), 'An Integrated Corpus and Genre Analysis Approach to Writing Research and Pedagogy: Development of Graduate Student Genre Knowledge', doctoral diss., The Pennsylvania State University, University Park.

Casal, J. E. and J. J. Lee (2019), 'Syntactic Complexity and Writing Quality in Assessed First-Year L2 Writing', *Journal of Second Language Writing*, 44: 51–62.

Casal, J. E., X. Lu, X. Qiu, Y. Wang and G. Zhang (2021), 'Syntactic Complexity across Academic Research Article Part-Genres: A Cross-Disciplinary Perspective', *Journal of English for Academic Purposes*, 52: 100996.

Charles, M. (2007), 'Reconciling Top-Down and Bottom-Up Approaches to Graduate Writing: Using a Corpus to Teach Rhetorical Functions', *Journal of English for Academic Purposes*, 6: 289–302.

Deng, Y., L. Lei and D. Liu (2021), 'Calling for More Consistency, Refinement, and Critical Consideration in the Use of Syntactic Complexity Measures for Writing', *Applied Linguistics*, 42 (5): 1021–7.

Garside, R. (1987), 'The CLAWS Word-Tagging System', in R. Garside, G. Leech and G. Sampson (eds), *The Computational Analysis of English: A Corpus-Based Approach*, 30–41, London: Longman.

Granger, S. (1997), 'On Identifying the Syntactic and Discourse Features of Participle Clauses in Academic English: Native and Non-Native Writers Compared', in A. Jan, I. de Mönnink and W. Herman (eds), *Studies in English Language and Teaching: In Honor of Flor Aarts*, 185–98, Amsterdam: Rodopi.

Greenbaum, S. (1996), *The Oxford English Grammar*, Oxford: Oxford University Press.

Hardie, A. (2012), 'CQPweb—Combining Power, Flexibility and Usability in a Corpus Analysis Tool', *International Journal of Corpus Linguistics*, 17 (3): 380–409.

Huddleston, R. and G. Pullum (2005), *The Cambridge Grammar of the English Language*, Cambridge: Cambridge University Press.

Johns, T. (1986), 'Micro-Concord: A Language Learner's Research Tool', *System*, 14 (2): 151–62.

Klein, D. and C. Manning (2003), 'Accurate Unlexicalized Parsing', in *Proceedings of the 41st Meeting of the Association for Computational Linguistics, Morristown, NJ*, 423–30, Stroudsburg: Association for Computational Linguistics.

Kyle, K. (2016), 'Measuring Syntactic Development in L2 writing: Fine Grained Indices of Syntactic Complexity and Usage-based Indices of Syntactic Sophistication', doctoral diss., Georgia State University, Atlanta, GA.

Kyle, K. and S. A. Crossley (2018), 'Measuring Syntactic Complexity in L2 Writing Using Fine-Grained Clausal and Phrasal Indices', *The Modern Language Journal*, 102 (2): 333–49.

Leech, G., R. Hoogenraad, D. Birch and D. Birch (1984), *English Grammar for Today: A New Introduction*, London and Basingstoke: The Macmillan Press.

Levy, R. and G. Andrew (2006), 'Tregex and Tsurgeon: Tools for Querying and Manipulating Tree Data Structures', in *Proceedings of the 2006 Conference on Language Resources and Evaluation*, 2231–4, Paris: ELRA.

Li, Y., L. Nikitina and P. N. Riget (2022), 'Development of Syntactic Complexity in Chinese University Students' L2 Argumentative Writing', *Journal of English for Academic Purposes*, 56: 101099.

Liu, P., X. Huang and S. Liu (2015), 'Constructing an Agricultural Research Article Corpus of English', *Corpus Linguistics* [in Chinese], 2 (2): 97–106.

Lu, X. (2010), 'Automatic Measurement of Syntactic Complexity in Child Language Acquisition', *International Journal of Corpus Linguistics*, 14: 3–28.

Lu, X., J. E. Casal and Y. Liu (2020), 'The Rhetorical Functions of Syntactically Complex Sentences in Research Article Introductions', *Journal of English for Academic Purposes*, 44: 100832.

Malá, M. (2010), 'Syntactic Functions of Finite and Non-Finite Clauses in Academic English', *Discourse and Interaction*, 3 (1): 73–85.

Martínez, M. Á. (2012), '-ing Supplementive Clauses and Narrative Discourse Referents', *International Journal of English Studies*, 12 (2): 73–91.

Parkinson, J. and J. Musgrave (2014), 'Development of Noun Phrase Complexity in the Writing of English for Academic Purposes Students', *Journal of English for Academic Purposes*, 14: 48–59.

Quirk, R., S. Greenbaum, G. Leech and J. Svartvik (1985), *A Comprehensive Grammar of the English Language*, London: Longman.

Shadloo, F., H. S. Ahmadi and B. Ghonsooly (2019), 'Exploring Syntactic Complexity and its Relationship with Writing Quality in EFL Argumentative Essays', *Topics in Linguistics*, 20 (1): 68–81.

Staples, S., G. T. Laflair and J. Egbert (2017), 'Comparing Language Use in Oral Proficiency Interviews to Target Domains: Conversational, Academic, and Professional Discourse', *The Modern Language Journal*, 101 (1): 194–213.

Xu, J. and L. Wu (2014), 'Web-Based Fourth Generation Corpus Analysis Tools and the BFSU CQPweb Case', *Computer-assisted Foreign Language Education* [in Chinese], (5): 10–15.

Xu, X. and J. Xu (2017), '40 Years of Corpus Application to Foreign Language Teaching in China', *Foreign Language Education in China (Quarterly)* [in Chinese], 10 (4): 62–8.

Yin, S., Y. Gao and X. Lu (2021), 'Syntactic Complexity of Research Article Part-Genres: Differences between Emerging and Expert International Publication Writers', *System*, 97: 102427.

Ziaeian, E. and S. E. Golparvar (2022), 'Fine-Grained Measures of Syntactic Complexity in the Discussion Section of Research Articles: The Effect of Discipline and Language Background', *Journal of English for Academic Purposes*, 57: 101116.

6

Applying Complex Dynamic Systems Theory in EAP Curriculum Design and Teaching Practice

Challenges and Possibilities

Rosmawati

Introduction

The increasingly wider integration of Complex Dynamic Systems Theory (CDST) into the fields of applied linguistics and second language acquisition has advanced our understanding of the complexity of language use and language learning processes at the conceptual, methodological and empirical levels through the rich scholarship published in the past two decades or so (e.g. Fogal and Verspoor 2020; Han 2019; Hiver and Al-Hoorie 2020). This theory, however, has enjoyed a significantly smaller scale of adoption in the English for Academic Purposes (EAP) enterprise, leading to a much more modest repertoire of CDST-inspired EAP publications, if any. Despite the valuable contributions CDST has made in applied linguistics, education and related disciplines, researchers and practitioners in the EAP field seem to have reservations about the practicality of the application of this theory as well as its pedagogical value for EAP. There could be many possible reasons behind these doubts. For one thing, CDST emphasizes interconnectedness among components of a system and does away with simple causal relationships. This very frequently prompts instantaneous scepticism due to the easily foreseeable complications in its operationalization in research and teaching. Moreover, as CDST is deeply rooted in hard sciences, a lot of its methodologies are heavily based in mathematics and/or advanced statistics, which requires a retraining, frequently with a steep learning curve, for many researchers and practitioners in soft sciences.

In the first part of this chapter, I will discuss these possible reasons in detail and will try to dispel the doubts and worries over embracing CDST in EAP. I argue that CDST can be a compatible metatheory which can be fruitfully applied into both EAP research and practice. I will then demonstrate, in the second part of this chapter, the possibilities of CDST application in exploring two constructs in EAP (i.e. complexity and accuracy) and will refer to two of the main tenets in CDST, that is, non-linearity and variability, to show how this theory could reshape our perception of learners' developmental stages. I will also discuss the implications this new perception might have on EAP research and teaching. I will conclude this chapter by suggesting several practical examples of how CDST can compatibly be applied into the EAP enterprise, both in its research and teaching sides.

Complex Dynamic Systems Theory: An overview

Originating from the field of hard sciences, Chaos/Complexity Theory (CT) was first introduced into the field of applied linguistics through the work of Larsen-Freeman (1994, 1997). Chronologically, this was coincidental with the publication of Smith and Thelen's (1993) and Thelen and Smith's (1994) seminal books on Dynamic Systems Theory (DST) and its applications in behavioural sciences. CT and DST are closely related, as they are part of the grand paradigm of complexity sciences (Castellani and Gerrits 2021) and share, to a great extent, similar underpinning concepts, understandings and methodologies. Due to this overlap, the two theories were used rather interchangeably during the early days of their inception into the field of applied linguistics and were only recently combined into a hybrid label – CDST – upon de Bot's (2017) suggestion.

In her seminal paper, Larsen-Freeman (1997) drew the parallels between language learning process and a complex system, noting that both comprise many interconnected components that interact with each other over time and, as a result, shape the overall behaviour of the system. She gave an example of how the process of second language acquisition is driven by many interacting factors, such as the first language (L1), the second language (L2), the input, the feedback, the context, the age and aptitude of learners, their motivation and their learning strategies (Larsen-Freeman 1997). All these factors are interrelated; they are inherently dynamic, and their interaction also changes with time – hence as a whole, this is a complex dynamic system. She advocated that the language learning process is similar to, and should therefore be considered, a complex dynamic system as it has the characteristics of such a system – being complex, dynamic and non-linear. In the same paper, she discussed twelve features of a complex dynamic system, that is, dynamic, complex, non-linear, chaotic, unpredictable, sensitive to initial conditions, open, self-organizing, feedback sensitive, adaptive, strange attractors and fractal shape, which have since then been the theme(s) of investigation in many CDST-inspired studies in applied linguistics (e.g. Fogal 2019), second language learning (e.g. Chan, Verspoor and Vahtrick 2015), L2 writing development (e.g. Rosmawati 2020), education (e.g. van Vondel et al. 2017) and educational psychology (e.g. Hilpert and Marchand 2018), for instance.

In the first fifteen years or so following its introduction into the field of applied linguistics, CDST was frequently labelled as a paradigm-shifting metatheory (de Bot 2008; Larsen-Freeman 2013b) due to its strikingly different epistemological and ontological underpinnings, which intentionally or not sent a rather uncongenial, if not supercilious, message to the well-established enterprise warranting a plan to shift the research paradigm in the field. As a result, this theory did not receive much welcome from the field and was instead met with much scepticism, if not resistance. Fellow researchers and practitioners had their reservations and were rather hesitant in taking the first dive to adopt this theory in their work. It took about a decade before this theory saw some uptakes in the field. The first empirical study that was based on this theory was Larsen-Freeman's (2006) paper on the emergence of developmental patterns in learners' data, which successfully demonstrated the potential this theory had to offer for the study of language acquisition. The following years saw a gradual uptake in the field through several publications, empirical or otherwise, in *Bilingualism: Language and Cognition*, volume 10, issue 1, in 2007; *The Modern Language Journal*, volume 92, issue 2, in 2008; and *Language Learning*, volume 59, special issue in 2009, as well as Larsen-Freeman and Cameron (2008), hence marking the start of the wider diffusion of this theory into applied linguistics and its related (sub)fields.

This theory made a substantial step forward at the methodological level through the publication of an edited volume that discussed a collection of methods and techniques, illustrated with detailed examples, that one could use when exploring second language development from the DST perspective (Verspoor, de Bot and Lowie 2011). This was followed by a rapid uptake in the field of L2 developmental research, particularly in the domain of L2 writing, where this theory has since flourished conceptually, methodologically and empirically (Fogal and Verspoor 2020). Popular themes explored in CDST-inspired studies include, among others, non-linearity[1] (e.g. Rosmawati 2014; Spoelman and Verspoor 2010), variability[2] (e.g. Huang, Steinkrauss and Verspoor 2021; Lesonen et al. 2022), developmental transitions[3] (e.g. Hepford 2020; Nitta and Baba 2014) and emergence[4] (e.g. Bassano and van Geert 2018; Lowie 2017). Though not necessarily always, many of these studies employ highly advanced statistical methods and/or mathematical modelling techniques to process language developmental data, visualize patterns of interaction, detect signs of development and capture the process of emergence. Some examples include Caspi (2010) and Lowie et al. (2011), who make use of a mathematical model based on precursor interactions to describe the interactions between connected growers and successfully modelled vocabulary growth; Baba and Nitta (2014), who use the change point analysis to detect phase transitions in the development of writing fluency; Rosmawati (2016), who applies the critical moment method (variability analysis) to detect transitional jumps in the development of complexity, accuracy and fluency in L2 advanced writing in English; and Evans and Larsen-Freeman (2020), whose use of bifurcation analysis successfully visualizes the emergence of several syntactic structures in the language production of a learner.

More recently, applied linguists are also starting to investigate the perhaps least popular and most under-researched tenet in Larsen-Freeman's (1997) list, that is, the fractal[5] property of language and language learning. Lowie, Plat and de Bot (2014), for example, explore the self-similar pattern of variability in a longitudinal data set collected over a period of six years through a word-naming experiment and find evidence of the existence of pink noise, which bears the signature of fractals, in their data set. Similarly, looking at his data set of naturalistic spoken outputs of an L2 learner over one year, Evans (2020) studies the variance in this time-series data set across different temporal scaling and finds evidence of self-similarity in the development trajectory of his participant. Taking a step further, Rosmawati and Lowie (under review) test their hypothesis about the multifractal nature of language through exploration of the distribution of three syntactic structures (finite verb phrases, noun phrases and head nouns) in English texts and find evidence of multifractality in the distributions of these structures. These studies not only lend support to CDST's tenet of fractality in language but also offer a novel perspective on understanding language development through exploring the changes in the (multi)fractal properties of syntactic complexity.

Owing much to the fruitful works of its zealous proponents, CDST has flourished well in applied linguistics and its related (sub)fields. In their scoping review, Hiver, Al-Hoorie and Evans (2021) found a pool of 488 reports of CDST-inspired studies published within twenty-five years (from 1994 to 2019) in their first round of screening the database search results, 158 of which were then included in the final analysis. The yearly breakdown of the publication years shows that the last decade has seen an upsurge in these scholarly outputs and celebrated the eventual growth of this theory out of its infancy in these fields. A similar finding is also reported in Fogal (2022), whose timeline mapping of CDST-inspired L2 writing studies also shows a higher density of publications in the last decade. Three decades after its first introduction to the field of applied linguistics, CDST has now been well integrated into the field and is now known more widely as an ecological approach (Larsen-Freeman 2020) or a pragmatic transdisciplinary framework (Hiver, Al-Hoorie and Larsen-Freeman 2022) for studying development that not only offers a new way of thinking and understanding the complex phenomena related to language and language learning but also enriches the fields through the methodological expansion it has introduced into these disciplines to study these phenomena.

Turning to the EAP enterprise, it is not difficult to notice that CDST has not enjoyed a similar scale of uptake, most likely due to the reluctance and reservations in the field, which have led to the scarcity of CDST-inspired EAP publications. In the next section, I will discuss some of the possible reasons behind this reluctance and try to dispel some common uncertainties EAP practitioners and researchers may have about this theory.

EAP and CDST: Challenges

The slow diffusion of CSDT into the EAP field might be due to many reasons. Among them the following challenges may constitute the main hurdles, even for those who are the least conservative in their thoughts: (1) the strikingly different epistemology and ontology CDST is based on, (2) the practical challenges in applying this theory and (3) the doubt over the pedagogical value of this theory. I will argue that while these challenges are obvious, they do not necessarily make a strong ground for not adopting CDST. This is particularly so in light of the contributions this theory has made to applied linguistics and its subfields. In this section, I will discuss some of the possible ways these challenges could be overcome in order to help dispel the doubts and worries over embracing CDST in EAP.

The (Seemingly) Radically Disparate Epistemological and Ontological Roots

The slow integration of CDST into the EAP field might be due to the rather terrifying first impressions that the CDST scholarship gives. CDST, as a metatheory, appears strikingly different from many of the object theories in applied linguistics and its related disciplines, including EAP. CDST shares the epistemological and ontological roots with other theories within the broad paradigm of complexity sciences. Common to all theories within this broad paradigm is their departure from the reductionism, which was, and sadly might still be, a common practice in many scientific pursuits. CDST, on the contrary, emphasizes the interconnectedness among the components in a complex dynamic system, as well as the soft assembly between the system and its environment (Larsen-Freeman 2013a). In other words, a complex dynamic system not only has highly interconnected components that are in themselves complex and dynamic but is also soft assembled[6] and interacting with its spatiotemporal contexts. From a CDST perspective, it is the interaction among these components and between the system and its environment that drives the overall development of the system. In other words, the development of a learner's language system is the combined result of the interactions between multiple factors (such as cognitive capacities, L1, etc.) and the learner's immediate contexts (e.g. exposure to L2 uses, interaction with teachers and peers, etc.). Therefore, in the CDST perspective, it is inefficacious, if not impossible, to reduce this complexity into one, or few, factor(s) in the pursuit of establishing a linear causal relationship. CDST urges for a reconsideration of the real nature of complex phenomena, including those related to language teaching and learning, and argues that these complex phenomena are wicked[7] (Hiver, Al-Hoorie and Larsen-Freeman 2022) and therefore cannot easily be reduced to a simple and linear causal relationship.

Moreover, CDST's perspective on variability and its role in development is largely different from how variability has traditionally been treated in non-CDST research. While variability is discarded as noise in the data in the more traditional non-CDST research, variability is elevated to the centre of attention in CDST-inspired research as it is the source of information on the development of the system itself (van Dijk, Verspoor and Lowie 2011; Verspoor, Lowie and de Bot 2020). According to CDST, the development of a complex dynamic system is, to a large extent, driven by the dynamic interactions among its interrelated components and between the system itself and its environment. Such interactions will certainly produce variability in the outward behaviour of the system, and therefore in the CDST perspective, variability is an inherent property of a complex dynamic system (Verspoor, Lowie and van Dijk 2008). The amount of variability will be even larger when the system is undergoing a developmental transition as the system restructures internally for a new attractor state (Lowie and Verspoor 2015; Verspoor, Lowie and de Bot 2020). Hence, the change in the magnitude of variability is considered a potential indicator of development, as larger variability is usually seen preceding a transitional jump/development of the system (Verspoor and de Bot 2022). Therefore, in the CDST's tenets, variability is not only an inherent property of any complex dynamic system but is also an indicator of the development of such a system (Lowie and Verspoor 2015; Verspoor et al. 2017; Verspoor, Lowie and de Bot 2020).

These two points are but small examples of how different CDST's epistemological and ontological underpinnings are. Since CDST postulates the interconnectedness and the ever-changing nature of the components in complex dynamic systems, it gives the impression of a very complex (if not complicated) design when operationalized in research and pedagogy. Its strong focus on variability, which is the messy part of the data, gives a further impression that if one is to adopt CDST into their research, they need to be ready to deal with this messiness. These dismal impressions frequently lead to a sceptical stance and doubt over the possibility of a real-life operationalization of such a complex design in either research or teaching or both. Moreover, adopting a CDST perspective usually entails a need to move away from reductionism, which has been a common practice in the scientific community for centuries, giving the impression that one would need to abandon their disciplinary beliefs and part with their usual research or teaching practices in order to convert to CDST, which certainly adds to the reservations one already has over this new metatheory.

While there is no denying that CDST has introduced a revolutionary perspective to the ways language learning and development can be investigated and understood, it is not true that CDST overthrows any existing theoretical frameworks nor does one need to reject their own past practice in research or teaching in order to adopt this metatheory. In fact, CDST is an integrative transdisciplinary framework (Hiver, Al-Hoorie and Larsen-Freeman 2022) that not only aligns well with but also complements many of the existing practices. Hilpert and Marchand (2018) demonstrate, from an ontological perspective, the close alignment between the nature of reality in education and a complex systems approach to studying it, noting the values of this approach and the means it provides for investigating 'underexplored elements of existing theory' (2018: 185). They encourage researchers and reviewers to keep an open mind to the new forms of evidence that are reached through the complex systems approach as these new findings can be used to make inferences that can help provide 'a more complete picture of learning in context' (2018: 199).

This chapter argues that the nature of constructs in EAP aligns well with the epistemological and ontological underpinnings in CDST and can therefore be fruitfully studied from a CDST perspective. In a later section of this chapter, examples of the development of syntactic constructs that are related to EAP will be presented and discussed from a CDST perspective to demonstrate the compatibility of this theory with EAP studies.

The Practical Challenges in Applying CDST

Another possible reason behind the reservations that EAP researchers and practitioners have regarding CDST is perhaps related to the methodological challenges that come with embracing this theory. Since CDST posits on the interconnectedness and the dynamic nature of the components in dynamic systems, the designs and methodologies that follow from these assumptions lead many of the CDST-inspired studies to employ a time-intensive or relation-intensive approach (or both) in their data collection and analysis. The time-intensive approach is usually employed in dynamic-dominant research that focuses on understanding the dynamics of development, interactions and emergent outcomes while the relation-intensive approach is generally deployed in studies that aim at discovering and understanding the underlying structure(s) of a complex system or of a dynamic relation (Hiver, Al-Hoorie and Evans 2021). Common to these two approaches is their focus on changes in the system, which is one of the core tenets in the CDST approach. In order to understand the behaviour of a complex dynamic system, it is necessary to explore its changes over time. CDST posits that a complex dynamic system is soft assembled with its spatiotemporal contexts and is to be explored, studied and explained within these contexts. Hence, the component of time is generally inherent to most CDST-inspired studies, and it is not uncommon to see that many CDST-inspired studies were of longitudinal nature, some spanning years of observation (e.g. three years of observation in Rousse-Malpat, Steinkrauss and Verspoor 2019). However, such a research design might, at its face value, seem to be practically incompatible with the content-rich and usually fast-paced nature of EAP classrooms.

Moreover, a lot of CDST-inspired studies engage with the use of advanced statistical methods (e.g. Monte-Carlo simulation, non-linear regression, etc.) that frequently require trainings beyond those commonly offered in applied linguistics postgraduate studies. This might present a barrier to those who do not have a strong background in advanced mathematics/statistics and may present a steep learning curve for those who brave the challenge (Kostoulas and Mercer 2018). This difficulty, however, is not unique to the EAP enterprise. Even in applied linguistics, where CDST has bloomed relatively well, there is a scarcity of resources that provide methodological guidance to researchers wanting to embark on their CDST journey. Many of the designs and methodologies that are currently used in CDST-inspired studies are borrowed from adjacent fields as well as distant disciplines. While such a practice of borrowing across disciplines is not uncommon, the translation of these borrowed methodologies into the practically viable application in applied linguistics research has not been extensive nor made accessible to peers without similar levels of background training in these methodologies. At the time of writing this chapter, there are only a few resources on research methods in CDST available (e.g. Hiver and Al-Hoorie 2020; Verspoor, Bot and Lowie 2011). The paucity of such literature is certainly a roadblock in the diffusion and adoption of CDST in both applied linguistics and EAP.

However, this chapter argues that these methodological challenges should not prevent one from embracing a powerful metatheory that has been shown to benefit applied linguistics in many ways, particularly in advancing our understanding of the process of language development. Proponents of CDST are putting their best in producing such resources. This joint effort is evident in many CDST-dedicated sessions at international conferences, including the recent Association Internationale de Linguistique Appliquée (AILA) 2020 World Congress (postponed to 2021) as well as the American Association for Applied Linguistics (AAAL) 2023 conference and the AILA 2023 World Congress, where there were specific colloquiums and symposiums that focused on CDST-inspired research methodologies. A recent book by Hiver and Al-Hoorie (2020) also provides a very comprehensive discussion on research methodologies in applied linguistics that are consonant with CDST. Hence, given time, there will certainly be more resources created in the field to guide those eager to adopt this theory into their research practice.

The Doubt over the Pedagogical Values of CDST

A question that CDST scholars frequently encounter is, 'So, what does CDST have to offer to practical classroom teaching that is not already known to the field?' This question does not come only from practitioners but also from fellow researchers. The doubt over the pedagogical values of CDST is shared as well in applied linguistics (Kostoulas and Mercer 2018). This is perhaps due to the scantiness of explicit conversation, in the field, on the direct application of this theory in teaching practices. The paucity of such literature is rather unsurprising. CDST is not a pedagogical approach per se – it is a metatheory, and like any other metatheory, it operates more at the ontological and epistemological levels. It offers 'an ontological position for understanding the social sphere in complex and dynamic terms' (Hiver and Al-Hoorie 2020: 20) and an epistemological frame to understand the nature of realities around us. It is from these ontological and epistemological standpoints that CDST scholars derive appropriate methodologies and suitable methods to study the complex world within this paradigm. It is, therefore, seemingly rather distant from pedagogy or at least so at this current stage of CDST integration into applied linguistics and its related subfields.

As CDST is a relatively young metatheory in applied linguistics, much of the earlier literature inspired by CDST revolved around drawing parallels between the ontological and epistemological roots of CDST and the theoretical concepts in the discipline. It was only in the last decade that a surge in the methodology-related CDST literature was evident (Fogal 2021). While this surge signals a positive trend in the adoption of CDST, it might still take a while before the drip-down towards research methods and pedagogy might materialize. Even in the mother field of applied linguistics, there is still a lack of clarity and consensus on research designs and methodologies that merit adoption into empirical studies underpinned by CDST. It will take time for the field to explore the potential of this metatheory and to decide on what direction it will want to take moving forward.

Giving a quick and explicit answer to the question on the pedagogical contribution of CDST is therefore not easy or straightforward. Larsen-Freeman (2013b) notes that CDST provides a new way of thinking. Bringing this new way of thinking into teaching involves, for example, the understanding that '[t]eaching does not cause learning; learners make their own paths' (Larsen-Freeman 2013a: 82). While this understanding does not necessarily dictate pedagogy, it certainly prompts a reconsideration of approaches to teaching and learning. Pedagogical approaches that align with the CDST tenets, according to Larsen-Freeman (2013a: 83), 'would not be curriculum-centred nor learner-centred, but it would be learning-centred – where the learning guides the teaching and not vice versa'. Therefore, while CDST does not directly contribute to classroom teaching techniques, it does offer a paradigm in which teaching practices can be reconsidered and reformulated to align better with the nature of realities in teaching and learning.

In the following section, I will demonstrate how the CDST approach can be compatibly applied in EAP and argue that this combination will benefit both research and teaching in the EAP enterprise.

Exploring the Compatibility between CDST and EAP

Using linguistic complexity and accuracy as examples, in this section I will demonstrate how *non-linearity* and *variability*, two popular concepts in CSDT, could reshape our understanding of learners' development stages and discuss its implications on research and teaching. For illustration, a data set comprising written production of an advanced student writer is used in this chapter to demonstrate how the concepts in CDST materialized in learners' development.

Data Set

The data set comes from one student writer, Arun (pseudonym), whose writing during his course of postgraduate study (majoring in TESOL education) in a higher education institution in Australia was collected as part of a larger project[8] on the dynamic development of and interaction among the constructs of complexity, accuracy and fluency (CAF) in advanced academic writing in English as an L2. As part of his course, Arun had to write two to three academic essays as assignments for each of the units of study he was enrolled in. With his consent, these essays were then collected at the end of each of the two semesters and made up the data set for the project. Arun had Thai as his L1 and an IELTS score of 7.0 at the beginning of the data collection period. No proficiency benchmarking was done at the end of the data collection period.

A total of twenty essays (of approximately 55,000 words) were collected from Arun over the course of two academic semesters. A purposive sampling of 200 words per essay was applied to the data set with the following rationale: (1) to filter out paragraphs with dense quotations, (2) to control for text length for the purpose of better comparability among texts and (3) to reduce the possible inflation effect in some of the measures that are highly sensitive to text length. The resulting 4,000-word sub-corpus of Arun's samples was included in the final analysis. These samples were then coded with a set of CAF measures (see Rosmawati 2016 for a complete list of these measures), several of which are used in this chapter for the purpose of illustrating the traits of non-linearity and variability in the learner's developmental path (see Table 6.1).

Non-Linear Trend and Variability in Development

When the data set was mapped into a time-series graph, it became clear that the constructs under observation developed in a non-linear way. Arun's syntactic

Table 6.1 Constructs measured in this study

No	Construct	Measure	Operationalization	Obtained From
1	syntactic complexity (sentence level)	finite verb token ratio	words/finite verbs	manual coding[1]
2	syntactic complexity (clausal level)	index of subordination	dependent clauses/t-units	manual coding[1]
3	syntactic complexity (phrasal level)	mean length clause	words/clauses	manual coding[1]
4	complex nominal use	index of complex nominalization	complex nominals/t-units	manual coding[1]
5	lexical diversity	measure of textual lexical diversity (MTLD)	mean length of sequential word strings with a given type-token ratio value	Text Inspector (Weblingua Ltd 2014)
6	academic word use	academic word list (AWL) word ratio	AWL words/total words	Vocabprofile (Cobb n.d.)
7	accuracy	error-free clause (EFC) ratio	EFC clause/total clause	manual coding[2]

[1] Intercoder reliability at 95% and the disagreement was resolved through discussion.

[2] Intercoder reliability at 78% and the disagreement was resolved through discussion that involved a third coder.

complexity as measured at the sentence level, for example, developed in the following manner (see Figure 6.1).

As can be seen from Figure 6.1a, the ratio of words to finite verbs (W/FV), which is considered a good measure of syntactic complexity at the sentential level in advanced L2 writing, developed in a non-linear fashion. Not only were there sharp peaks and deep valleys, the development still manifested a non-linear trend even after a three-window moving average smoothing line was fitted to the data set. For the purpose of juxtaposing, a linear trend line was added to this data visualization to highlight the stark comparison between the common assumption of linear development and the messy and non-linear developmental trend in the actual data.

Similarly, such non-linearity was also manifested in the measures of syntactic complexity at the clausal and phrasal levels in Arun's writing. Figure 6.1b shows the non-linear development of the index of subordination, which is one of the measures of syntactic complexity at the clausal level, and Figure 6.1c shows the non-linear development of mean length clause, which is one of the measures of syntactic complexity at the phrasal level. Both measures developed in a non-

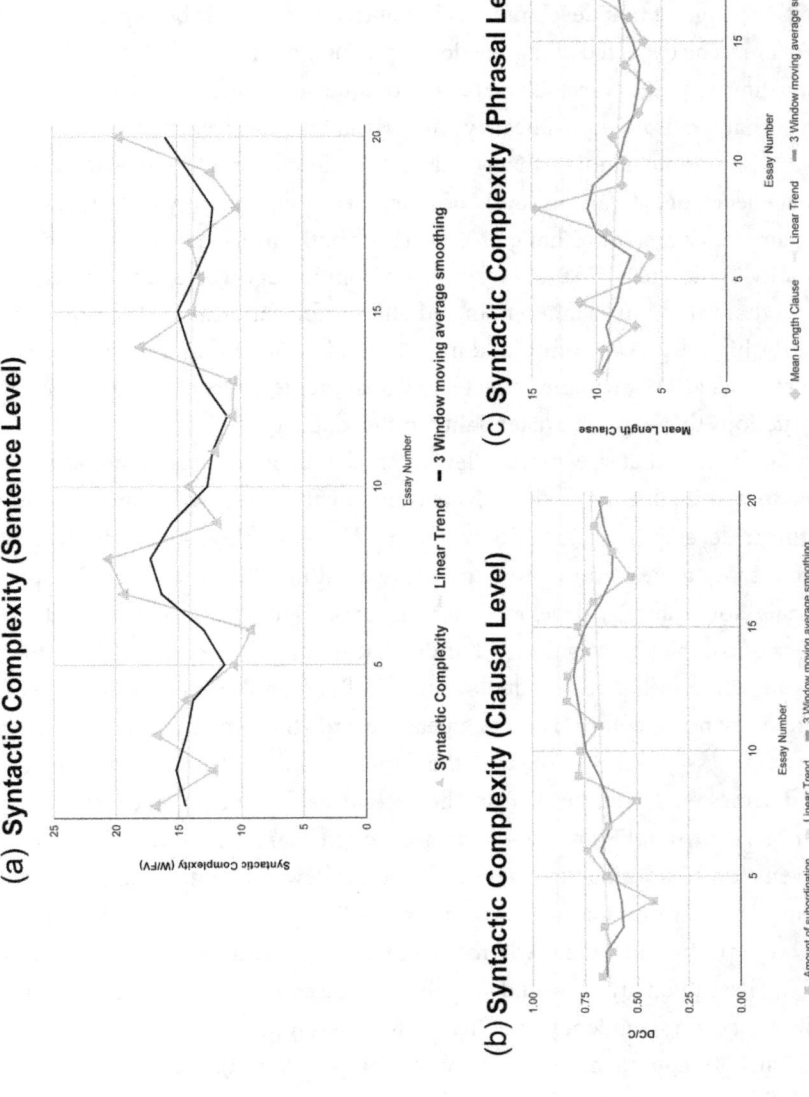

Figure 6.1 Non-linear development of syntactic complexity at (a) the sentence level, (b) the clausal level and (c) the phrasal level.

linear fashion, and their pattern of development was very different to each other. Index of subordination fluctuated to a higher degree, which resulted in a larger bump in the three-window smoothing trend line. At the phrasal level, such a bump was relatively smaller due to the smaller degree of fluctuations in the measure of the Mean Length Clause. In other words, the amount of variability was larger in syntactic complexity at the clausal level than at the phrasal level. All of these suggest that development ebbs and flows, and that both progress and regress are to be expected along the developmental path.

Non-linearity and variability are not unique to Arun's data set as shown in this chapter. Both non-linearity and variability have been reported, and analysed, in many studies that tracked the development of constructs in language learning, at various levels of granularity and a variety of time length. For example, Chang and Zhang (2021) report both intra- and inter-individual variability in their participants' listening developmental trajectories and support the idea that variability is inherent in and offers information about development. Similarly, high degrees of intra- and inter-individual variability are identified by Lesonen et al. (2022), who investigate how beginner learners of Finnish develop constructions that express existentiality in the language.

For measures that are more relevant to the EAP settings, such as those related to nominalization, lexical diversity, use of academic words and accuracy, non-linear development was also evident in Arun's writing. As can be seen in Figure 6.2a–d, none of these measures developed in a linear fashion. Complex nominals, for example, developed non-linearly. Figure 6.2a showed that the number of complex nominals per T-units that Arun produced in the first three essays he wrote in his postgraduate study declined and dropped to the lowest level in essay no. 3, before rising to a peak towards the end of the first semester (i.e. around essay nos. 8–10), and then this construct fluctuated less in the second semester, as can be seen in the second half set of the data. The other constructs shown in Figure 6.2 also went through a large amount of fluctuation and even after smoothing lines were added to the developmental graphs, it is still evident that their development was in no way linear. Along the developmental paths were peaks and valleys where a large amount of variability could clearly be seen. These fluctuations would very likely be discarded in studies that employ measures of central tendency as well as a linear assumption of development, and within such an approach, the measures of complex nominals/t-units as well as lexical diversity would be assumed to have been stagnant given their rather flat linear trend lines, while the measure on the use of academic words would be said to have regressed due to the downward trend in its linear trend line. However,

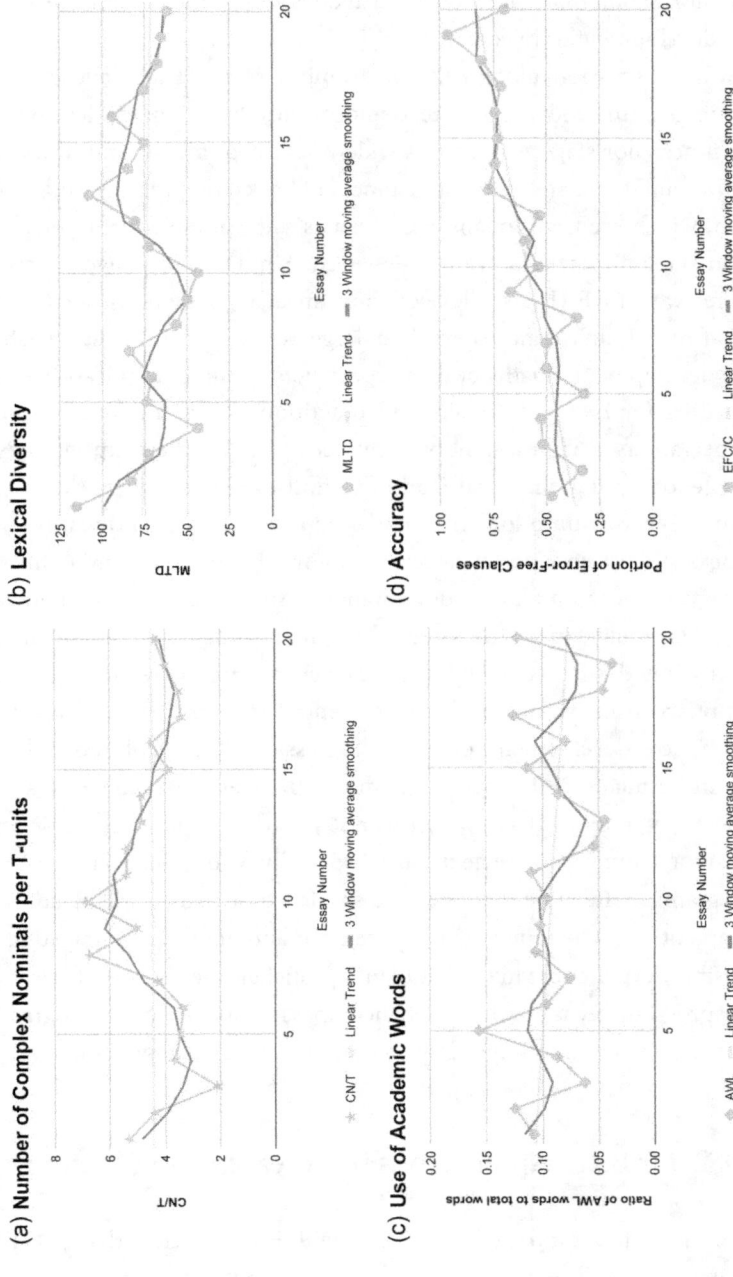

Figure 6.2 Non-linear development of (a) the use of nominalization, (b) lexical diversity, (c) the use of academic words and (d) accuracy.

these assumptions were not necessarily true, nor were they descriptive of Arun's development. A CDST approach to describing development provides more nuanced information than a linear approach does, due to the inherent variability along the developmental trajectory.

The earlier discussion, along with the examples from Arun's data set as well as the findings in the wider literature, demonstrates that language development is neither linear nor stage-wise as was widely assumed. It ebbs and flows from time to time, and there are frequent instances of backslides, regress, stagnations and so on, which are traditionally perceived as unfavourable for development but are an integral part of development itself. Similarly, language constructs that are relevant to EAP also develop non-linearly, as demonstrated by the examples from Arun's data. There is a large degree of inherent variability along the developmental paths of these constructs. A direct implication of this understanding for EAP researchers and practitioners is perhaps the need to adjust expectations. EAP researchers might need to adjust their expectations in, for example, designing empirical studies to find evidence of proficiency gain as the more linear assumptions frequently employed in conventional research might not be robust enough to detect or capture this inherent variability that is necessary in accounting for development. Similarly, EAP teachers also need to adjust their expectations regarding their students' development and not feel frustrated when encountering learners whose scores of proficiency tests (expressed usually with measures of central tendency) seem to indicate stagnant or slow development, or worse, regression. It is highly possible that there are more nuanced fluctuations than captured in those linear measures, and the learners' interlanguage system is not yet at the point where it is ready for a transitional jump into the next stage. Especially within the contexts of EAP, where programmes are rather intensive and short in time span, it will be necessary for EAP practitioners to adjust their expectations and not be discouraged to not see any visible development in their students' proficiency test scores at the end of their EAP programme, as development encompasses more than just progress (or increase in scores) but also inherently includes regress and stagnancy.

CDST for EAP: Applications in Research and Teaching

Having discussed the compatibility of CDST with EAP, it is clear that CDST has a lot of potential to offer for the EAP enterprise. Not only does it provide a novel angle into understanding how language development unfolds, but it also offers a set of highly advanced statistical tools and analyses that are not overused already in the field. It hence has the potential for uncovering information in the data set that is otherwise not explored when using common techniques. Interested readers are referred to Hiver and Al-Hoorie (2020) as well as Verspoor, de Bot and Lowie (2011) for a comprehensive discussion of these methods, techniques and tools. In this section, I will briefly point out several of these methods and tools that can be readily applied into EAP research and discuss some teaching practices that align with CDST and that can be applied in EAP classrooms.

Research Methods

Certainly, adopting a CDST approach entails the adaptation of research designs and methodologies to align with the tenets of CDST. However, this does not necessarily mean that the currently available research methods are not compatible with CDST. In fact, the opposite is true. There are many classroom-oriented research methods that are consonant with CDST and could be compatibly applied to EAP research. Action research, for example, which is quite commonly used by many practitioner-researchers including those in EAP, is a research method that is compatible with CDST. In action research, teachers try out a certain pedagogical strategy, say for example teaching how to write the introductory paragraph(s) of an essay or report through the CARS model's rhetorical moves approach instead of a systemic functional linguistic genre-based approach, to see how this new strategy improves the quality of students' writing. This aligns well with the tenets of CDST, whereby the teachers' action of trying out a new strategy is introducing a perturbation into the class as a system. It is very likely that this perturbation will lead to noise in the system. The teacher-researcher then observes the emergence of change in this system in order to inform their next pedagogical decisions (Larsen-Freeman 2016). Therefore, action research is a research method that can be readily used in CDST-inspired EAP research.

A very similar approach is that of the formative experiment (Reinking and Bradley 2008), in which the researcher uses a retrodictive approach to investigate the adaptations necessary to achieve a pedagogical goal without the pre-emptive attempt to control the context and situation of the classroom in the process of achieving that goal – making this method another CDST-compatible research method. In the context of EAP research, a formative experiment approach can be used, for example, in researching how students learn and use hedging in their writing through observing the ecological dynamics of an intensive academic writing course. In such a formative experimental study, the researcher looks back at the data (which may comprise not only the written outputs from the students but also the teaching materials, survey results about students' exposure to the language outside the classrooms, lesson observation videos, etc.) and tries to look at the dynamic interactions among the many factors/components identified in the data set in order to arrive at a more holistic understanding of the students' learning. Eventually, through analysing these interactions, the researcher would be able to better identify potential adaptation strategies to improve students' learning experiences and enhance their mastery of hedging in academic writing.

Beyond research methods, CDST also provides tools to study the dynamics of development through visualization and methodological/statistical tools to measure/detect changes. These tools can certainly be used in the EAP research enterprise too. When investigating learners' mastery of rhetorical moves in academic writing in an EAP course, for example, the progmax-regmin graph (van Geert and van Dijk 2002) can be used to visualize the changes in the uses of these moves over time showing the periods when the uses are relatively stable and the periods when larger variability is detected. Knowing these periods will help the researcher and the teacher in having a better guess at the factors that might have caused these changes and in conceiving a corresponding intervention strategy if considered necessary. If a further exploration into the data is desired, the critical frequency method (van Geert and van Dijk 2002) can then be used to detect if this period of large variability signifies a transitional jump in the learners' developmental paths. This will help the researcher and teacher understand the seemingly inconsistent performance of the students and make a better-informed pedagogical decision for the students.

The vast repertoire of methods and tools that are compatible with CDST and hence used in CDST-inspired research is, however, beyond the discussion of this chapter. Interested readers can refer to Hiver and Al-Hoorie (2020) for a comprehensive review of both qualitative and quantitative research methods that are consonant with CDST and to Verspoor, de Bot and Lowie (2011) for a detailed discussion and hands-on demonstration of techniques and tools available for CDST-inspired studies of language learning. These methods and tools can certainly be compatibly applied to and complement the current EAP research.

Teaching and Learning

Despite not being a pedagogical approach, CDST does have implications for teaching and learning. In this section, I will briefly point out three of them. First, the notion of classroom as a complex dynamic system that is soft assembled with its spatiotemporal context has strong implications on how teachers view the classroom and subsequently on how they conduct their teaching. Mercer (2013) argues that teachers with this understanding will consider each classroom a unique complex dynamic system that emerges from the interactions among all its components and therefore refrain from generalizing beyond the spatiotemporal contexts of a specific classroom. Perhaps not novel to any teachers, there is no one-size-fits-all approach in teaching, and CDST particularly emphasizes the importance of understanding a classroom within its contexts, hence making each classroom a unique one. Teachers are encouraged to 'engage in a form of ethnographic analysis' (2013: 381) to look at each of their classrooms-in-progress and decide on what works best in each situation. When a teaching strategy works for one class but not the other, teachers can, for example, have conversations with the students, or ask the students to write a reflection on their learning experience, or observe the students when they are studying independently (with their consent, of course) in order to get a better understanding of what could have caused the success/failure of the teaching strategy. This certainly aligns with what EAP teachers have been doing in their classrooms where they adapt their teaching to the dynamics of the classroom accordingly.

The other tenet of CDST that has a strong implication on teaching and learning is the emergent property of a complex dynamic system. Larsen-Freeman (2013a: 77) argues that 'it is not necessary to posit a central rule-governed mental grammar that applies in a top-down manner'. Given sufficient input in which the target language feature is salient and contingent enough, learning will emerge. This tenet has a direct implication on teaching. Instead of assuming a predetermined natural order of development for learners, teachers are encouraged to adopt an ecological approach to teaching (Kramsch 2008) that creates sufficient affordances for learning to emerge. This means situating the learning in an authentic context – the teachers' role in the learning process is to afford a construct's salience and cue contingency to perturb the learners' system enough for it to move towards the acquisition of this new construct or, in the dynamic parlance, towards the emergence of this new system. This is very much in line with a dynamic usage-based (DUB) approach to language teaching (Verspoor and Hong 2013; Verspoor and Phuong Nguyen 2015). This approach does not assume the existence of Universal Grammar; instead, it puts a strong emphasis on the frequency of input as well as on forms at all levels of language. The DUB approach encourages the use of authentic input in a sufficient and meaningful way, where relevant language constructs should be made clear enough through scaffolding (hence, salience) and be encountered enough to be remembered (hence, contingency) to lead to emergence. Such a close alignment between the principles of the DUB approach and the tenets of CDST makes this approach a rather popular one for CDST-inspired language classrooms.

Finally, with the understanding of non-linearity and variability as inherent properties of development, teaching materials should ideally be designed in a way that allows learners to not only meaningfully revisit a newly learned construct multiple times (Larsen-Freeman 2013a) but also to have various chances of receiving and acting on feedback they receive in their learning. Learning develops in a non-linear way, and it is not uncommon that learners may slide back to their previous state and hence will need to revisit the newly learned construct in order to learn it again before this can be internalized into their system. There will be many trial-and-error phases during this process, which results in a high degree of variability in the system, but this is not to be so readily discarded. According to CDST, variability is the expression of development, and hence teachers should refrain from labelling students' inconsistent performance as failures in learning and instead create a learning environment where learners can revisit the newly learned construct as many times as necessary for learning to emerge.

Conclusion

The uptake of CDST in the EAP enterprise has not caught up with the recognition this metatheory has gained in applied linguistics and its related disciplines. This chapter has discussed three possible reasons behind this slow diffusion and argued that CDST is as compatible with EAP as it is with applied linguistics. As much as the CDST approach has enriched the scholarship of language teaching and learning and added to the wealth of research methodologies available in applied linguistics and second language developmental studies, it can certainly be fruitfully applied into EAP research and teaching. Some examples of classroom-oriented research methods as well as recommendations on its pedagogical implications are given in this chapter. Researchers and practitioners in the EAP field are invited and warmly welcomed to jump on this metatheory ship and benefit from it.

Notes

1 Non-linearity is the CDST's tenet that development is not always one-directional (upward or forward) – it can sometimes slide backwards or get stagnant as well. In

contrast with the rather conventional understanding of progress (and only progress) as development, CDST sees development as being non-linear and acknowledges that regress and stagnation are inherent features of development.

2 Variability is the outcome of the not-necessarily-always-consistent behaviours of the system. In language learning, variability includes both the inter-individual and the intra-individual variability. While the former refers to the differences observed among the behaviours of a group of language learners, the latter is about the differences observed in the behaviours of an individual across different occasions of observation. The inconsistency in the observed behaviours is generally referred to as variability.

3 Developmental transitions refer to the jumps from one stage of development to the next.

4 Emergence refers to the process in which order or pattern(s) emerges from chaos or disorganized behaviours.

5 Fractal is a geometric concept to refer to self-similar shapes, such as the Sierpinski Triangle, the snowflake and so on.

6 Soft assembly refers to the idea that behaviours emerge from the interactions between an individual and its immediate contexts.

7 A wicked problem is one that is challenging and very difficult to solve because of its multiple interdependent and interacting factors that are complex in nature.

8 This project was approved by the Human Research Ethics Committee (HREC) of the University of Sydney (Ref: GD/ADS).

References

Baba, K. and R. Nitta (2014), 'Phase Transitions in Development of Writing Fluency from a Complex Dynamic Systems Perspective', *Language Learning*, 64 (1): 1–35.

Bassano, D. and P. van Geert (2018), 'New Perspectives on Input-Output Dynamics: Example from the Emergence of the Noun Category', in M. Hickmann, E. Veneziano and H. Jisa (eds), *Sources of Variation in First Language Acquisition: Languages, Contexts, and Learners*, 201–18, Amsterdam: John Benjamins Publishing Company.

Caspi, T. (2010), 'A Dynamic Perspective on Second Language Development', PhD diss., University of Groningen.

Castellani, B. and L. Gerrits (2021), 'Map of the Complexity Sciences', LLC, *Art and Science Factory*. Available online: https://www.art-sciencefactory.com/ complexity -map_feb09.html (accessed 13 June 2022).

Chan, H., M. Verspoor and L. Vahtrick (2015), 'Dynamic Development in Speaking versus Writing in Identical Twins', *Language Learning*, 65 (2): 298–325.

Chang, P. and L. Zhang (2021), 'A CDST Perspective on Variability in Foreign Language Learners' Listening Development', *Frontiers in Psychology*, 12: 601962.

Cobb, T. (n.d.), *VocabProfilers* [computer program]. Available online: at https://www.lextutor.ca/vp/ (accessed 7 June 2015).

de Bot, K. (2008), 'Introduction: Second Language Development as a Dynamic Process', *The Modern Language Journal*, 92 (2): 166–78.

de Bot, K. (2017), 'Complexity Theory and Dynamic Systems Theory: Same or Different?', in L. Ortega and Z. Han (eds), *Complexity Theory and Language Development: In Celebration of Diane Larsen-Freeman*, 51–8, Amsterdam: John Benjamins Publishing Company.

Evans, D. (2020), 'On the Fractal Nature of Complex Syntax and the Timescale Problem', *Studies in Second Language Learning and Teaching*, 10 (4): 697–721.

Evans, D. and D. Larsen-Freeman (2020), 'Bifurcations and the Emergence of L2 Syntactic Structures in a Complex Dynamic System', *Frontiers in Psychology*, 11: 574603.

Fogal, G. (2019), 'Tracking Microgenetic Changes in Authorial Voice Development from a Complexity Theory Perspective', *Applied Linguistics*, 40 (3): 432–55.

Fogal, G. (2021), 'L2 Writing Scholarship from a Complexity Theory Perspective: An Overview of Fifteen Years of Research', *AILA2021*, Groningen, The Netherlands, 15–20 August.

Fogal, G. (2022), 'Second Language Writing from a Complex Dynamic Systems Perspective', *Language Teaching*, 55 (2): 193–210.

Fogal, G. and M. Verspoor, eds (2020), *Complex Dynamic Systems Theory and L2 Writing Development*, Amsterdam: John Benjamins Publishing Company.

Han, Z., ed. (2019), *Profiling Learner Language as a Dynamic System*, Bristol: Multilingual Matters.

Hepford, E. (2020), 'The Elusive Phase Shift: Capturing Changes in L2 Writing Development and Interaction between the Cognitive and Social Ecosystems', in G. Fogal and M. Verspoor (eds), *Complex Dynamic Systems Theory and L2 Writing Development*, 161–82, Amsterdam: John Benjamins Publishing Company.

Hilpert, J. and G. Marchand (2018), 'Complex Systems Research in Educational Psychology: Aligning Theory and Method', *Educational Psychologist*, 53 (3): 185–202.

Hiver, P. and A. Al-Hoorie (2020), *Research Methods for Complexity Theory in Applied Linguistics*, Bristol: Multilingual Matters.

Hiver, P., A. Al-Hoorie and R. Evans (2021), 'Complex Dynamic Systems Theory in Language Learning: A Scoping Review of 25 Years of Research', *Studies in Second Language Acquisition*, 44 (4): 913–41.

Hiver, P., A. Al-Hoorie and D. Larsen-Freeman (2022), 'Towards a Transdisciplinary Integration of Research Purposes and Methods for Complex Dynamic Systems Theory: Beyond the Quantitative-Qualitative Divide', *International Review of Applied Linguistics in Language Teaching*, 60 (1): 7–22.

Huang, T., R. Steinkrauss and M. Verspoor (2021), 'Variability as Predictor in L2 Writing Proficiency', *Journal of Second Language Writing*, 52: 110787.

Kostoulas, A. and S. Mercer (2018), 'Reflection on Complexity: TESOL Researchers Reflect on Their Experiences', *Theory and Practice of Second Language Acquisition*, 4 (2): 109–27.

Kramsch, C. (2008), 'Ecological Perspectives on Foreign Language Education', *Language Teaching*, 41 (2): 389–408.

Larsen-Freeman, D. (1994), 'On the Parallels between Chaos Theory and Second Language Acquisition', Second Language Research Forum, Montreal, Canada, 6–9 October.

Larsen-Freeman, D. (1997), 'Chaos/Complexity Science and Second Language Acquisition', *Applied Linguistics*, 18 (2): 141–65.

Larsen-Freeman, D. (2006), 'The Emergence of Complexity, Fluency, and Accuracy in the Oral and Written Production of Five Chinese Learners of English', *Applied Linguistics*, 27 (4): 590–619.

Larsen-Freeman, D. (2013a), 'Complexity Theory', in S. Gass and A. Mackey (eds), *The Routledge Handbook of Second Language Acquisition*, 73–87, Hobeken: Taylor and Francis.

Larsen-Freeman, D. (2013b), 'Complexity Theory: A New Way to Think', *Revista Brasileira de Linguística Aplicada*, 13 (2): 369–73.

Larsen-Freeman, D. (2016), 'Classroom-Oriented Research from a Complex Systems Perspective', *Studies in Second Language Learning and Teaching*, 6 (3): 377–93.

Larsen-Freeman, D. (2020), 'Foreword: Taking the Next Step', in P. Hiver and A. Al-Hoorie (eds), *Research Methods for Complexity Theory in Applied Linguistics*, vii–ix, Bristol: Multilingual Matters.

Larsen-Freeman, D. and L. Cameron (2008), *Complex Systems and Applied Linguistics*, Oxford: Oxford University Press.

Lesonen, S., R. Steinkrauss, M. Suni and M. Verspoor (2022), 'Variation and Variability in L2 Learning Trajectories: Learning the Finnish Existential Construction', *Journal of the European Second Language Association*, 6 (1): 1–17.

Lowie, W. (2017), 'Emergentism: Wide Ranging Theoretical Framework or Just One More Meta-Theory?', *Recherches en didactique des langues et des cultures*, 14: 1–9.

Lowie, W., T. Caspi, P. van Geert and H. Steenbeek (2011), 'Modeling Development and Change', in M. Verspoor, K. de Bot and W. Lowie (eds), *A Dynamic Approach to Second Language Development: Methods and Techniques*, 99–121, Amsterdam: John Benjamins Publishing Company.

Lowie, W., R. Plat and K. de Bot (2014), 'Pink Noise in Language Production: A Nonlinear Approach to the Multilingual Lexicon', *Ecological Psychology*, 26 (3): 216–28.

Lowie, W. and M. Verspoor (2015), 'Variability and Variation in Second Language Acquisition Orders: A Dynamic Reevaluation', *Language Learning*, 65 (1): 63–88.

Mercer, S. (2013), 'Towards a Complexity-Informed Pedagogy for Language Learning', *Revista Brasileira de Linguística Aplicada*, 13 (2): 375–98.

Nitta, R. and K. Baba (2014), 'Self-Regulation in the Evolution of the Ideal L2 Self: A Complex Dynamic Systems Approach to the L2 Motivational Self System', in Z. Dörnyei, P. MacIntyre and A. Henry (eds), *Motivational Dynamics in Language Learning*, 367–96, Bristol: Multilingual Matters.

Reinking, D. and B. Bradley (2008), *On Formative and Design Experiments: Approaches to Language and Literacy Research*, Amsterdam: Teachers College Press.

Rosmawati, R. (2014), 'Dynamic Development of Complexity and Accuracy: A Case Study in Second Language Academic Writing', *Australian Review of Applied Linguistics*, 37 (2): 75–100.

Rosmawati, R. (2016), 'Dynamic Development and Interactions of Complexity, Accuracy, and Fluency in ESL Academic Writing', PhD diss., University of Sydney.

Rosmawati, R. (2020), 'Profiling the Dynamic Changes of Syntactic Complexity in L2 Academic Writing: A Multilevel Synchrony Method', in G. Fogal and M. Verspoor (eds), *Complex Dynamic Systems Theory and L2 Writing Development*, 109–31, Amsterdam: John Benjamins Publishing Company.

Rosmawati, R. and W. Lowie (under review), 'Multifractal Analysis of the Distribution of Grammatical Constructions in English Texts'.

Rousse-Malpat, A., R. Steinkrauss and M. Verspoor (2019), 'Structure-Based or Dynamic Usage-Based Instruction: Long-Term Effects on (Morpho)Syntactic and Lexical Complexity in Writing Samples', *Instructed Second Language Acquisition*, 3 (2): 181–205.

Smith, L. B. and E. Thelen (1993), *A Dynamic Systems Approach to Development: Applications*, Cambridge, MA: MIT Press.

Spoelman, M. and M. Verspoor (2010), 'Dynamic Patterns in Development of Accuracy and Complexity: A Longitudinal Case Study in the Acquisition of Finnish', *Applied Linguistics*, 31 (4): 532–53.

Thelen, E. and L. B. Smith (1994), *A Dynamic Systems Approach to the Development of Cognition and Action*, Cambridge, MA: MIT Press.

van Dijk, M., M. Verspoor and W. Lowie (2011), 'Variability and DST', in M. Verspoor, K. de Bot and W. Lowie (eds), *A Dynamic Approach to Second Language Development: Methods and Techniques*, 55–84, Amsterdam: John Benjamins Publishing Company.

van Geert, P. and M. van Dijk (2002), 'Focus on Variability: New Tools to Study Intra-Individual Variability in Developmental Data', *Infant Behaviour and Development*, 25: 340–74.

van Vondel, S., H. Steenbeek, M. van Dijk and P. van Geert (2017), 'Ask, Don't Tell: A Complex Dynamic Systems Approach to Improving Science Education by Focusing on the Co-Construction of Scientific Understanding', *Teaching and Teacher Education*, 63: 243–53.

Verspoor, M. and K. de Bot (2022), 'Measures of Variability in Transitional Phases in Second Language Development', *International Review of Applied Linguistics in Language Teaching*, 61 (1): 85–101.

Verspoor, M., K. de Bot and W. Lowie, eds (2011), *A Dynamic Approach to Second Language Development: Methods and Techniques*, Amsterdam: John Benjamins Publishing Company.

Verspoor, M. and N. Hong (2013), 'A Dynamic Usage-Based Approach to Communicative Language Teaching', *European Journal of Applied Linguistics*, 1 (1): 22–54.

Verspoor, M., W. Lowie, H. Chan and L. Vahtrick (2017), 'Linguistic Complexity in Second Language Development: Variability and Variation at Advanced Stages', *Recherches en didactique des langues et des cultures*, 14: 1–27.

Verspoor, M., W. Lowie and K. de Bot (2020), 'Variability as Normal as Apple Pie', *Linguistics Vanguard*, 7 (s2): 20200034.

Verspoor, M., W. Lowie and M. van Dijk (2008), 'Variability in Second Language Development from a Dynamic Systems Perspective', *The Modern Language Journal*, 92 (2): 214–31.

Verspoor, M. and H. Phuong Nguyen (2015), 'A Dynamic Usage-based Approach to Second Language Teaching', in T. Cadierno and S. W. Eskildsen (eds), *Usage-Based Perspectives on Second Language Learning*, 305–28, Berlin: De Gruyter Mouton.

Weblingua Ltd. (2014), *Text Inspectors* [computer program]. Available online: http://textinspector.com/multi (accessed 7 June 2015).

Part III

Appropriateness to Academic Rhetorical Conventions

7

How Does Academic Writing Produced for the Abstracts of Articles in More and Less Prestigious Journals Reflect Grice's Maxims?

Mark Wyatt

Introduction

Clear, focused, well-balanced and convincing writing is characteristic of successful academic communication. In contrast, writing couched in obscure language that appears irrelevant, that offers too much or too little information or that makes assertions that on available evidence appear too confident or too cautious risks provoking negative reactions in writing instructors and journal editors. One way of exploring such problems in writing from a pragmatic perspective is through the lens of Grice's (1975) Cooperative Principle and its maxims of quantity, quality, relation and manner. The Cooperative Principle is based on the idea that, when interacting, people generally seek to cooperate to achieve shared purposes or at least try to move the conversation in a mutually acceptable direction, one which might evolve during the conversation itself. Adhering to Grice's (1975) four maxims facilitates the fulfilment of the Cooperative Principle.

However, as Grice (1975) points out, many exchanges in the real world are not cooperative. Indeed, even in situations where one interlocutor is cooperative, the other may nevertheless choose to opt-out and therefore not seek to build mutual understanding. Another scenario when interlocutors meet is that the speaker might face a clash between maxims, unable to fulfil one in favour of another. Alternatively, the skilled communicator may deliberately *flout* maxims for particular effects, while the less skilled communicator may try unsuccessfully to adhere to them and, in this failed process, unintentionally *violate* them. In the latter situation, in the assumption that the speaker is trying, though unsuccessfully, to adhere to the maxim, their audience may seek clarification (Lovejoy 1987).

Grice's (1975) work in this area of pragmatics has been enormously influential, with his original chapter on this topic cited over 47,000 times. However, the focus of the citing research has predominantly been on oral interaction. Applications of the Cooperative Principle and the four maxims to the teaching of academic writing have been comparatively rare, with some exceptions (e.g. Lovejoy 1987; Nunn 2009; White 2001; Wyatt and Nunn 2018). And yet, as Lovejoy (1987: 12) explains, the Cooperative Principle can be very usefully applied to writing:

> One of the advantages of Grice's theory is that it helps students to understand that writing, like speaking, is a cooperative effort. The Cooperative Principle operates between writer and reader just as it does between speaker and hearer. It defines for the student the relationship between writer and reader, and it enables the student, when faced with a writing task, to conceptualize an audience.

Such a conceptualization can be highly beneficial, enabling novice writers to position themselves in relation to their readers (White 2001). A longer-term outcome can be the growth of transferable pragmatic competence in students (Nunn and Deveci 2019), so it is clearly worth developing.

This consideration has informed practitioner research. Specifically, to raise awareness among undergraduates as to how the Cooperative Principle is realized in writing, instructors have used academic essays (Lovejoy 1987), business correspondence involving the handling of complaints (White 2001) and academic articles including abstracts (Wyatt and Nunn 2018). Such awareness raising is vital. As Lovejoy (1987) explains, it can be challenging for the novice writer to conceptualize an audience that is not physically present during the drafting/writing process and is therefore unable to question any violations of the maxims that might occur. Any questions that the reader might wish to ask need to be anticipated by the writer so that the writing process itself needs to be highly reflective if the writing then produced is to be clear and coherent.

Accordingly, various strategies have been employed by writing instructors utilizing Grice's (1975) maxims to help their students conceptualize an audience. These include providing questions and prompts, such as generic evaluative comments for students to use when evaluating their own first drafts, such as 'People won't see why this is important' (Lovejoy 1987: 14); questions designed to help students identify a reader's likely concerns that need to be addressed (White 2001); or, with regard to critical reading skills development, questions inviting students to consider how well a research article has established and maintained relevance and used relevant literature to construct an argument (Wyatt and Nunn 2018). Such strategies can encourage students to engage deeply with the text rather than focus on surface features, as various authors (Lovejoy 1987; White 2001; Wyatt and Nunn 2018) argue. Students are then more likely to be able to 'honour or flout the maxims of quality, quantity, relation and manner in ways which are compatible with effective written communication in English' (White 2001: 68).

The aim of this chapter is to demonstrate how these maxims can be applied to the analysis of writing produced for abstracts in more and less prestigious journals and to raise implications for pedagogy and research. The text is structured in the following way. Having outlined the focus, I next discuss Grice's (1975) maxims in more detail, considering how they can be applied for analytical purposes. I then outline the research methodology employed, present and discuss findings and finally conclude, acknowledging limitations and offering recommendations.

Grice's Maxims Used to Support the Evaluation of Journal Article Abstracts

While my focus here is on using Grice's (1975) maxims to analyse journal article abstracts, I should acknowledge that the notion of analysing abstracts will immediately conjure up for some readers the work of John Swales and colleagues on genre analysis (Swales 1990), particularly regarding abstracts, on which they have provided advice (e.g. Swales and Feak 2009). So I must emphasize that, although my analysis draws on an understanding of abstract as a genre and on the framework of metadiscourse (Hyland 2019), these perspectives are backgrounded. My central concern is with using Grice's (1975) maxims.

Briefly, though, applied linguists such as John Swales and Ken Hyland have provided useful insights into how abstracts tend to be structured in different disciplines, for example, often following 'a rhetorical macrostructure broadly corresponding to the organisation of the paper itself' (Hyland 2004: 67) by containing up to five broad rhetorical moves: Introduction, Purpose, Method, Product and Conclusion (Hyland 2004: 67). The interactive and interactional features of metadiscourse have also been described (Hyland and Tse 2004); interactive resources include transitions, such as *in addition*, and frame markers, such as *to conclude*; interactional resources include hedges to express caution, boosters to express confidence, attitude markers to express feelings, engagement markers to build a relationship with the reader and self-mentions to highlight the author's involvement.

Unfortunately, though, although 'the early aims of genre analysis were to help demystify academic conventions rather than provide a fool proof sequential formula' (Nunn and Deveci 2019: 280), some of the emerging quantitative research that has focused on genre and metadiscourse has been rather disappointing by focusing on surface features of text rather than engaging deeply with it (Hyland 2019). Consequently, as Nunn and Deveci (2019: 280) argue, 'a principled alternative approach to only following a given sequential "move-step" structure as a kind of template' is needed to support writers in developing skills that they can apply to new contexts and new genres as they engage with new readers. Hence the focus here on Grice's (1975) Cooperative Principle and maxims, which seem to offer such an alternative. In the following subsections, I discuss the applicability of Grice's (1975) maxims to the evaluation of journal article abstracts, starting with Relation, after Lovejoy (1987), who also accorded this maxim primary consideration. While all the maxims are important in both speech and writing, it seems especially crucial that writers, operating across time and space, can demonstrate that what they have to say is relevant to the reader.

Maxim of Relation

In discussing his Relation Maxim 'Be relevant', Grice (1975: 46) highlights that what may be considered to be of relevance depends on the context and the stage of a conversation. For example, a jovial *Happy New Year!* might seem highly relevant as a greeting in early January in countries following the Gregorian Calendar when the interlocutors are meeting in the new year for the first time. However, in other circumstances, for example, in mid-conversation or in mid-February, the utterance might seem oddly irrelevant, and the hearer may suspect either an ironic flouting of the Relation Maxim or a socially inept violation of it.

The Relation Maxim can be applied to academic writing in various ways. Firstly, given that the reader might ask *Why is the topic of the article important?*, it can help to commence an abstract with a highly focused introduction. Establishing relevance might be achieved, for example, through problematizing, either directly or indirectly, thereby demonstrating that 'matters are not so clear, nor so simple, nor so unimportant as generally thought' (Swales and Feak 2009: 23). So, problematizing seems to be one way of establishing relevance, justifying the need for the research that is then going to be reported on. However, of course, there are other strategies to get the reader's attention at the start of the abstract. For example, this can be done with reference to a real-world situation or common practice (Swales and Feak 2009). Alternatively, the writer might assume that their audience is already familiar with the background to their study, wants to avoid 'being too obvious' (Lovejoy 1987: 14) and might start with the aims of the research or with researcher action.

Regardless of how it is done, once established, relevance needs to be maintained through each stage of the abstract, to hold the reader's attention. Engagement markers bringing the reader into the writer's world and attitude markers that might connect with the reader's feelings can help build relevance. A conclusion (if present) might then specifically address the question readers often ask before leaving the abstract: *Why is the study significant?* After analysing a small corpus of abstracts, Swales and Feak (2009) divided them into those that offered 'definite and upbeat conclusions, often stressing the utility or applicability of the reported results' (2009: 21), those that offered 'general implications' and those with even vaguer endings (2009: 22). These authors argue: 'Obviously, . . . it is better to try to say something meaningful' (2009: 23). It is likely that the more specific conclusions better meet the Relation Maxim.

Maxim of Quantity

Regarding the quantity of information provided in discourse, Grice (1975: 45) offers two interrelated submaxims: 'Make your contribution as informative as is required (for the current purposes of the exchange)' and 'Do not make your contribution more informative than is required'. We have probably all been in situations when we would have liked a speaker we are interacting with to elaborate more on their key arguments or to curtail talk that seemed excessive and led to us feeling distracted.

The key issue for researchers operationalizing this maxim in academic writing, then, is whether or not an appropriate quantity of information (sufficient but not excessive) has been provided at each stage of the argumentation (Lovejoy 1987; Nunn 2009). For an example of this being applied, a student cited in Wyatt and Nunn (2018: 371), who had been invited to consider the Quantity Maxim in this way, dissected an overlong section of text she had identified in an academic article and reflected later: 'I realized that providing information blindly weakens the article enormously.'

Since the abstract needs to serve as a screening device for busy readers seeking to process just some of the millions of academic articles published every year (Swales and Feak 2009), one might question how much information is required. For instance, Swales and Feak (2009) imply that methods moves are sometimes overlong. Meanwhile, an abstract that was analysed in a whole class tertiary setting, as reported in Wyatt and Nunn (2018: 369), 'contained detailed findings that somehow seemed to miss the big picture and . . . [it was agreed, would likely] quickly be forgotten if the reader chose to engage with the whole article'. Looking at the Quantity Maxim from another perspective, is any key information omitted that, if included, would help the abstract communicate better overall?

Maxim of Quality

Grice (1975: 46) explains that with regard to quality, the maxim 'Try to make your contribution one that is true' is supported by two specific submaxims: 'Do not say what you believe to be false' and 'Do not say that for which you lack adequate evidence'. So, for example, when I am being asked by a student for what seems the umpteenth time *How many references should we include in our assignment?*, and I reply something like *762* while keeping a poker face, I am flouting the Quality Maxim for humorous effect (in this case to illustrate that perhaps the number in itself is inconsequential, as I then truthfully go on to explain).

So, the Quality Maxim relates to conveying truthfulness, which can be achieved in academic journal abstracts in various ways. An important consideration for the writer is to decide on their degree of confidence in the facts and evidence at their disposal. Are categorical statements reflecting low modality or cautious statements characterized by hedging more in order? The writer might wish to convey sincerity (White 2001) through boosters, attitude markers and self-mentions, but cautious language may also be needed for this, and to express 'a suitable degree of deference and modesty to the audience' (Hyland and Milton 1997: 183). The reader assessing the writer's truthfulness may react negatively to statements that seem too confident or too weak. For example, the verb *prove* may seem too strong a lexical choice for the evidence available or an expression such as *our results may possibly hint at* may seem so tentative a judgement that it is not really genuine. The reader is functioning to some extent as a critical co-analyst through every stage of the abstract and so is considering how the topic is introduced in relation to current concerns in the literature (does the writer have a firm enough grasp of this to convey sufficient authority and credibility?), the degree of robustness and transparency in the description of the article's methodology, the level of self-confidence shown in the way findings are presented, whether there is any commitment to act on these findings where appropriate and whether any limitations that have become evident are acknowledged.

The Quality Maxim is sometimes violated. For example, an abstract analysed in Wyatt and Nunn (2018) gave an impression of bias, since the abstract seemed to privilege one ethnic group, described in more detail and in positive terms, over another (also found in the same national context), which was positioned negatively in the abstract. Moreover, this impression of bias was accentuated by overgeneralizing and a lack of hedging.

Maxim of Manner

Grice's (1975: 46) final category centres on the maxim: 'Be perspicuous', that is, lucid, clear. The submaxims include: 'Avoid obscurity of expression; Avoid ambiguity; Be brief (Avoid unnecessary prolixity); Be orderly'. In speech, frequent interjections such as *Sorry?* or *Could you say that again, please?* will provide the speaker with rapid feedback that their output needs to be clearer, as too much of the message is being lost.

The Manner Maxim might be realized in academic journal abstracts in various ways. Clearly, lexical choices should be appropriate if the Manner Maxim is being adhered to, with unnecessarily obscure technical terms avoided wherever possible, particularly perhaps in an abstract where they might not be defined. Moreover, if adherence to the Manner Maxim is a goal, grammatical structures should also not be unnecessarily complex. Unfortunately, though, as Hyland (2002: 351) explains, students are too often encouraged to see academic writing as 'a kind of impersonal, faceless discourse', through which they should pursue the illusion of objectivity through relentless avoidance of the first person and active voice, with compensatory overuse of the passive. However, overuse of the passive can lead to the development of convoluted prose, which thus violates the Manner Maxim (Wyatt and Nunn 2018).

Even if active voice is not almost completely avoided, the Manner Maxim can still be violated through unnecessarily verbose prose, characterized by superfluity and repetition. However, skilful use of interactive resources may help the text cohere. For example, transitions and frame markers can provide helpful signposting. Unfortunately, though, if transitions are inappropriately used, the effect might be opacity; for example, when the logical link is contrastive but the author uses *moreover*; the reader will need to re-read. The misuse of linking words can reduce coherence (Lei 2012).

Linguistic errors in general might have a negative impact on intelligibility. While academic English as a Lingua Franca rather than Standard English seems an appropriate goal (Flowerdew 2019), it will not be realized by texts including run-on sentences in which meaning breaks down. Furthermore, examples of seemingly careless linguistic errors in a published abstract might be distracting. Having discussed how Grice's (1975) maxims can be used to evaluate academic journal article abstracts, I now turn to the research methodology.

The Present Study

My study is guided by the following research question: In the field of applied linguistics, do the abstracts of articles in more prestigious journals tend to adhere more closely to Grice's maxims than those in less prestigious journals and violate them to a lesser extent?

To address this question, I created a corpus of 113 abstracts, 57 abstracts from more prestigious journals and 56 abstracts from less prestigious journals. The corpus consisted of 21,446 words. I appreciate that this is a smaller corpus than that of El-Dakhs (2018), who analysed 400 abstracts, and Saidi and Talebi (2021), who examined 171 of them. Both these studies compared abstracts from more and less prestigious journals but engaged only in the kind of quantitative analysis that has been criticized elsewhere (e.g. Hyland 2019; Nunn and Deveci 2019) and earlier. Unlike these researchers, I determined to examine the abstracts closely in depth to support qualitative analysis, and a corpus of just over 20,000 words seemed optimal, since I would need to engage several times at least in careful re-reading and coding.

When considering which journals to include in the sample, I excluded those that require structured abstracts, which specify the elements to be included. I also looked for balance in the selection of the abstracts to compare. With this in mind, I considered the focus of the journals (i.e. relating to applied linguistics from both practical and theoretical perspectives) and the length of the abstracts required (anywhere from about 150 to 250 words). The more prestigious journals I selected included: *ELT Journal (ELTJ)*, *System*, *Language Teaching Research (LTR)*, *TESOL Quarterly (TQ)* and *Applied Linguistics (AL)*. These journals are all very well known around the world. They are also in the top quartile of those recognized by journal ranking system Scimago (i.e. Q1).

The less prestigious journals I selected were *Arab World English Journal (AWEJ)* and *MEXTESOL Journal (MJ)*. These journals are both open access and linked to specific regions but are also different in certain ways. *AWEJ*, which is unranked by Scimago, charges authors 300 USD per accepted paper (a practice which more prestigious journals in our field tend not to follow) and has consequently been described as predatory (e.g. Markowitz, Powell and Hancock 2014). *MJ*, in contrast, does not charge authors, and has a mission to interest English language teachers around the world in research through publishing good-quality and highly ethical practical and theoretical articles. It is ranked by Scimago, though relatively lowly (Q2 now for Linguistics and Language, up from Q4 in 2020, but still Q4 for Education; it was Q4, i.e. in the lowest quartile, in both categories when selected for this corpus). Both *AWEJ* and *MJ* tend to publish many articles per issue.

To ensure as fair a comparison as possible, after selecting the journals for the corpus, I analysed all abstracts in the issue that was current on 31 July 2021 in each of the seven journals, regardless of whether or not an empirical study was being reported on. My reasoning here was that literature reviews and opinion pieces might still wish to demonstrate through their abstract that the topic was relevant to the audience and the arguments were worth listening to; they would still be trying to attract the reader.

My procedure was as follows: First, I anonymized the data (copying and pasting the abstracts into a Word file without article titles or authors and then labelling the abstracts M1–M57 and L1–L56, the M and L here signifying *More* and *Less* prestigious journal sources). I then coded the data manually, which involved various readings, during which I made notes with regard to linguistic features. While doing this, I tried to remain reflexively sensitive as to the judgements I was making, recognizing that they were shaped by my life experiences and views, which are supportive of academic English as a Lingua Franca understandings. I now present my findings, organized around Grice's (1975) maxims, in the order discussed earlier.

Findings

In relation to each maxim, I first present and discuss examples of it being violated and then examples of it being adhered to. I then discuss pedagogical implications.

To What Extent Is the Maxim of Relevance Met in the Corpus?

Establishing Relevance or Not

An issue with some of the less prestigious journal abstracts is that their openings signal an apparent lack of awareness of their audience, for example:

(1) Competency-Based Learning implementation has become a necessity at the Northern Border University (NBU), the kingdom of Saudi Arabia (KSA). However, there are still a lot of implementation challenges that need to be faced. (L1)

I should acknowledge first that, on the positive side, aspects of this opening may appeal to readers interested in competency-based learning and challenges in implementing this approach. Furthermore, it is evident that the writer is attempting to build relevance through problematizing. However, while these aspects of the opening support reader engagement, there is another issue. Featuring the name of a university little known outside Saudi Arabia so prominently early in the abstract suggests that the conceptualized audience may primarily be readers already very familiar with that context, such as faculty employed there. One can imagine such an opening working very well in an in-house presentation to the university's staff. However, this information of only very local relevance might effectively close the door to an international audience that is assuming that what follows is also likely to be of very local relevance. Such parochialism can be a barrier to publication in itself (Farley 2018), but this kind of issue of not conceptualizing the needs of an international audience from the start is quite common among the less prestigious journal abstracts. See also:

(2) The English syllabus provides the students of the Maritime Vocational Schools (MVS) with necessary Maritime English (ME) competence compatible with the International Maritime Organization (IMO) curriculum, or the Indonesian Seafarers Quality Standard System (QSS) Curriculum (adapted from the IMO, in an Indonesian context). The gap in the ME learning process which represents a crucial problem in the Indonesian MVS is the availability of a syllabus for the subject. This study aims to evaluate ... (L41)

Here, while the writer might have something very interesting to say about the need for a syllabus for Maritime English to address miscommunication problems at sea, the writer seems unaware of how to reach out to an international audience in a way that is going to bring them onboard. One can visualize a more skilled writer bringing the specific problem to life for readers interested in English for Specific Purposes curriculum design. However, the abstract starts in a way that assumes a local reader, perhaps a colleague in the same department, rather than an international audience.

So, a problem with some of the less prestigious journal abstracts is that they might immediately discourage an international readership through being too parochial. Other abstracts, though, start in a way that is so vague that a connection with the reader is not really established. Example 3 is illustrative of this phenomenon.

(3)　Second language classroom interaction has unique characteristics. The purpose of this paper is to describe … (L46)

Here, there does not seem to be enough precise information to establish relevance, not for an audience of applied linguists anyway. The opening sentence is in fact a truism, that is, a statement that is so obviously true that it offers nothing insightful or interesting. Another example of such a phenomenon, embellished by a cliché, is provided by Example 4:

(4)　As the world we live in has become more digitalized, challenges are occurring left and right, especially in the education field. (L26)

The tone here seems too conversational (so also violating the Manner Maxim), while no relevant information is provided. After the opening sentence, the reader still has no idea what the article is about other than educational challenges, of which there are of course rather many. An opening such as this does not encourage the reader to read on.

These kinds of issues were not noted in the sub-corpus of more prestigious journal article abstracts to the same extent. However, I did feel that some of them could have done more to build relevance through greater contextualization or problematization in the opening sentence, as in:

(5)　We examined the relationship between C-test and criterion-test scores to better understand the C-test construct. (M26)

While I appreciate that the author here might have been writing for an audience already familiar with the background to their research, I wonder nevertheless whether by contextualizing the development or use of the C-test or highlighting possible misunderstandings with its use, they could have done more to reach out to readers unfamiliar with but potentially interested in the topic.

In many cases, though, a consideration of how to engage the audience is highly apparent in the opening sentences of more prestigious journal article abstracts, for example:

(6)　Antiracism constitutes an important component of social justice in ELT. Yet, discussing racism is often evaded, leaving the concept of racism inadequately understood. (M1)

Here, the writer is reaching out to a large and likely growing community of professionals around the world who are concerned about social justice in ELT and are at least interested in or, quite likely, committed to the need to tackle racism. The opening sentence, then, is likely to capture many readers' attention. The consciousness-raising introduced in the opening sentence is then followed by expert problematization, highlighting inadequate current understanding that the article will no doubt address. The reader interested in this topic will very likely read on.

Another example of an effective opening is provided by Example 7:

(7) Assigning homework is a common practice of teachers internationally. However, we know little about teachers' perceptions of the qualities of good homework. This article reports on . . . (M7)

Here, a deceptively simple, descriptive opening sentence concerning the everyday seeks to connect, appealing to *common practice*. It highlights shared experience *internationally*. The inclusive *we* at the beginning of the second sentence strengthens the relationship with the reader, as the writer guides us into a brief problematizing statement and then the aim.

Maintaining Relevance or Not

Of course, it is not enough simply to establish relevance. Relevance needs to be maintained. However, maintaining relevance is not achieved very well in all the less prestigious journal article abstracts, for example:

(8) Although many studies have examined the ability of admission tests and High School General Point Averages to predict academic performance, they are not in agreement whether or not, these two measures are an entirely sufficient criterion to foretell college learning success. In addition, there seems to be a gap in the literature concerning using the type of high school (private or public) a student attends as a supportive measure to the two criteria mentioned above. This study tried . . . (L24)

Here, relevance is successfully established in the first sentence, but unfortunately this sense of relevance is then dissipated in the second sentence. The first sentence sets up variables to consider (prior performance and subsequent academic success) and highlights that to date researchers have not been able to agree, thus indicating that there is a gap to explore. However, the second sentence then introduces a related but different problem, and by the time the reader has decoded it, the first problem might seem fuzzier and the likely focus of the article less clear. This problem could have been avoided, actually, by replacing the whole of the second sentence with five words after *success*: . . . *success in different kinds of environment*. So, there is an issue with the Manner and Quantity Maxims as well as the Relation Maxim being violated, although I am primarily interested here in relevance being lost. Such issues were not evident in the more prestigious journal abstracts.

Underlining the Significance of the Study or Not

As noted earlier, after maintaining relevance throughout the abstract, the writer may choose to offer a conclusion that emphasizes why the study is significant and worth reading and therefore why the reader should access the article in full. If a conclusion is highly specific rather than vague, as Swales and Feak (2009) note, this might engage the reader more fully.

My re-readings of abstracts in both sub-corpora revealed that vague conclusions that do little to build rapport with the reader were present in both though more evident in the less prestigious journal article abstracts. Examples of vague conclusions include:

(9) These findings hold some notable pedagogical implications. (M15)
(10) The findings are followed by some implications for teaching and learning. (L14)

Curiously, the use of a positive attitude marker (*notable*) in Example 9 might offset the vagueness of the statement about implications to some extent. However, to really engage the reader, the researcher could provide some examples of the pedagogical innovations needed. Meanwhile, Example 10 is even less engaging than Example 9, without the attitude marker and with passive voice. As they stand, these conclusions do not seem to fulfil the Relation Maxim.

In contrast, examples of specific conclusions in the corpus are as follows:

(11) The study demonstrates the high feasibility of using the flipped classroom for primary English education and its great potential for providing students with personalized learning, developing their self-regulated learning and active learning skills. (M4)
(12) We suggest that happy and resilient teachers who enjoy their profession constitute the very basis of students' progress, as the positive emotional atmosphere they establish in the classroom is a pre-condition for linguistic and psychological growth. The new 9-item scale is recommended for future research on FLTE. (M16)

(13) Finally, the paper discusses pedagogical implications that may help educators at health science universities develop in-house entrance tests in place of standardized tests, which often do not address context, curriculum, or program objectives. (L4)

These specific conclusions argue persuasively for the significance of the research reported on. Interactional resources present that build relevance include boosters, as in *high (feasibility), great (potential), very (basis)*, while a natural emphasis falls on *not* in *do not address*. Boosters are balanced, though (with *demonstrates*, not *proves*, used), and hedges are employed, as in *(we) suggest, may (help educators)*. The hedges in these instances precede the boosters, allowing the researchers to first position themselves as careful scientists reasoning plausibly. The boosters then highlight their confident commitment to the insights their research has generated. Hyland (2019: 62) explains that, by closing down alternative perspectives, boosters 'construct rapport by marking involvement with the topic and solidarity with an audience, taking a joint position against other voices'. The self-mention in Example 12 (*we suggest*), which is, in fact, the only self-mention in that particular abstract (M16), emphasizes the researchers' commitment to building rapport. The presence of such specific conclusions, together with a genre-appropriate use of interactional resources such as hedges, boosters and self-mentions, seems to help these researchers fulfil the Relation Maxim.

Pedagogical Implications

As we have seen earlier, success in fulfilling the Relation Maxim seems to vary considerably within the corpus. From a pedagogical perspective, there may be various implications for practice in supporting less skilled writers to connect better with their audiences, and advice in this area provided by Lovejoy (1987), White (2001) and Wyatt and Nunn (2018), which is alluded to earlier (in the chapter's introduction), offers a good starting point. The most crucial issue is to encourage novice writers to adopt a reflective stance, which generic comments and questions that support reflective writing practice can help develop through their introduction in a whole class setting, followed by practice. Novice writers need to have the tools to use to interrogate their own writing against the Relation Maxim, so it seems crucial to introduce these tools throughout the further and higher education institutes where less skilled writers aiming to write for publication either study or work. In such settings, novice writers' reflective work can be supported ideally not just directly by EAP practitioners individually themselves but also by a sympathetic and supportive audience of their peers in a safe environment. The EAP practitioner can therefore work to create an appropriate atmosphere characterized by positive group dynamics in which sharing and learning from others through appropriate activities takes place. For example, workshops on writing for postgraduate students or novice researchers in further and higher education institutes could employ interactive revision tasks incorporating peer review, using participants' abstracts.

During the workshop, the researcher and reviewer (who could later switch roles) could be told to imagine a reader who is interested in the topic (e.g. competency-based learning – Example 1 or Maritime English – Example 2) but has very limited knowledge of the local context and local challenges. Which information would be most relevant to the reader to bring the local issues to life? The educational level of the reader should be considered too. How is the reader going to feel if the information provided is too vague (as in Examples 3 and 4)? The next consideration is how to maintain relevance. Peer reviewers in the workshop situation could be asked to highlight any point during the text when they started to lose concentration (as in the second sentence of Example 8) and why. Finally, they could consider whether the conclusion was specific enough to make them feel they wanted to read the full article (as in Examples 11–13). Such activities could raise consciousness of how to better connect with the audience, establishing and maintaining relevance throughout. I now turn to the Quantity Maxim.

To What Extent Is the Maxim of Quantity Met in the Corpus?

Ideally, as noted earlier, sufficient but not excessive information will be provided in the abstract. We have already seen, though, while discussing the Relation Maxim, that too much or too little information is sometimes provided. Example 8 violates the Quantity Maxim as well as the Relation Maxim in excessively problematizing; the vague conclusions offered in Examples 9 and 10 not only fail to engage the reader, violating the Relation Maxim, but also fail to provide sufficient information.

Quantitative research (e.g. El-Dakhs 2018) suggests that abstracts published in less rather than more prestigious applied linguistics journals tend to be top-heavy, with more emphasis on introductions, aims and methodology than on findings and conclusions. Such a tendency is also evident in my corpus. Too many of the less prestigious journal article abstracts do not seem to devote sufficient space to findings and conclusions. An extreme example is provided by the last two sentences of L5:

(14) Three experimental groups, 34 students in total, studying in their final year of Bachelor studies within the Subject Areas of Applied Mechanics and Industrial Engineering, participated in the methodological experiment. The conducted experiment confirmed the efficiency of the methodology proposed. (L5)

There are various issues here that relate to the Quantity Maxim. First, we have been told very little about *the methodology proposed* in the first three-quarters of the abstract (and the information provided is also not very clear, an issue with regard to the Manner Maxim). Second, we need more information about the *efficiency* of the conducted experiment – *efficient* in what ways? Third, the information about the students' *subject areas* seems excessive since it does not seem to connect with other parts of the abstract. Of course, there are other issues with the abstract that relate to the Relation Maxim, but the overriding issue for me is imbalance (top-heavy overall, with individual parts containing too much or too little information).

There are also instances in the more prestigious journal abstracts of the Quantity Maxim being violated, though these seem comparatively less frequent. However, one abstract reporting on findings (M55) completely omits any reference to methods, which is unfortunate since some information would be beneficial. Mostly, though, the more prestigious journal abstracts are better balanced overall, which may partially reflect sometimes skilful embedding of one move within another, as in Example 15, where Method is embedded in Purpose before Product:

(15) Taking a comparative ethnographic approach, it analyses how the same cohort of students behave in two English language courses taught by two teachers: one from the local non-western context and the other from the western context. The findings indicate that seemingly collaborative behaviour can mask sites of resistance and ideological struggles. (M19)

Referring lightly to a well-established methodological approach here allows the writer to devote more space to findings and conclusions, which account for over two-thirds of the abstract. Well-developed conclusions that emphasize relevance, as in Examples 11 and 12, are, as already noted, quite frequent in the more prestigious journal abstracts.

Pedagogical Implications

Developing reflective skills is crucial for the fulfilment of the Quantity Maxim, as for others, and so the support in this direction offered by Lovejoy (1987),

White (2001) and Wyatt and Nunn (2018) is as relevant here as for the Relation Maxim. Novice writers need to think very carefully about how much information to include at each stage of the abstract, and EAP practitioners thus have a role in supporting the growth of reflective practice in this area.

A further challenge for less skilled writers is achieving balance within the word limit (particularly since word limits for abstracts can be strict). As we have seen, some of the less prestigious journal abstracts are top-heavy (as in Example 14), which might suggest that some of the writers may have run out of words and then concluded quickly. If that is the case, a clear implication is the need for more practice of producing abstracts. For example, in a workshop situation, novice writers could be asked by EAP practitioners to produce an abstract with no word limit or a high word limit, and then edit it down (e.g. to 300 words) and then again, to 200 or 150 words, while ensuring that they retained the most important content in a balanced way. I now turn to the Quality Maxim.

To What Extent Is the Maxim of Quality Met in the Corpus?

As noted earlier, greater truthfulness might be conveyed if the writer adopts an appropriate degree of modality, given the strength of the evidence and their stance, and also manages to avoid sounding biased. While many of the abstracts in the corpus do fulfil the Quality Maxim, there are nevertheless some issues, particularly in the sub-corpus of less prestigious journal abstracts.

One of the issues relates to insufficient hedging. For example, one writer overgeneralizes while providing background information:

(16) Second year students cannot decode and scrutinize a short text. (L6)

This is a rather censorious statement to make about all second-year students. Similarly, another researcher, referring apparently to university students everywhere, informs us that:

(17) Synchronous and asynchronous classes were implemented by universities around the world during the COVID-19 pandemic. Students learning English as a Foreign Language (EFL) engaged in multiple practices when attending English writing classes in both modes. However, the practices they engaged in and the benefits they perceived were reportedly of limited benefit. (L7)

The researcher here is hedging to some extent through the use of *reportedly*, but the overgeneralization is so vast (effectively applied to hundreds of thousands of university students from around the world, many of whom would not have been asked for their opinions) that the Quality Maxim is clearly being violated.

Such issues are not entirely confined to the less prestigious journals, though. One abstract from the other sub-corpus concludes:

(18) Such a reading scheme has been proved to be a pedagogically appropriate approach for language development in academic contexts. (M11)

Proved, as noted earlier, is a very strong word. Reading back through the abstract, it does not seem justified. The study had explored how such schemes *can be incorporated*, and the findings, after implementation of the scheme, revealed that *twenty-six EFL university students* [who were investigated] *held quite positive attitudes* (M11). A modal expression such as *appears to be* would seem more appropriate than *has been proved*. The writer is perhaps arguing for the significance of their study in using *proved*, aiming to fulfil the Relation Maxim, but a lack of needed modality in this case compromises the Quality Maxim.

This is not to suggest in any way that writers should be overcautious, and, indeed, there are examples in the data of excessive hedging, for example:

(19) This study attempted to examine the relationship between . . . (L13)

In this case, *attempted to* seems unnecessary. It quickly becomes clear that the study in question certainly did examine the different relationships.

Many other abstracts, though, do strike an appropriate balance between cautious and bolder language to fulfil the Quality Maxim. For instance, in Example 20, we see hedging (*suggest*) combined effectively with other interactional resources, including boosters (*fully introduced; cannot expect*) and engagement markers (*not only should . . . but they should also*), to make a point forcefully:

(20) The findings suggest that without having been fully introduced to this approach, one cannot expect teachers to perform well in a task-based classroom. Hence, not only should stakeholders, administrators, and teacher educators consider offering teaching practicum opportunities, but they also should include . . . (L38)

Pedagogical Implications

Novice writers need support in reflecting on the quality of their evidence, which suggests the EAP practitioner has a key role in asking probing questions in a way sensitive to the novice writer's feelings. Giving sufficient time for reflection and providing sufficient space are also crucial. It may then be useful to share with novice writers prompts suggested by Lovejoy (1987: 14) such as: 'People won't believe this; I'm over-generalizing here' and 'I need to evaluate my facts and weigh my sources'. These could be used for individual reflection before any subsequent discussion. If they had engaged in such reflection themselves, one can imagine the authors of Examples 16–18 expressing themselves differently. Writers with the temptation to overgeneralize could be invited to consider further questions, such as *How do I know this?* and *What is the basis for this assertion?*

In the kind of workshop scenario organized by the EAP practitioner for postgraduate students discussed earlier, peers/peer reviewers could very usefully pose questions to a colleague, such as *Why do you think this?* or *How confident are you that. . .?*, while examining every segment of the text. Care should also be taken by the EAP practitioner to establish the kind of trusting environment in which such criticism is seen as constructive, though. Otherwise, such dialogues, no matter how well motivated, could undermine confidence, with novice writers, who nevertheless need to be prepared for the world of publishing, on the defensive. I now discuss the Manner Maxim.

To What Extent Is the Maxim of Manner Met in the Corpus?

If writing is unclear, potentially valuable content fails to reach its intended audience. Unfortunately, though, lengthy, sometimes convoluted, confusing and awkwardly phrased sentences are a feature of various abstracts in the less prestigious journals. Consequently, intelligibility, which should be a goal of academic English as a Lingua Franca (Flowerdew 2019), suffers. Example 21, for example, starts in the following way:

(21) The paper represents a fragment of a multi-year project focused on everyday speech interaction and, particularly, on verbal mechanisms of granting speech efficiency and effectiveness. The introductory statement of the research is more precise the speaker organizes his/her message verbally, the easier it is understood by the listener. Special attention is paid to the methodological approach to verbal identification of literary characters' social strata. (L31)

While Example 21 starts intelligibly, meaning soon breaks down, not helped by an apparent run-on sentence, which then needs to be re-evaluated in light of a comparative expression (*the easier it . . .*). The reader might then wonder whether a definite article, as in *the more precise,* had been intended, but if so, what does one do with the first part of that sentence (*The introductory statement . . .*), and how does the second sentence connect to the third? Better coherence and cohesion are clearly needed here.

Sometimes the Manner Maxim is violated not through obscurity of meaning but through excessive wordiness, as in:

(22) Yet, not much spotlight and acknowledgment were given to the learners with Autism in their voyage of English language learning. In conjunction to that, this paper intends to investigate the obstacles that the learners with Autism face in their English as secondary language learning. In addition to that, teachers are not to be forgotten as teachers are also believed to be playing a role in learners with Autism's English as a second language (ESL) learning process which is why this research also intends to investigate the challenges faced by the teachers who are in charge of teaching learners with Autism. (L2)

While this ninety-nine-word section of the abstract contains minor grammatical errors, the key issue is that it could easily be rewritten in under twenty-five words, as here: *English language learners with Autism face challenges, which have been neglected. This study investigates these challenges and those faced by their teachers.* Economy of expression is required to fulfil the Manner Maxim.

Elsewhere in the corpus, the passive seems overused, as in:

(23) In the course of the research, theoretical, empirical, and statistical methods have been used. Various approaches to identifying the assessment criteria have been thoroughly analyzed. Seven criteria to assess the monologue production skills, five primary and two secondary ones, have been suggested. The allocation of the points by every criterion according to the devised scales have been elucidated. (L5)

The text here is intelligible but rather stilted, with consistent use of the present perfect passive requiring readers to almost approach the English used here as another Germanic language, as they wait for the main verb at the end of each sentence. However, it would be relatively easy to rephrase such text, incorporating the active voice so that the text flowed more smoothly and clearly, for example, *After analysing various approaches . . ., we developed criteria to assess . . . and explain how.*

In the less prestigious journal abstracts, while there are various linguistic features that do not conform to American/British Standard English, some of these affect intelligibility much less than others. Creative vocabulary use, missing articles and omitted third person *-s* may perhaps be deemed perfectly acceptable from a lingua franca perspective, together with unexpected plurals, as in *motivations* in:

(24) However, such a program can only succeed if teachers mediate their learners' social identities and motivations for sustained second language learning. (L36)

However, some linguistic features demand careful re-reading. Inappropriate use of interactive resources, such as transition markers for example, can cause the reader difficulty. In the corpus, *moreover* (L32), *additionally* (L42), *furthermore* (L51) and *therefore* (L53) are all misused. *Moreover*, for example, suggests addition. However, in Example 25, the information provided after *moreover* does not obviously add to the information preceding it, which is about *discussions* and *interviews*; reference to another method if appropriate, such as *observations*, would provide such addition. The writer needed to connect the information (about inspiring background reading or analytical techniques?) in another way.

(25) Qualitative data was gathered through the implementation of a triangulation strategy that incorporated focus-group discussions and individual interviews. Moreover, the research takes inspiration from the work of MacIntyre (1994) and MacIntyre and Charos (1996), who focused on learners' readiness to speak as the conceptual basis for their studies. (L32)

However, no such linguistic issues are evident in the more prestigious journal abstracts.

Pedagogical Implications

The linguistic features highlighted earlier in relation to the Manner Maxim carry various implications for EAP practitioners. Novice writers' overuse of the passive, for example (23), and misuse or overuse of transition markers (25) could reflect the learning materials they have used and the ways they have been taught (Hyland 2002; Lei 2012). It can be very good practice for EAP practitioners to refer to academic sources such as Hyland (2002) and Lei (2012), rely less on the sometimes inauthentic teaching materials they have been provided and make their own comparisons between the authentic output of published experts and novice writers and so let their reading guide their pedagogy.

Work can also be done in class in supporting novice writers to develop smooth, cohesive sentences balancing active and passive, as discussed earlier in the analysis of Example 23, and in reducing wordiness, an issue highlighted in relation to Example 22. So, students can be asked in a teaching situation to combine simple sentences cohesively and to express content concisely.

Self-monitoring is also crucial, as discussed earlier in relation to other maxims, with prompts useful for this. Peer feedback and autonomy supportive (peer) tutoring are also needed. Novice writers need to be asked: *What do you mean here?* (if presented with text such as Example 21) or *How can you better connect the ideas?* (if there are issues with coherence and cohesion, as in Example 25). So, university writing centres providing academic support, including peer tutoring, can play a vital role in helping novice writers fulfil the Manner Maxim.

Conclusions

I set out to analyse academic writing produced for the abstracts of articles in more and less prestigious journals, using Grice's (1975) maxims of Relation, Quantity, Quality and Manner as a framework. Grice's maxims have been underexploited for such a purpose but can clearly be of use, as I hope this small-scale study shaped inevitably by my own perspectives demonstrates. The study raises distinctive pedagogical implications of potential benefit not only to novice researchers trying to get published but also to their supervisors, EAP practitioners and researchers. Moreover, while I should acknowledge that the convenience sample of journal article abstracts delimited the primary focus here, we should remember that Grice's (1975) maxims can be used to support writing at various levels, as researchers, including Lovejoy (1987), White (2001) and Wyatt and Nunn (2018), have illustrated. Rather than focusing on academic writing through a narrow quantitative lens, a problem highlighted by Nunn and Deveci (2019), more teacher-researchers could embrace Grice's (1975) maxims as an analytical framework to inform their pedagogy.

References

El-Dakhs, D. A. S. (2018), 'Comparative Genre Analysis of Research Article Abstracts in More and Less Prestigious Journals: Linguistics Journals in Focus', *Research in Language*, 16 (1): 47–63.

Farley, A. F. (2018), 'NNES RAs: How ELF RAs Inform Literacy Brokers and English for Research Publication Instructors', *Journal of English for Academic Purposes*, 33: 69–81.

Flowerdew, J. (2019), 'The Linguistic Disadvantage of Scholars Who Write in English as an Additional Language: Myth or Reality', *Language Teaching*, 52: 249–60.

Grice, H. P. (1975), 'Logic and Conversation', in P. Cole and J. L. Morgan (eds), *Syntax and Semantics, Vol. 3: Speech Acts*, 41–58, New York: Academic Press.

Hyland, K. (2002), 'Options of Identity in Academic Writing', *ELT Journal*, 56 (4): 351–8.

Hyland, K. (2004), *Disciplinary Discourses*, Michigan: University of Michigan Press.

Hyland, K. (2019), *Metadiscourse*, 2nd edn, London: Bloomsbury.

Hyland, K. and J. Milton (1997), 'Qualification and Certainty in L1 and L2 Students' Writing', *Journal of Second Language Writing*, 6 (2): 183–205.

Hyland, K. and P. Tse (2004), 'Metadiscourse in Academic Writing: A Reappraisal', *Applied Linguistics*, 25 (2): 156–77.

Lei, L. (2012), 'Linking Adverbials in Academic Writing on Applied Linguistics by Chinese Doctoral Students', *Journal of English for Academic Purposes*, 11: 267–75.

Lovejoy, K. B. (1987), 'The Gricean Model: A Revising Rubric', *Journal of Teaching Writing*, 6 (9): 9–18.

Markowitz, D. M., J. H. Powell and J. T. Hancock (2014), 'The Writing Style of Predatory Publishers', *Paper Presented at the 121st ASEE Annual Conference and Exposition*, Indianapolis, 15–18 June 2014.

Nunn, R. (2009), 'Developing Pragmatic Competence for Critical Academic Reading', in R. Cohen (ed.), *Explorations in Second Language Reading*, 117–31, Alexandria: TESOL International Publications.

Nunn, R. and T. Deveci (2019), '"Holistic Argumentation Creation": Integrated Principles for Helping Graduate Students Create a Journal Paper', in J. N. Corcoran, K. Englander and L. M. Muresan (eds), *Pedagogies and Policies for Publishing Research in English*, 266–83, New York: Routledge.

Saidi, M. and S. Talebi (2021), 'Genre Analysis of Research Article Abstracts in English for Academic Purposes Journals: Exploring the Possible Variations across the Venues of Research', *Education Research International*, 2021: 3578179.

Swales, J. M. (1990), *Genre Analysis*, Cambridge: Cambridge University Press.

Swales, J. M. and C. B. Feak (2009), *Abstracts and the Writing of Abstracts*, Michigan: University of Michigan Press.

White, R. (2001), 'Adapting Grice's Maxims in the Teaching of Writing', *ELT Journal*, 55 (1): 62–9.

Wyatt, M. and R. Nunn (2018), 'Exploring Academic Writing with Grice', *The Journal of Teaching English for Specific and Academic Purposes*, 6 (3): 365–75.

Evaluative Genres of Research Communication

Article Comments and Peer Reviews from Linguistic and Pedagogical Perspectives

Tatyana Yakhontova

Introduction

The importance of feedback literacy of both students and researchers has been recently emphasized in the literature (Carless and Boud 2018; Gravett 2021). To develop such literacy, that is, to learn how to understand and process various forms of feedback, it is important to possess at least some knowledge of the conventions of those genres which are targeted at evaluating the work of others.

Although evaluation is an inherent characteristic of any type of academic writing (Hyland and Diani 2009), certain genres of research communication are quite straightforward and explicit in providing assessment. Due to their important, often gatekeeping function, such genres are vital for sustaining research and ethical standards of academic communities in various disciplines. The most prominent and widespread of them have already attracted the attention of applied linguists; in particular, a noticeable amount of research has focused on various features of book reviews (Diani 2009; Motta-Roth 1996; Shaw 2009), review articles (Azar and Hashim 2019; Noguchi 2006) and peer reviews (e.g. Hyland and Jiang 2020; Paltridge 2017; Yakhontova 2019). However, some evaluative or, as they are also called, review genres remain underinvestigated, probably because of their relatively infrequent use.

One of such genres is the so-called article comments (Belcher 1995) or a response to the previously published article. The article comments genre seems to have some common features with the peer review, although a public character of the former and 'hidden' nature of the latter suggests that they may exhibit some interesting differences on the various levels of their texts. Therefore, in this chapter the generic structure and evaluations in the texts of the article comments genre will be analysed and discussed. Since comparison can usually yield deeper and more interesting results, the identified features of the article comments texts will be considered against the more or less congeneric corpus of peer reviews. More broadly, this exploratory study aims to enhance our vision of the communicative characteristics, language features and functioning of evaluative research genres and to provide the material utilizable for pedagogical purposes. Such a material can be effectively used in EAP and doctoral writing courses to help students master evaluative genres and develop critical writing skills.

Article Comments and Other Evaluative Genres

Article comments are relatively short responses which appear in journals as reactions to the papers which were published earlier, often in the same journal. As Belcher (1995: 144) indicated, such responses mostly discuss the validity of new knowledge claims raised in the article under consideration and provide a personal opinion of the contribution made by its authors. Article comments are written by researchers who are experts in the area and are therefore 'challenged by the latest findings' (Belcher 1995: 144). Furthermore, such authors (henceforth, commentators) seem to be driven by the desire to publicly express their thoughts provoked by the considered article and to raise an imaginary dispute with its author and other members of the appropriate research community. As Hyland and Diani rightly indicate, such a dispute allows the commentator to create a '"research space" for his or her own views' (2009: 3) and thus to make his/her research voice heard. As it would be expected, the instances of this genre include critique as a mandatory component which, according to Belcher's observations (1995: 148), can sometimes appear as a direct attack.

Despite their potential interestingness for journal readership, the exemplars of the article comments genre are not frequently found in journals. Their inclusion seems to depend upon the editorial policies: some journals prefer to publish such articles more often, while others do this only occasionally or do not publish them at all. Perhaps it is due to their limited appearance on journal pages that the article comments have not yet attracted the attention of linguists (apart from Belcher's chapter where they are briefly considered). This is somewhat surprising, especially if we take a look at its closest 'relative' – the peer review or referees' report.

The peer review is an unpublished pre-publication review which evaluates research articles submitted to journals. Such reports are usually anonymous, although nowadays certain journals support open peer review process, in which the identities of reviewers and reviewees can be disclosed to each other and to the public. The pre-publication review aims to evaluate and thus to ensure the appropriate standards of research to be published as well to protect research territories from low-quality publications. At the same time, reviewers usually motivate researchers to improve their work by providing specific recommendations, thus making their reports somewhat educative. These communicative orientations form three intertwined purposes of the peer review: (1) gatekeeping, (2) evaluative and (3) didactic (Yakhontova 2019: 68).

In contrast to article comments, the traditional (anonymous) review addresses quite a limited audience – the author of the manuscript, the editor of the journal and the other reviewer/s (who might get access to reviews of each other when revision is recommended or a final decision has been made). Therefore, the peer review is a 'hidden', or occluded, in Swales's (1996) terms, genre. Nevertheless, its texts have already been studied by a cohort of researchers in the field of applied linguistics who focused on their various aspects, such as move structure (Kourilova 1998; Fortanet 2008; Mason and Chong 2022; Tharirian and Sadri 2013; Yakhontova 2019), typology of reviewer's remarks (Belcher 2007; Gosden 2003; Hyland and Jiang 2020; Mungra and Webber 2010; Samraj 2016; Paltridge 2015), evaluative language and strategies of evaluation (Fortanet-Gómez 2008; Hewings 2004; Johnson and Roen 1992; Yakhontova 2019) and linguistic construction of reviewers' identities (Englander and López-Bonilla 2011; Matsuda and Tardy 2007).

However, the most comprehensive, monographic publication on the peer review belongs to Paltridge (2017), who provided a thorough, multiperspectival analysis of peer reviews, which was further developed in his subsequent publications (2019a, 2019b, 2020). In this book, Paltridge also shares recommendations on reviewer teaching and mentoring assuming that 'training in peer review is an important part of researcher development' (2017: 145). This didactic orientation was also explored by other researchers who underscored a useful role of peer reviewing in enhancing students' critical appraisal and writing skills and preparing them for future academic careers (see e.g. Ball 2013; Gaynor 2020; Sandstrom 2021).

Thus, as can be seen earlier, the amount of research on article comments and peer reviews strikingly differs even though they belong to one group of evaluative genres. Within this group, or constellation, they form complex relations and share overlapping features with other genres. Article comments, for example, obviously possess some common characteristics with such widespread formats as book reviews and review articles, while peer reviews exhibit similarities not only with these genres but also with such a type of evaluative texts as teacher responses to student writing (called 'end comments' by Smith 1997). All of these genres share an evaluative function; however, the book review, review article and article comments appeal to a quite broad audience, while the 'hidden' genre of the reviewer's report (as well as end comments) addresses only several readers. This factor as well as the differences in the communicative purposes may be assumed to leave imprints on the structure and discourse of article comments and peer reviews which will be analysed further in the chapter.

Corpora and Methodology

The research reported in this chapter is a qualitative study (with some incorporated quantitative data) which combines genre-based and functional linguistic perspectives. A genre-based approach is effective in identifying text macrostructures and showing the role of context in their formation, while functional linguistic analysis helps to reveal the role of linguistic parameters in implementing communicative tasks of the texts and ensuring their adequate interpretation.

The study of the prominent features of article comments has been carried out based upon a corpus of thirty texts which provide remarks and criticism on the research articles in the fields of linguistics and language teaching. It should be noted that compiling such a corpus was not a straightforward task as the exemplars of this genre rather rarely appear on the pages of scholarly journals. The major part of the corpus therefore consists of the article comments extracted from the two journals which seem to favour this genre more than other ones – *TESOL Quarterly* (thirteen texts) and *Applied Linguistics* (thirteen texts). To reach a sufficient number of thirty items, four more texts have been added to the corpus; they were found in such journals as *Linguistics* (three texts) and *Journal of English for Academic Purposes* (one text). It should be noted that the texts selected for the study were identified as article comments based on the presence of the words *reply, response, reaction, comments on* or a sentence *a reader responds* in their titles. The article comments which comprise the corpus were selected from the above journals' issues covering the period of 2006–18. This rather long time span appeared to be inevitable since article comments are quite irregularly published. The total length of the compiled corpus is 57,616 words, with the length of individual texts ranging from 559 to

6,164 words. For ease of referencing, all texts in this corpus were consecutively labelled (e.g. AC-1, AC-2, etc.).

The second corpus utilized in this study consists of texts of peer reviews. The purpose of involving this corpus was to provide a comparative and, therefore, vivid basis for distinguishing and characterizing genre features of the article comments. The corpus includes seventeen texts previously studied in Yakhontova (2019) with thirteen more added to make up a number of thirty equal to that of the article comments corpus. Due to the difficulties in accessing the texts of this occluded genre, it appeared to be impossible to compile an entirely new corpus.

All the texts of peer reviews analysed in the study evaluated research articles (more precisely, their initial versions) submitted to international journals in the fields of linguistics and language teaching. The texts in the corpus resulted from the procedure of double-blind review, in which the identities of reviewer and author are concealed from each other. All the texts recommended revising, although in many cases it was unclear what type of revision (major or minor) was meant. As in the case with the article comments corpus, the texts of reviews were collected during a rather long period of 2006–22, the reason for this being a 'hidden' nature of this genre and necessity to solicit the texts in quite different ways (e.g. via personal contacts). The total length of the corpus is 21,962 words, with the length of individual texts ranging from 116 to 2,385 words. The texts in this corpus were also consecutively labelled (as PR-1, PR-2, etc.).

The analysis of the article comments texts and their comparison with those of peer reviews followed three main stages. At the first stage, the main research attention was concentrated on the semantic and functional organization of the texts, which was interpreted as a series of consecutive moves in the spirit of Swales's (1990) genre analytical model. The overall procedure applied at this stage followed the one adopted in Yakhontova (2019) and Yakhontova and Ivantsiv (2021): the texts were segmented based on detailed top-down reading of the texts for shifts in topics and relevant linguistic signals. A communicative function for each fragment was identified with due regard to the global characteristics of the texts. The revealed moves were labelled using the names of their underlying functions. Then, the most conspicuous linguistic features of each move were briefly outlined.

At the second stage, explicit evaluations in the texts of both genres were considered. Evaluative words, that is, the lexemes in which evaluation is an intrinsic and explicit aspect of meaning (Warren 2006), are key components of evaluative acts (Hewings 2004). Following Shaw (2009: 219), evaluative acts in the context of the present research are defined as textual fragments (sentences or less) which contain at least one evaluative word and are uniform in polarity (either positive or negative). Since evaluative acts referentially differ, evaluations were considered based on the typology of evaluative acts (Yakhontova 2019) which includes

1. article-oriented acts aiming to evaluate various aspects of the commented or reviewed article;
2. author-oriented acts which assess the actions or activities of the author of the commented/reviewed work;
3. commentator- and reviewer-oriented acts showing intellectual and emotional states of the commentator or reviewer caused by the commented or reviewed article;
4. context-oriented acts which evaluate other research papers, methods or approaches and thus create the context against which the commented or reviewed article is evaluated.

Proceeding from this typology, the evaluative lexemes and evaluative acts were identified in the texts and quantitatively and qualitatively analysed to reveal the peculiarities of their functional roles in the article comments and peer review genres.

Formal Layout and Functional Organization

Article Comments

Article comments are texts of medium length embracing about five journal pages on average. All texts in the corpus are accompanied by titles and lists of references and, frequently, by such additional textual elements as abstracts, acknowledgements, biodata and/or notes (which will not be considered in the chapter due to space limitations). The analysis of the main bodies of the texts has allowed identifying a number of semantic and functional elements or moves (see Table 8.1).

Table 8.1 Moves and their quantitative distribution in the texts of article comments

No.	Moves	Number (out of 30)
1.	Overviewing the research topic of the commented article	10
2.	Introducing the commented article	30
3.	Announcing major points of criticism	16
4.	Critique/Comments	30
5.	Summarizing the commentator's opinion	21
6.	Providing implications for further research	15

The first revealed move (found, however, only in ten texts) was labelled as Overviewing the research topic of the commented article. It embraces either several sentences, paragraphs or even pages which familiarize the reader with the research area and/or particular theme covered by the article which will further be commented on, for example:

(1) On the surface level, producing vocabulary lists is easy. The task that once involved an enormous effort and countless hours of meticulous manual counting (cf. West 1953) can today be achieved in a matter of seconds using current language corpora and corpus software. However, the vocabulary list is only meaningful if several key methodological and conceptual questions are addressed before it is produced. (AC-19)

The communicative function of this move is obvious – to prepare the recipients for thematically adequate perception of the article comments text.

The second move labelled as Introducing the commented article has been found in all thirty texts. It aims to let the reader know about the main content and/or ideas of the article which will further be discussed and criticized. The move includes either a description of the article or only indication of its main ideas or those aspects which will be considered in the comments, for example:

(2) In their recent FORUM contribution, Slabakova et al. (2014) argue that there are a number of misunderstandings with regard to generative theories about second language acquisition (SLA). The crux of the article is to be found in its final sentence: 'Generative SLA research should no longer be considered on the fringe of SLA research.' In my opinion, this points to a different kind of problem from the ones identified by these authors. (AC-15)

The third move identified in the texts of the corpus can be labelled as Announcing major points of criticism. The move was found in sixteen texts, where it is formulated either as an explicit statement of personal opinion or as a research-related action to be undertaken in the text, or as both, as in the following example:

(3) In this response to Zuengler and Miller, *I argue* that, rather than separately, the two theories developed antithetically (e.g., *langue* and *parole*) and *suggest* that in SLA, incommensurability actually led to the cognitive perspective being dominant over SCT. Then *I point out*

assimilative developments in both theories as they enter their third generation and *briefly explain* the advantages of a sociocognitive approach *to reveal* how it offers the best of both worlds. (AC-28)

This extract, typical in many respects of the move being considered, builds upon different categories of verbs (as suggested by Hyland 2002) which allow the author to take a clear stance towards the commented article. First, the assurance discourse verb *argue* (Hyland 2002: 121) is used, which signals the evaluative attitude of the author and his/her taking responsibility for the formulated claim. The created impression of authoritative stance is further reinforced by such verbs as *suggest, point out, explain* and *reveal*, which establish the author's position alternative to that in the commented article and open, in this way, a communicative space for criticism and expression of personal views. It should be noted that disagreement and criticism announced in this move concern the global research issues tackled upon in the commented articles, for example, theoretical assumptions and implications, validity of claims or chosen methodological approaches.

The fourth move of article comments is frequently developed as cycles of comments, each of them discussing one issue. These cycles can be united under one label of the Critique/Comments move which occurs in all texts of the corpus and therefore can be treated as an obligatory one. In the samples in the corpus, the cycle begins with a summary of the issue to be criticized or commented on followed by its discussion, for example:

(4) Methodologically speaking, the way the authors calculate subordination – normalized frequency (per 1,000 words) for each specific dependent structure – is certainly not comparable with the measures conventionally used to show the amount of subordination, such as C/TU. (AC-4)

In Example 4, the criticism is based upon the indication of errors made by the authors of the article. Other ways of discussing the commented research (often in a rather essayistic way) revealed in the corpus include research literature analysis, appeals to shared knowledge, personal views and, certainly, logical argumentation, which plays an important role in research thinking and construction of appropriate texts. In the samples of the corpus, the arguments (results of the argumentation process) used by the commentators seem to generally reflect the premise-based model identified by Walková and Bradford (2022) in soft disciplines. Its structure includes individual claims supported by evidence, either in pre- or postposition. In the following example, evidence follows the claim made by the author of the article comments:

(5) I argue below that universal comparative concepts and language-particular descriptive categories are each highly problematic in and of themselves. It is only by means of working out the interplay between the language-particular and the language-independent that we can hope to understand either. (AC-25).

The other two elements of the argument, counterarguments and rebuttals, are also prominent in the texts of the article comments, for instance:

(6) Hence, there are awkward gaps in familiar paradigms. It could be that the subject forms and object forms are subsumed under the subject forms, and equally the nominal use of the possessive pronouns *mine, yours, hers, his, ours, theirs* would be subsumed under the use as an adjective. This, however, would be inconsistent since all other lexical items are accounted for according to their grammatical category. (AC-17)

Here, the potential counterargument to the author's claim is rebutted with the help of the contrastive conjunction *however*. Overall, the language of concession as well as that of contrast is abundant in Critique/Comments.

This move, which occupies the largest part of the article comments textual space, is followed in the texts of the corpus by two more moves which may be labelled as Summarizing the commentator's opinion (found in twenty-one texts) and Providing implications for further research (present in fifteen texts). The moves can appear in the texts either separately or together. In the majority of cases, they follow the order of occurrence indicated earlier, although in three texts this order is reverse.

A conspicuous feature of the Summarizing the commentator's opinion move is the combination of the evaluation targeted at the commented work with the assertion of his/her research views and beliefs, for example:

(7) the study the authors conducted is not capable of answering development-related questions and is mathematically questionable when comparing subordination across the two registers examined. For subordination, we have developmental evidence for finite subordination in writing, and we still need to understand the developmental patterns concerning nonfinite subordination in writing. (AC-4)

As can be seen from the preceding example, the commentator's negative evaluation of the considered and commented paper (provided in the first sentence) gives rise to the formulation of his/her own claims and appeal to the research community. This appeal is also visible in the final move, where the implications for subsequent studies in the area are provided:

(8) Further research is required to build on recent studies that interweave micro- and macrolevels of analysis (Duff, 2002) and thus provide the foundation for a holistic understanding of language learners' spoken participation in academic communities of practice. (AC-30)

Overall, the move structure of the article comments genre does not seem to be rigid, allows variations and favours cyclic development. Nevertheless, the organization of the article comments clearly includes three parts: Introduction with three possible moves – Overviewing the research topic of the commented article, Introducing the commented article and Announcing major points of criticism; Critique/Comments tending to appear as cycles; and Conclusion which embraces the Summarizing the commentator's opinion and Providing implications for further research moves. This textual organization of the article comments somewhat resembles the structure of research articles, this being also characteristic of some other evaluative genres (Diani 2009).

Peer Review

Peer reviews in the compiled corpus are also relatively short texts (of the length varying from one to five pages). Like article comments, they may be either formally structured or unstructured; those structured show the presence of the textual parts with such subheadings as *General comments* (or *Main points*), *Specific comments* (or *Other comments*) and *Conclusion*. However, structuring in the texts of peer reviews is less elaborate than that in article comments, this undoubtedly resulting from the 'hidden', less formal character of the genre. In view of this, it is obvious that peer review texts do not contain such textual elements as abstracts and rarely include titles or lists of references.

The functional organization of peer reviews has been interpreted in terms of three moves (see Table 8.2) – Summarizing reviewer's opinion; Providing critical comments, remarks and recommendations; and Providing reviewer's final recommendation (for discussion concerning the correlation of this structure with those identified by other researchers, see Yakhontova 2019).

In the first move (found in twenty-nine texts out of thirty), reviewers express their overall opinion of the articles under review either by indicating their

Table 8.2 Moves and their quantitative distribution in the texts of peer reviews

No.	Moves	Number (out of 30)
1.	Summarizing reviewer's opinion	29
2.	Providing critical comments, remarks and recommendations	30
3.	Providing reviewer's final recommendation	4

positive features and then switching to criticism or summarizing their content and ideas followed by critical evaluation, for example:

(9) The article presents an interesting and innovative topic, dealing with a not so well-known genre, which makes it fresh and different. References are up to date and the author offers a complete literature review. However, the paper shows some serious weaknesses that would need to be addressed for eventual publication. (PR-18)

Overall, this move essentially resembles the Introducing the commented article move found in the article comments texts, the main difference here being a more formal tone of article comments, which introduce the commented articles by naming their author and/or by providing appropriate bibliographic information. It should also be noted that peer reviews do not contain any move which would be similar to the Overviewing the research topic of the commented article move found in article comments. While the presence of this move in article comments adds to their formal tone and makes them partially look like research texts, its absence in peer review texts, vice versa, testifies to their less formal and pragmatic character, that is, orientation at being more 'quick' and specific in evaluating the reviewed work.

The second move – Providing critical comments, remarks and recommendations – is present in all the texts of the corpus. It is pragmatically the most important part of peer reviews, their quintessence, as it fully realizes its three intertwined communicative functions – gatekeeping, evaluative and didactic. However, while article comments provide cycles of criticism which concern theoretical or methodological aspects of the considered article or validity of new knowledge claims it raises, peer reviews seem to focus on a quite wide spectrum of the reviewed work's characteristics ranging from chosen theoretical frameworks and literature reviews to interactive properties of texts and their layout and/or language (for a thematic typology of reviewer's comments, see Yakhontova 2019: 75). Here are some examples of the reviewers' critical remarks focusing on the ways of expression, review of the literature and textual organization:

(10) These axiomatic statements are clear and carry little useful information. (PR-28)
(11) The author makes a review of the existing literature in the Introduction section, pointing out the several perspectives adopted in previous publications. However, none of these studies has been discussed in some depth. (PR-15)
(12) Paragraph two of 'Conclusions and implications': this is a very short paragraph and it highlights some findings that were not sufficiently detailed in findings. (PR-24)

Furthermore, while the Critique/Comments moves in the article comments texts are marked by reflections, peer reviews are rather straightforward and specific in providing directions for further revision, often in a quite didactic way, for example:

(13) I think the easiest way to do this would be to move the theoretical discussion from the end upward. (PR-20)
(14) It is imperative that the latest sources about citations/references related to the topic of this article be included. (PR-30)
(15) After that, make the interpretation of your results, and acknowledge your limitations. (PR-15)

These three examples represent a scale of reviewers' recommendations ranging in straightforwardness and intensity from a mild, indirect suggestion with the modal verb *would* (13) to a strong recommendation linguistically based on a *that*-clause with the stance adjective *imperative* (14) and explicit order or command expressed by the imperative form of the verbs *make* and *acknowledge* (15). However, all of them, as Paltridge rightly states, are directions 'with the intended effect being the making of, usually, very specific changes to the submission' (Paltridge 2015: 119). Such recommendations are absent in the texts of article comments which provide only evaluation, without any direct recommendations.

Finally, peer reviews exhibit presence of one more move, Providing reviewer's final recommendation (found, however, only in four texts), for example:

(16) The article is publishable after minor corrections. (PR-12)

This move can be treated as being somewhat analogous to the Summarizing the commentator's opinion move in article comments, although a substantial difference between them arises from a highly specific and concise character of the former and a much broader expression of the latter, which includes not only evaluation of the commented article but also the assertion of the commentator's personal views and beliefs. Notably, the texts of peer reviews do not contain the move which would resemble the final one (Providing implications for further research) found in the texts of the article comments genre.

Evaluations in Article Comments and Peer Reviews

Evaluation lies at the core of such genres as article comments and peer reviews as they are explicitly targeted at evaluating the work of others. In broader terms, article comments and peer reviews provide a legitimate space for academics to express personal viewpoints, to test the validity of knowledge claims and interpretations of other researchers and thus to support and reinforce the values of the research communities to which they belong.

Following the analytical framework described in the Corpora and Methodology section of this chapter, evaluative words (adjectives, nouns, verbs and adverbs) were identified in the texts. The lexical units not referring to a commented or reviewed paper or its author, to the commentator or reviewer and to methodological context were excluded from the list. The quantitative characteristics of the use of evaluative words in the texts of both genres are shown in Table 8.3.

Although the absolute number of evaluative items and their occurrences in the texts of article comments is somewhat larger than those used in the texts of peer reviews (as can be seen from Table 8.3), the texts of the latter group seem to be much more loaded with evaluative words given the number of items per 1,000 words. The texts of peer reviews even produce the impression of being densely 'packed' with explicit evaluations, which, however, seem to be dispersed in the texts of article comments. In both groups, the words of positive evaluation dominate, one reason for this being the exclusion of positive evaluative words with negation (which convey a negative evaluation in the mitigated form) from the list. On the other hand, several researchers have already noticed that positive evaluations generally tend to be more numerous in evaluative texts (Giannoni 2007; Moreno and Suarez 2008) as their authors try to soften face-threatening situations to maintain academic politeness and intend to use negative evaluations as marked devices to produce a strong rhetorical effect (Shaw 2009). It should be also taken into account that the considered corpus of peer reviews does not include those which recommend

Table 8.3 Quantitative distribution of evaluative words in the texts of article comments and peer reviews

Evaluative Words	Article Comments Texts				Peer Review Texts		
	Number	Occurrences	Items Per 1,000 Words		Number	Occurrences	Items Per 1,000 Words
Words of positive evaluation	237	430	7.5		204	693	27.9
Words of negative evaluation	203	358	6.2		80	183	7.4
Total	440	788	13.7		284	876	35.3

rejection of a paper and may thus be assumed to contain a significant amount of negative evaluations.

Then, the four types of evaluative acts occurring in the texts of the genres under consideration were quantitatively analysed (see Table 8.4). The results provided in Table 8.4 reveal some interesting characteristics typical of the texts of each genre in question. First, the number of article-oriented evaluative acts is more or less alike in both groups of texts even though article comments are much longer and tend to evaluate considered articles in a more detailed way. At the same time, the texts of article comments contain conspicuously more context-oriented acts (see, for instance, Example 4), this meaning that commentators are obviously interested in discussing relevant methodological issues while reviewers seem not to find this important. Also, commentators tend to evaluate more their own ideas and mental states as well as actions of the authors of considered articles. Overall, the total number of evaluative acts in the texts of article comments is almost twice as large as that in peer reviews, although the number of occurrences of evaluative words is comparable in both groups of texts (see Table 8.3). In other words, evaluative acts in article comments tend to include considerably less evaluative items than those in peer reviews. Such quantitative data additionally support the previous observation on the dispersed character of evaluations in the texts of article comments and their remarkable density in peer reviews.

Further consideration of the use of evaluative words and acts of different types and their distribution across the moves shows both similar and dissimilar features of their functioning. In the article comments texts, positive context-oriented acts appear in the first (Overviewing the research topic of the commented article) move found in one-third of the corpus, for example:

(17) Content and Language Integrated Learning (CLIL) . . . is also becoming more *prominent* in theoretical and applied debates on foreign language (FL) learning. (AC-22)

Table 8.4 Quantitative distribution of the types of evaluative acts in the texts of article comments and peer reviews

Types of Evaluative Acts	Article Comments	Peer Reviews
Article-oriented acts	291	331
Author-oriented acts	60	13
Commentator- and reviewer-oriented acts	132	64
Context-oriented acts	239	33
Total	**722**	**387**

Such evaluative acts foreground the importance of the research topic covered in the commented article and therefore positively highlight the intention of the commentator to consider and discuss it.

In the second and third (Introducing the commented article and Announcing major points of criticism) moves in the article comments and the first (Summarizing reviewer's opinion) move in peer reviews, both positive and negative article-oriented evaluative acts are quite prominent. They appear in concessive 'praise-criticism' constructions which signal that 'the writer tends to be cautiously criticizing someone' (Bruce 2014: 92), for example:

(18) Stuart Webb and John Macalister's 'Is Text Written for Children Useful for L2 Extensive Reading' (2012) reports on corpus-derived analyses comparing texts written for children, language learners, and older readers to make claims regarding their relative value in extensive reading programs and language pedagogy. Although I find their *results sound and practical, their article still invites some further comment*. (AC-1)

This logical relationship quite frequently operates as an organizational principle of review texts on different levels of their organization (Shaw 2009: 231).

In the texts of article comments, such juxtaposed evaluative acts sporadically coexist with negative commentator-oriented ones which reveal and emphasize the intellectual and emotional reactions of commentators provoked by the articles under consideration, for example:

(19) what *troubles* me and maybe other readers is that the study reported in the article is not itself a developmental study. (AC-4)

Such evaluative acts with negative polarity immediately establish the critical tone of the texts (this being more characteristic of article comments than peer reviews, which seem to adhere only to the 'praise-criticism' pattern, at least, in the studied corpus).

In the fourth (Critique/Comments) move, a widespread strategy of criticizing or commenting based on the use of evaluative acts consists in sharing some issues raised in the considered work and further evaluating them:

(20) Guilloteaux and Dörnyei's second student motivated behavior is *participation*. . . . A first problem is that this variable *confounds* two very different phenomena: oral participation in the classroom and concentrated effort on an individual assignment. It would *surely be better* to distinguish these. I know of no work in L2 classroom research that has

examined how students engage with independent classroom assignments, so I will not comment on this. However, there is a *considerable* body of work that has examined oral participation in the classroom. Presumably, the choice of this variable was informed by the assumption that the more students participate in the classroom, the more they will learn. However, there is in fact *very slender* evidence to suggest that sheer quantity of participation in the classroom benefits language learning. . . . Arguably, then, what we need to know is what motivates students to participate with these qualitative behaviors rather than focusing just on the quantitative aspect of participation. (AC-7)

In Example 20, article- and context-oriented evaluative acts are embedded into lengthy discussions. They are marked by rather slow flow which seems to be caused by the commentator's intention to highlight or explain some important issues or to express a personal viewpoint. In other words, the critique here opens a space for the commentator to make a mini literature review, provide his/her own interpretations and arguments and, as can be seen from the last sentence, even to appeal to his/her research community by indicating future research trends. Therefore, evaluative acts in article comments seem to realize a *dual* function: on the one hand, they express negative (or positive in some situations) attitude to various aspects of the commented work and, on the other, they are used as starting points for further consideration of the research problems raised in the commented articles and/or expression of personal ideas or beliefs.

Quite on the contrary, evaluative acts in the context of peer reviews appear to be quite purposeful and committed to one function – to thoroughly evaluate (by mostly criticizing) the reviewed work. They seem to follow each other rather quickly without leaving much space for explanations, justifications or personal opinions (although these are also present in the peer review texts, however, in a much shorter and less elaborated form). Furthermore, while article comments critically scrutinize the ideas or research methodology in considered articles, peer reviews provide evaluation of all possible aspects of the reviewed work ranging from ideas to language and technical points, for example:

(21) There is certain *vagueness* when it comes to the way quantitative differences are reported. . . . The phrase 'a bit shorter' is somewhat *unscientific* as is 'seems to be statistically insignificant'. (PR-10)

Not surprisingly, the second move of the peer review texts produces the impression of being loaded with evaluative acts and looks to be straightforwardly critical. At the same time, such acts in the pragmatically comparable move of the article comments (Critique/Comments) seem to occur sporadically, this effect being largely created and supported by lengthy argumentative, reflexive and descriptive paragraphs, in which evaluative acts look to be somewhat 'dissolved'.

In both groups of texts, however, negative evaluation is realized with the help of the linguistic devices which mitigate critical pathos. The use of such devices is typical of the texts of evaluative genres, especially of the public ones like article comments, whose authors speak as members of research communities and 'often strive to side-step personal attacks and avoid antagonizing colleagues by balancing critique with collegiality' (Zou and Hyland 2020: 99). However, they are also quite common in the texts of peer reviews, this being not surprising as all texts in the corpus are minor or major revision reviews which, according to Paltridge's (2017) observations, tend to employ criticism-softening devices.

Zou and Hyland (2020: 102–3) have suggested the mitigation model which includes such types of mitigation as praise-criticism pairs, hedging, personal responsibility, other attribution (as a contrast to personal responsibility), illocutionary signalling, indirectness and critical (i.e. rhetorical) questions. However, the fourth and second moves of the considered texts show the prevalence of the mitigation technique not mentioned by these authors, which consists in using the words of positive evaluation with negation instead of incorporating their lexical synonyms with negative polarity, for example:

(22) Regarding the development in subordination accounting for both finite and nonfinite dependent clauses as Biber et al. define it, because previous writing studies *have not explicitly* examined it we *do not yet have a good* answer about the associated developmental patterns. (AC-4)
(23) Table 3 is *not quite clear*. . . . This is *not quite a typical* presentation method for this type of data. (PR-5)

The evaluative acts exemplified earlier (context- and article-prominent, respectively) soften straightforward judgements, making them more polite.

At the same time, such a mitigation strategy as the use of praise-criticism pairs (identified by Zou and Hyland 2020) is particularly prominent in article comments. It is based upon different combinations of praise or agreement with criticism, as the following examples demonstrate:

(24) I agree that learners are unpredictable, but through observation and investigation, research may be able to lessen the possibilities. . . . I

agree that induced vocabulary salience deserves more attention from researchers; however, it can be researched in its own right. (AC-2)

(25) Such, at any rate, are the perils of using the GSL as a foundation on which to build more specialized lists. What might be extremely useful for many practitioners, then, would be the production of a face-lifted GSL. (AC-8)

Example 24 exemplifies 'agreement-criticism', while the one following it provides a 'criticism-suggestion' (Diani 2017) pair. Such a way of commenting establishes a balance between negative evaluation and professional involvement and solidarity and minimizes a face-threatening act of criticism. A noticeable peculiarity of such pairs is their recurrency within the textual boundaries of the Critique/Comments move in the texts of article comments. As can be seen from Examples 20 and 24, the 'praise-criticism' and 'agreement-criticism' pairs appear in cycles, thus unravelling and maintaining a debate over various issues arising from the commented article. In this debate, the points causing criticism are not only evaluated but also used to voice the commentator's ideas, as can be vividly seen from the above examples. At the same time, such pairs are infrequent in the comparable move of peer reviews, where they never appear in cycles and contain specific comments and suggestions rather than expression of the reviewer's ideas, for example:

(26) The literature review (and, in fact, the first half of the paper) discusses many important topics that are relevant to study. However, the organization of this information should be carefully evaluated and perhaps re-conceptualized. (PR-6)

As can be seen, a quite specific reviewer's recommendation in this excerpt sharply contrasts with rather broad statements made by the commentator in the earlier examples.

'Praise-criticism' pairs are also found in the fifth and sixth – Summarizing the commentator's opinion and Providing implications for further research – moves of the article comments, where they typically embrace evaluative acts of all types. Alternatively to this strategy, the commentators may provide only negative or only positive evaluation (depending on their dominant opinion) of the commented articles with embedded personal ideas or statements (see Example 7). As to peer reviews, they provide short and concise article-oriented evaluations in the Providing reviewer's final recommendation move without any personal reflections, broad generalizations or appeals, for example:

(27) In sum, the article is an *inspiring study* and a *meaningful contribution* to the fields of mass media discourse and genre analysis. (PR-11)

Finally, it should be noted that the texts of both genres contain episodic evaluative comments which may be labelled, following Hyland and Jiang, as 'highly critical and hurtful' (2020: 1) or 'particularly savage or wounding' (2020: 3), for instance:

(28) What for me is so distinctive, and so disturbing, about this article is its *epistemological intolerance*. There is here *a sort of fundamentalism*: a *zealous adherence* to a way of conceiving of the world based on an unthinking trust in the wisdom of the pronouncements of some guru, sage, or prophet. (Al-14)

(29) The opening sentence . . . is a very poor beginning as it adds nothing new worth saying. (PR-9)

In the example from the article comments text, a critical attitude of the commentator is elegantly expressed in a stylistically rich language, while in that from a peer review it is realized in a plain and straightforward way, thus being in line with a more pragmatic style of peer review writing. Both cases, however, exemplify sporadic attacks more uncommon than common for the texts of both genres which generally tend to adhere to polite, face-saving strategies of evaluation.

Conclusion

The article comments genre is a rather rare representative of evaluative genres, which play a significant role in academic communication since 'they assess the value of research and provide a platform for members in a community to engage with each other's ideas and analyses in conventional fora' (Hyland and Diani 2009: 1). As this study has shown, it has both similar and dissimilar features with its 'relative' – the peer review, which also targets at evaluating articles although unpublished ones.

The semantic and functional structure of the article comments texts is more elaborated and includes six functional moves, in contrast to peer reviews, which consist of only three ones. This, however, is not surprising as article comments appear in journals and therefore bear resemblance with other types of published research work which are marked by a sufficiently high level of elaboration and formality. At the same time, the texts of both genres exhibit the presence of a common functional move aimed at critiquing the commented or reviewed work (labelled as Critique/Comments and Providing critical comments, remarks and recommendations). This move seems to be determined by the central – evaluative – function of both genres. However, its textual development in the article comments is more complex and less straightforward: critical remarks appear in cycles and are based upon argumentation supported by short literature analyses, appeals to shared knowledge and expression of personal views. Such remarks mostly focus on theoretical or methodological aspects of the commented article or validity of its new knowledge claims, in contrast to a similar move in peer reviews, which critically scrutinizes all aspects of the reviewed article including its language and/or deficiencies of formatting. Furthermore, while three moves (Introducing the commented article, Announcing major points of criticism and Summarizing the commentator's opinion) in the article comments structure semantically correlate with the first (Summarizing reviewer's opinion) and third (Providing reviewer's final recommendation) moves in peer reviews, the former genre exhibits two additional moves (which have been labelled in this chapter as Overviewing the research topic of the commented article and Providing implications for further research moves). These moves bring the article comments closer to the genre of the research article, make it more formal and allow commentators to suggest ideas and appeal to their research communities, these features not being characteristic of peer reviews, which strive to provide specific and pragmatically valuable remarks and recommendations.

As to evaluation, it is most prominently realized in article comments in the form of explicit evaluative acts which, being placed at the beginning of paragraphs, perform a role of starting points for lengthy discussions marked by reflexivity and rather elaborate argumentation. Also, inside the paragraphs criticism is often presented in the mitigated form, as 'praise-criticism', 'agreement-criticism' or 'criticism-suggestion', combinations which appear as cycles in the Critique/Comments and other moves. The constant recurrency of such pairs enables the commentator not only to politely and professionally maintain the debate but also to effectively use it for articulation of his/her own ideas. This is not case of the peer review, where evaluations are specific, generally not repeated and rarely occur as concessive contrast statements (with the exception of the first move where they play a role of the standard beginning). Overall, the texts of peer reviews seem to be heavily loaded with explicitly evaluative words which are more dispersed in the lengthy article comments texts. Harsh criticism is, however, only sporadic in the texts of both genres.

The conspicuous and distinguishing features of the article comments genre summarized earlier stem from its communicative orientation which includes not only an obvious evaluative function but also additional ones which may be formulated as follows: (1) to make one's own research voice heard and (2) to claim a visible place in a research community. Further research, however, is needed to provide a richer linguistic justification of these functions as the study presented in this chapter is only an exploratory one.

Pedagogical Implications

The conducted research provides a significant amount of linguistic data which can be used to develop feedback literacy, that is, 'the understandings, capacities and dispositions needed to make sense of information and use it to enhance work or learning strategies' (Carless and Boud 2018: 1315) in university settings.

Since the study generally follows a genre-centric research perspective, the obtained results can be utilized to provide a holistic vision and to explain an overall organization of evaluative texts. The data related to evaluations in article comments can be helpful for developing students' abilities to make and express judgements about the work of others in a rhetorically appropriate and acceptable form. Furthermore, all the findings on the features of peer reviews can be used in training sessions for beginning reviewers and can thus provide an adequate linguistic response to Paltridge's (2017) call to support such important training and development courses. It is worth emphasizing that even though the ability to critically evaluate requires awareness of sociorhetorical context, developed thinking skills and experience, didactic transmission of linguistic data and their successful mastery forms an unavoidable stage in the development of writers as research critics and reviewers.

References

Azar, A. S. and A. Hashim (2019), 'The Impact of Attitude Markers on Enhancing Evaluation in the Review Article Genre', *GEMA Online® Journal of Language Studies*, 19 (1): 153–73.

Ball, C. (2013), 'Adapting Editorial Peer Review of Webtexts for Classroom Use', *Writing and Pedagogy*, 5 (2): 301–16.

Belcher, D. (1995), 'Writing Critically across the Curriculum', in D. Belcher and G. Braine (eds), *Academic Writing in a Second Language: Essays on Research and Pedagogy*, 135–54, Norwood: Ablex.

Belcher, D. (2007), 'Seeking Acceptance in an English-only Research World', *Journal of Second Language Writing*, 16: 1–22.

Bruce, I. (2014), 'Expressing Criticality in the Literature Review in Research Article Introductions in Applied Linguistics and Psychology', *English for Specific Purposes*, 36: 85–96.

Carless, D. and D. Boud (2018), 'The Development of Student Feedback Literacy: Enabling Uptake of Feedback', *Assessment and Evaluation in Higher Education*, 43 (8): 1315–25.

Diani, G. (2009), 'Reporting and Evaluation in English Book Review Articles: A Cross-Disciplinary Study', in K. Hyland and G. Diani (eds), *Academic Evaluation: Review Genres in University Settings*, 87–104, Houndmills: Palgrave Macmillan.

Diani, G. (2017), 'Criticism and Politeness Strategies in Academic Review Discourse: A Contrastive (English-Italian) Corpus-based Analysis', *Kalbotyra*, 70: 60–78.

Englander, K. and G. López-Bonilla (2011), 'Acknowledging or Denying Membership: Reviewers' Responses to Non-anglophone Scientists' Manuscripts', *Discourse Studies*, 13 (4): 395–416.

Fortanet, I. (2008), 'Evaluative Language in Peer Review Referee Reports', *Journal of English for Academic Purposes*, 7: 27–37.

Fortanet-Gómez, I. (2008), 'Strategies for Teaching and Learning an Occluded Genre: The RA Referee Report', in S. Burgess and P. Martín-Martín (eds), *English as an Additional Language in Research Publication and Communication*, 19–38, Bern: Peter Lang.

Gaynor, J. W. (2020), 'Peer Review in the Classroom: Student Perceptions, Peer Feedback Quality and the Role of Assessment', *Assessment & Evaluation in Higher Education*, 45 (5): 758–75.

Giannoni, D. S. (2007), 'Metatextual Evaluation in Journal Editorials', *Textus*, XX (1): 57–82.

Gosden, H. (2003), '"Why not Give us the Full Story?": Functions of Referees' Comments in Peer Reviews of Scientific Research Papers', *Journal of English for Academic Purposes*, 2: 87–101.

Gravett, K. (2021), 'Learning from Feedback via Peer Review: Using Concept Maps to Explore the Development of Scholarly Writing Literacies', in L. M. Muresan and C. Orna-Montesinos (eds), *Academic Literacy Development: Perspectives on Multilingual Scholars' Approaches to Writing*, 265–84, Cham: Palgrave Macmillan.

Hewings, M. (2004), 'An "Important Contribution" or "Tiresome Reading"? A Study of Evaluation in Peer Reviews of Journal Article Submissions', *Journal of Applied Linguistics*, 1 (3): 247–74.

Hyland, K. (2002), 'Activity and Evaluation: Reporting Practices in Academic Writing', in J. Flowerdew, *Academic Discourse*, 115–30, London: Longman.

Hyland, K. and G. Diani (2009), 'Introduction: Academic Evaluation and Review Genres', in K. Hyland and G. Diani (eds), *Academic Evaluation: Review Genres in University Settings*, 1–14. Houndmills: Palgrave Macmillan.

Hyland, K. and F. Jiang (2020), '"This Work is Antithetical to the Spirit of Research": An Anatomy of Harsh Peer Reviews', *Journal of English for Academic Purposes*, 46: 1–13.

Johnson, D. M. and D. H. Roen (1992), 'Complimenting and Involvement in Peer Reviews: Gender Variation', *Language in Society*, 21 (1): 27–57.

Kourilova, M. (1998), 'Communicative Characteristics of Reviews of Scientific Papers Written by Non-native Users of English', *Endocrine Regulations*, 32: 107–14.

Mason S. and S. W. Chong (2022), 'Bringing Light to a Hidden Genre: The Peer Review Report', *Higher Education Research & Development*. Available online: https://doi.org/10.1080/07294360.2022.2073976 (accessed 20 December 2022).

Matsuda, P. K. and C. M. Tardy (2007), 'Voice in Academic Writing: The Rhetorical Construction of Author Identity in Blind Manuscript Review', *English for Specific Purposes*, 26: 235–49.

Moreno, A. I. and L. Suarez (2008), 'A Study of Critical Attitude across English and Spanish Academic Book Reviews', *Journal of English for Academic Purposes*, 7 (1): 15–26.

Motta-Roth, D. (1996), 'Same Genre, Different Discipline: A Genre-based Study of Book Reviews in Academe', *The ESPecialist*, 17 (2): 99–131.

Mungra, P. and P. Webber (2010), 'Peer Review Process in Medical Research Publications: Language and Content Comments', *English for Specific Purposes*, 29: 43–53.

Noguchi, J. (2006), *The Science Review Article: An Opportune Genre in the Construction of Science*, Bern: Peter Lang.

Paltridge, B. (2015), 'Referees' Comments on Submissions to Peer-reviewed Journals: When is a Suggestion not a Suggestion?', *Studies in Higher Education*, 40 (1): 106–22.

Paltridge, B. (2017), *The Discourse of Peer Review: Reviewing Submissions to Academic Journals*, London: Palgrave Macmillan.

Paltridge, B. (2019a), 'Looking Inside the World of Peer Review: Implications for Graduate Student Writers', *Language Teaching*, 52 (3): 331–42.

Paltridge, B. (2019b), 'Reviewers' Feedback on Second Language Writers' Submissions to Academic Journals', in K. Hyland and F. Hyland (eds), *Feedback in Second Language Writing: Contexts and Issues*, 2nd edn, 226–43, Cambridge: Cambridge University Press.

Paltridge, B. (2020), 'Engagement and Reviewers' Reports on Submissions to Academic Journals', *Journal of English for Research Publication Purposes*, 1 (1): 4–27.

Samraj, B. (2016), 'Discourse Structure and Variation in Manuscript Reviews: Implications for Genre Categorisation', *English for Specific Purposes*, 42: 76–88.

Sandstrom, K. H. (2021), 'Building Genre Knowledge through Peer Review: L2 Doctoral Students' Provision of Feedback in the Natural Sciences', *Journal of Writing Research*, 13 (2): 257–83.

Shaw, P. (2009), 'The Lexis and Grammar of Explicit Evaluation in Academic Book Reviews, 1913 and 1993', in K. Hyland and G. Diani (eds), *Academic Evaluation: Review Genres in University Settings*, 217–35, Houndmills: Palgrave Macmillan.

Smith, S. (1997), 'The Genre of the End Comment: Conventions in Teacher Responses to Student Writing', *College Composition and Communication*, 48 (2): 249–68.

Swales, J. M. (1990), *Genre Analysis: English in Academic and Research Settings*, Cambridge: Cambridge University Press.

Swales, J. M. (1996), 'Occluded Genres in the Academy: The Case of the Submission Letter', in E. Ventola and A. Mauranen (eds), *Academic Writing: Intercultural and Textual Issues*, 45–58. Amsterdam: Benjamins.

Tharirian, M. H. and E. Sadri (2013), 'Peer Reviewers' Comments on Research Articles Submitted by Iranian Researchers', *The Journal of Teaching Language Skills*, 5 (3): 107–23.

Walková, M. and J. Bradford (2022), 'Constructing an Argument in Academic Writing across Disciplines', *ESP Today*, 10 (1): 22–42.

Warren, B. (2006), 'Prolegomena to a Study of Evaluative Words', *English Studies*, 87 (2): 210–29.

Yakhontova, T. (2019), '"The Authors Have Wasted their Time . . .": Genre Features and Language of Anonymous Peer Reviews', *Topics in Linguistics*, 20 (2): 67–89.

Yakhontova, T. and O. Ivantsiv (2021), '"We are Strong Believers in the Power of the Avon Brand": Genre Features of International Cosmetics Companies' E-releases', *ESP Today*, 9 (2): 182–205.

Zou H. and K. Hyland (2020), 'Managing Evaluation: Criticism in two Academic Review Genres', *English for Specific Purposes*, 60: 98–112.

Conceptual Metaphors as a Resource to Build a Coherent Text

A Socio-Cognitive Approach to EAP

Tomoko Sawaki

Introduction

Academic writing genre analysis has been explored mainly from three traditions (Hyon 1996): English for Specific Purposes (ESP)/English for Academic Purposes (EAP), Systemic Functional Linguistics (SFL) and New Rhetoric. For all three traditions, a text is understood in relation to social practices and purposes. Cognitive aspects of genre, combined with the social ones, are also recognized to play a part to varying extents in the understanding of genre in these traditions; however, cognitive approaches are still underexplored despite the fact that cognitive-oriented theories and approaches have a potential to resolve issues in genre analysis and EAP pedagogies. This chapter argues that the cognitive orientation to genre, integrated with the structuralism of a semiotics orientation, another unexplored theory in EAP, can establish a flexible genre model. The chapter explores the cognitive aspects of genre, in particular, the role of conceptual metaphors (Lakoff and Johnson 1980) in constructing academic texts. It argues that a framework that can take into account linguistic, social and cognitive aspects of genre both in research and practices becomes possible by highlighting the role of conceptual metaphors.

The existing writing models link linguistic or text-type features to generic structure components. This results in inflexibilities when analysts encounter a new instance of genre, causing what Cope and Kalantzis (1993: 12) problematized as the infinite classifying of structural components 'which just don't seem to fit the generic descriptions'. As a step towards addressing this gap between theory, model and practices, I previously proposed a simple, flexible generic structure model for academic writing that allows the description of evolving, diverse academic writing genres (Sawaki 2014, 2016). The flexibility of the new model was enabled by the Paris School structuralism and the expanded application of the prototype theory to genre components. The extensive cognitive orientation this model deploys enables the concept of genre that can take into account linguistic and sociocultural variations in academic writing.

In the sections that follow, I first present the prototype theory, followed by genre frameworks with cognitive orientations. Then, the theories and concepts that the new model draws upon (conceptual metaphor, Paris School Structuralism and Greimassian binary generic structure model) are presented, followed by the presentation of the new model and its pedagogical implications.

Prototype Theory, Family Resemblance and Cognitive Aspects of Genre

Prototype approaches to categorization and the concept of family resemblance occupy a crucial foundation in the ESP/EAP genre tradition. I present the relevant history of the prototype theory and the concept of family resemblance, on which the new model is grounded.

The prototype approach to categorization was developed by Rosch (1975). Her categorization approach is contrastive to the classical Aristotelian one (Aristotle 1996). The Aristotelian categorization approach is characterized by categories defined by essential, definite criteria. For Aristotle, things can be determined by their essence, as essential properties of items are considered as everlasting properties of an entity. Based on definite conditions, Aristotelian categories hold that anything that has all the defining (essential) features of a category qualifies as its member whereas anything that lacks the defining features is disqualified from its membership. This means that all the members of a category have equal status and categories have clear boundaries in the Aristotelian approach.

Contrastively, Rosch's (1975) prototype categories are characterized by unequal membership statuses and fuzzy boundaries. Prototype categories have central and peripheral members, and there is always a chance for elements lacking in central properties to gain membership. Rosch's prototype categories draw on Wittgenstein's ([1953] 1958) family resemblance. Wittgenstein rejects the classic approach to word categorization that assumes the existence of a concrete definition of words and proposes that category members are loosely related to each other with family resemblance, which he explains by using the word *game* as an example, showing that there is nothing common in all games.

Some are entertaining, some competitive, some are played by skills, some by luck and so on. Between groups of games, in Wittgenstein's words, 'similarities crop up and disappear' and 'we see a complicated network of similarities overlapping and criss-crossing' (Wittgenstein [1953] 1958: para. 66–7). Wittgenstein goes on to point out that there are various resemblances between family members: some members share a feature (eye colour); other members share other features (hair colour, temperament, etc.); but there are no features that all the family members share. It is in this way that games are related to each other, too. Hence, Wittgenstein's categories are not discrete, since without a common feature, it is impossible to draw category boundaries. The understanding that fuzzy category boundaries provide the potential for new members that share some family resemblance features to be included enables genre analysis and teaching to gain flexibility, taking into account the evolution of genre.

Thus, the family resemblance approach to categorization set the ground for a shift from a definitional to a cognitive perspective to categorization. The concepts of prototype theory and family resemblance are often confused with each other. The major difference between these is that, unlike the family resemblance perspective, Rosch's (1975) prototype theory identifies unequal membership statuses – different degrees of centrality – in categories. Rosch's series of experiments demonstrated that category memberships are not uniform and that central members play a crucial role in people's cognition; for instance, Rosch showed that *chair* and *sofa* were rated by subjects as central examples of the category *furniture* whereas *fan* and *telephone* were not. The evidence formed the ground for the cognitive-based understanding of the prototype categories.

In linguistics, a line of cognitive linguistics research explored graded, overlapping, radial structures made up of central and peripheral members (Givón 1986; Lakoff 1987). Pragmatics also explored the idealized nature of our categorization, showing that our understanding of the world affects the category membership statuses. *Apples*, for instance, are central instances of *fruits* to people from some cultures, while to people from other cultures, *apples* are not a central member of the fruit category. Prototype categories and category membership statuses are not universal, and the prototype features are idealized depending on the shared knowledge of a specific community (Lakoff 1987). Crucially, hence, there are no superior or inferior idealizations among different communities. This idealized nature of prototype categories serves as a basis of the integration of cognitive and cultural aspects of genre for the new model.

There are different traditions within the prototype theory. The one that Swales's (1990) definition of genre is based upon is the dual theory (Armstrong, Gleitman and Gleitman 1983), which combines the Aristotelian classical categorization with the prototype categorization and family resemblance. The dual theory holds that certain properties shared by all or most of the category's members form a core in a category, serving as defining features, thus partly making it the classical Aristotelian category. However, the arrangement that the dual theory has made attracted criticisms. Laurence and Margolis (1999: 35) pointed out, for example, that the dual theory is not an advancement 'since it reinforces the difficulties that face the Classical Theory'. Swales (1990) draws on the prototype theory and family resemblance for genre definition and identification. Deploying the dual theory for genre categorization, Swales (1990: 52) places communicative purpose as the core, privileged and defining property of genre. Other properties such as structure, form, audience expectations and so on are not shared by all members, thereby forming family resemblance. This arrangement was meant to prevent the genre analysis from 'the unassailable classification of new instances', relaxing into 'the irresponsibility of family resemblance' (Swales 1990: 52).

Other genre frameworks characterized by cognitive orientations include Paltridge (1995, 1997) and Bruce (2008, 2009). These frameworks are in line with the present model in that cognitive aspects are understood to occupy an important place in genre. These two frameworks, in contrast to the present model that considers that social aspects of genre are contained in the cognitive ones, have detailed definitions of social and cognitive elements. Aspects that are included as cognitive aspects differ between the frameworks. In Paltridge's (1995, 1997) genre framework, the cognitive aspects are associated with the semantic domains concerning particular communicative events, including scenario, roles, macrostructure, discourse elements and relations, components of discourse elements, semantic relations and institutional understandings. These semantic domains are termed cognitive frames that are paired with interactional frames such as sender, receiver, message, channel, code, topic, setting and function. Paltridge considers that the notion of prototypicality provides crucial implications for genre and that genre assignment in typical genre instances is enabled by both pragmatic and cognitive aspects of sufficient similarity. On the other hand, Paltridge (1995: 404) argues that, with regard to atypical instances lacking in cognitive conditions that trigger a genre assignment, 'it is on the basis of pragmatic conditions alone that genre membership is assigned' as atypical instances that have particular pragmatic conditions, for example, a trustworthy setting, uttered by a well-known individual and so on, can still represent a genre. The framework, therefore, appears to view the interactional frames as having stronger autonomy than the cognitive ones.

Another socio-cognitive orientation of genre framework has been developed by Bruce (2008, 2009), who places the social aspects of genre at a higher level than the cognitive aspects. In this dual approach to genre, the upper levels of the model regulate the lower levels, aiming to account for the construction of knowledge process. Social genre relates to socially recognized constructs in terms of the text's social purpose, involving context, disciplinary knowledge, writer stance and content schemata, and hence includes the conventionalized staging of content in texts such as Introduction, Method, Results and Discussion. Social genre occupies the top level within the hierarchical framework and then comes cognitive genre. The cognitive genres or procedural knowledge relate to the rhetorical purpose of the text's segments (text types) such as argument, explanation, recount and description. At the bottom, regulated by the cognitive genre, comes the linguistic realization of the text. By including the cognitive genre level, the framework is meant to resolve the deterministic relationship between rhetorical organizations and linguistic features in genre theories of social orientation (SFL and ESP), which were previously problematized (Biber 1989; Paltridge 1997). Importantly, Bruce (2008) extensively refers to cognitive linguistic literature (Fillmore 1985a; Fauconnier 1985; Lakoff 1987; Lakoff and Johnson 1980) to highlight the knowledge structuring process of cognitive entities that serves as one of the bases for his hierarchical genre framework.

As can be seen, prior EAP studies agree that cognitive aspects of genre should occupy a part in genre analysis and at pedagogic settings. However, integrating cognitive and social or pragmatic aspects of genre has been particularly challenging, which, as Paltridge (1995) noted, has not yet been achieved in EAP research. Maintaining cognitive and social aspects apart, while having an understanding that these aspects impact each other, however, results in complexity in genre frameworks. The present model, therefore, proposes that cognitive elements that are idealized alone constitute genre's components to account for both social and cognitive aspects of text.

Theoretical Grounds

The model integrates theories and frameworks developed in cognitive linguistics and the Greimassian, Paris School structuralism. The integration enables flexible conceptualization of genre elements. The flexibility is ensured by the simple binary representation of genre elements that are not deterministically prefixed with specific lexicogrammatical or semantic features or with a specific linear sequence of generic structure components. The model also takes into account sociocultural and ideological variations of genre through the understanding that genre realizations are idealized. The description of sociocultural conceptualization of genre is further enabled by drawing on the prototype theory (Rosch 1975) and conceptual metaphor (Lakoff and Johnson 1980) developed in cognitive linguistics. The model considers that genre components are conceptual entities idealized by shared knowledge.

Binary Structure Model

In applied linguistics, structuralism is often viewed as synonymous with formalism. However, contrastive to formalism, the Paris School structuralism rejects cementing between form and content and instead highlights the meaning-making mechanism through the relationships between a text's elements that construct a whole text. This enables the flexibility of a generic structure model, without falling into deterministic descriptions of genre as well as genre components.

As Lévi-Strauss ([1958] 1983) pointed out, earlier structuralist generic structure frameworks represented with Propp's model of folktales (Propp [1928] 1968) still contained formalistic aspects, which was resolved in the Greimassian model. There are two major problems in Propp's formalistic generic structure analysis. One is the fixation between form and content. The other is fixed generic structure sequences. Propp ([1928] 1968) proposed that the folktales' structure consists of the same basic characters and plot and hence the function that a specific semantic participant (hero, villain, princess, etc.) realizes does not vary across folktales. Furthermore, these functions or events are linearly constrained. It is these features in Propp's model that Lévi-Strauss ([1958] 1983) criticized as formalistic. Lévi-Strauss ([1958] 1983) further pointed out that Propp's functions such as interdiction and violation, struggle and victory, in fact form pairs, with each of the paired elements corresponding to each other, thereby semiotically depending on each other to construct a story.

Responding to Lévi-Strauss's ([1958] 1983) criticism, Greimas ([1966] 1983) developed a binary generic structure model based on the structuralist perspective and resolved the issues with Propp's model. In this binary model, semiotically dependent elements that are diverse in lexicogrammatical, semantic and plot features are reduced into a pair of minimal functions – which represents a whole relational system of the text – that is free from lexicogrammatically, semantically and sequentially based definitions. This means that diverse elements, including those that will emerge in the future genre evolution, become analysable without complicating the model.

Instead of defining a text's components in terms of form and content, the model highlights the relationship between its binary components. Importantly, one of the grounds for the Greimassian model is Hjelmslev's ([1943] 1961) biplanar perspective, in which components on the content plane are mutually dependent in meaning-making. Greimas extended Hjelmslev's biplanar perspective to generic structure analysis. In the Greimassian binary model, schema or semiotic relationship between two components structures the text and makes meaning wherein components on the content plane are mutually dependent in meaning-making (Figure 9.1). This enables the flexibility of the model, free from lexicogrammatical, semantic and the linearly fixed generic structure sequences.

Greimas also proposed the Semiotic Square to sort out the logical relations between components. As surface-level discourse often appears complex, being realized by various linguistic features, newly encountered generic structure instances might pose complications in structural analysis. Placing such seemingly complex, unclear generic structure components on the Semiotic Square can clarify their underlying generic functions. Figure 9.2 represents the basic Semiotic Square developed by Greimas ([1966] 1983).

Four semes (the minimal unit of meaning) are mapped out on the Semiotic Square. 'S1'–'S2' and 'Not S1'–'Not S2' are in opposition to one another. 'S1'–'Not S1' and 'S2'—'Not S2' contradict one another. 'Not S1' can be 'S2' or something other than 'S1'. 'Not S2' can be 'S1' or something other than 'S2'. The first level of the square ('S1', 'S2') is for clear, pre-established categories, whereas the second

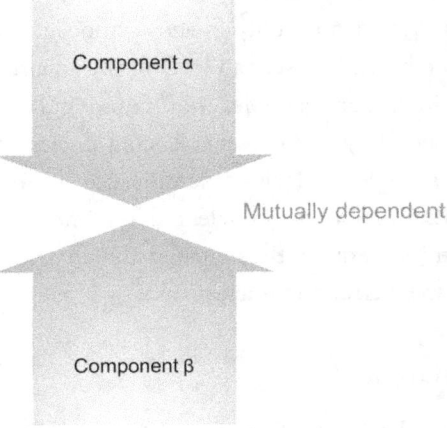

Figure 9.1 Hjelmslev's biplanar perspective to generic structure components.

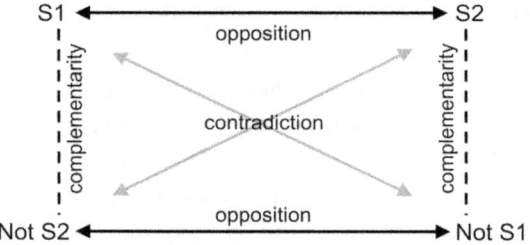

Figure 9.2 Basic Semiotic Square (based on Greimas [1966] 1983). Reprinted with permission from Sawaki, T. (2014). 'The CARS Model and Binary Opposition Structure', *The Public Journal of Semiotics*, 6(1), 73–90. https://doi.org/10.37693/pjos.2014.6.11945.

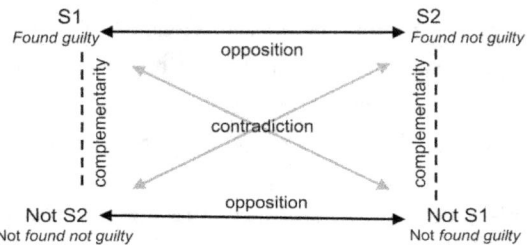

Figure 9.3 Verdicts on the Semiotic Square (based on Jackson 1985). Reprinted from Sawaki (2016).

level ('Not S1', 'Not S2') is for unclear, new cases. For example, Jackson (1985) analysed verdicts in legal discourse and described similarities and differences between clear 'found guilty' and 'found not guilty' cases and unclear cases. One of the Semiotic Squares that Jackson drew is presented in Figure 9.3.

The first level of the square, as Jackson pointed out, equates layperson categories, wherein 'found not guilty' means 'innocent', namely guilty versus innocent, one or the other. The second level of the square, on the other hand, represents ambiguities. For example, 'not found guilty' indicates that the defendant is possibly guilty or innocent. Placing unclear cases on the second level of the square enables a flexible identification of a newly identified set of realizations instead of forcing unclear cases into pre-established binary categories. The Semiotic Square thus enables the analysis of both similarities and differences between clear and unclear cases.

Cognitive Orientation

The model draws on the perspective of cognitive linguistics that meaning and form are conceptual structures. This view is extended to generic structure analysis in the model. That is, if meaning and form are conceptual, generic structure and components should also be conceptual. It is this extension that further enables the model's flexibility and the sociocultural description of genre. The crucial cognitive linguistic concepts for the model include conceptual metaphor and idealized cognitive model (ICM) (Fillmore 1975, 1982, 1985b).

As Fillmore (1975, 1982, 1985b) established, prototype categories are idealized and are abstractions from the real world, and hence, 'they do not capture all the complexity of reality, but provide a conceptual mould for flexibly dealing with that complexity' (Geeraerts 2010: 224). Lakoff (1987) showed the flexibility of such a conceptual mould in dealing with the complexity of reality with a number of examples. One of the examples, *lack*, which is one of the most prevalent conceptual components for the present model, is useful to understand how a conceptual mould functions. Lakoff pointed out that *lack* entails 'a background condition indicating that some person or thing *should have* something and a foreground condition indicating that that person or thing does *not* have it' (1987: 133). In the following example from a medical research article, *lack* entails two conditions: one, the background condition indicating that the use of the devices should be backed up by high-quality evidence to support their use (importance) and two, the foreground condition indicating that the devices do not have it (absence):

(1) The use of these devices has increased substantially in the past 15 years, despite being expensive, resource intensive, associated with major complications, and lacking high-quality evidence to support their use. (Combes et al. 2020: 199)

Lack can make meaning where there is a shared understanding that having high-quality evidence to support the use of devices is good. Importantly, *lack* is not a synonym for *not have* or *have*, not involved in the definitions of *not* and *have* (Lakoff 1987: 135).

Lakoff pointed out that *lack* is defined relative to the ICM (Fillmore 1975, 1982, 1985b, Lakoff 1987), a conceptual mould. ICM is understood as a cover term for models that connect the traditional semantics and pragmatics wherein cognitive semantics is concerned (Geeraerts 2010). That is, it is the basis of ICM that the understanding of the world varies among people of different cultures and times. As seen with the examples of idealized prototype of fruits, boundaries of such categories are fuzzy, and it is the conceptual moulds that enable us to process the complex realities. As ICMs are incongruent with the complex reality, being an abstraction from the world, they are an idealized knowledge structure, which at the same time promises the flexibility of the conceptual moulds. Meaning and our understanding of the world are inseparable; and hence, as cognitive semantics holds, the distinction between semantics and pragmatics is deemed irrelevant.

Conceptual metaphor theory (Lakoff and Johnson 1980) also plays a crucial role in the cognitive aspects of the present model. Importantly, this cognitive-oriented approach to metaphor holds that metaphors structure our abstract thinking. In the conceptual metaphor theory, two domains of metaphor are identified showing how the metaphorical expressions are embodied, which becomes useful to identify the role of conceptual metaphors in ICMs and the systematic structuring of text. For example, Lakoff and Johnson (1980) formulated that the sentence *He is going through a difficult stage in life* involves two conceptual domains, *life* and *journey*: the sentence is about life, expressed in terms of a journey, represented by *going through a difficult stage*. Lakoff and Johnson identified the conceptual domain *life* as a target domain and *journey* as a source domain. The source domain is utilized to construct an embodied metaphorical expression to understand the target domain. Conceptual metaphor is formulated as 'target domain is source domain' (Lakoff 1993: 207). Hence, LIFE IS A JOURNEY is the conceptual metaphor for the sentence *He is going through a difficult stage in life*. As shown later, JOURNEY conceptualization is also described in relation to the SOURCE-PATH-GOAL image schema (Johnson 1987, 1993) since it involves a starting point, trajectory and destination, as Johnson demonstrated that 'metaphorical systems are constrained by image-schematic structure in the source and target domains in our experience' (Johnson 1991: 15). Metaphorical systems are constrained by image-schematic structure and 'experiential groundings and imaginative projections prefigure certain fundamental logical relations' (Johnson 1991: 13).

Other conceptual metaphors Lakoff and Johnson (1980) identified include, for instance, THEORIES ARE BUILDINGS, for example, *Is that the foundation for your theory?*; AN ARGUMENT IS A CONTAINER, for example, *Your argument does not have much content*; and AN ARGUMENT IS A WAR, for example, *Your claims are indefensible*. As Lakoff and Johnson pointed out, our shared, conventionalized knowledge becomes obvious by analysing conceptual metaphors, since our everyday expressions are constrained by our shared experiences. Recent studies agree that the choice of which metaphors are selected to be used in interactional settings depends on cultural factors while metaphors originating from universal bodily experiences are shared across cultures (Kövecses 2005; Yu 2008; Ibarretxe-

Antuñano 2013). These studies indicate that our everyday expressions may change when our shared experiences and values change.

Along this line, metaphor research is further extended to the structure of a text (Kövecses 2002; Lakoff and Johnson 1980). For instance, Kövecses (2002) shows that a conversation can be metaphorically structured: the knowledge about the source domain can be taken over across sentences since our systematic deployment of image-schemata of the same source domain operates to refer to different aspects of specific target domains. Gibbs (1994) proposed that metaphors structure even legal reasoning and scientific theories, since thinking itself is figurative. Uniformly structured metaphorical entailments that are idealized through a shared understanding of the world can cohere a text. This further promises the new model to integrate the cognitive and pragmatic aspects of genre into textual function.

The Proposed Model

The proposed model integrates structuralism, cognitive linguistics and pragmatics. This integration aims to enable a flexible analysis of new and atypical genre components and effective synthetic presentation of genre to students.

The Binary Model with Cognitive-Oriented Components

The binary structure model for academic writing draws on Lévi-Strauss's ([1958] 1983) understanding of structure as not defined by its content and vice versa. While leaving the model's contents unspecific might seem problematic for the model's operationality, it is by leaving them undefined that the model achieves a diverse, evolving realization of genre. Yet, a text's components become analysable when they are viewed as a consequence of cognitive processing. The model holds that all the elements of genre are prototype entities, including structural components. The view that all the elements of genre serve as a conceptualized image is an extension of the previously established understanding that genre is a prototype entity (Swales 1990). The binary structure binds together prototype elements that are diverse in semantic, lexicogrammatical and pragmatic features to make the text's meaning.

In line with the Paris School structuralism, the model is based on the understanding in semiotics that form and content can make meaning when relationships between components are taken into account. That is, the model does not define a text's components in terms of form and content. Instead, it defines the relationship between its binary components. This enables the flexibility of the model, free from lexicogrammatical and semantic restrictions.

The two relational components I proposed (Sawaki 2014, 2016) for research genres are 'research' and 'the rest' (non-research). Elements that conceptualize 'research' include everything that presents the new research, such as research aim, research method, results, findings, interpretation and so on. 'The rest' includes everything else, such as research background, justifying research, justifying method, justifying interpretation, referring to and comparing with previous results, referring to and comparing with previous interpretation, justifying implications and so on. Importantly, 'research' and 'the rest' elements in isolation do not make meaning. Justifying research, for example, relies on research, and vice versa, forming a pair. Similarly, 'justifying method' and 'method', 'justifying interpretation' and 'interpretation', 'referring to and comparing with previous results' and 'results' and so on form pairs, each of the paired components corresponding to each other. All these pairs semiotically depend on each other to construct a whole text. Elements in 'research' and 'the rest' are semiotically dependent on each other, while being diverse in lexicogrammatical, semantic and text type features and sequential orders in generic structure components. Thus, 'research' and 'the rest' relationships operate across formal macro-sections and smaller units.

In contrast, models that restrict form and content do not have adequate flexibility to analyse diverse, newly discovered genre elements, causing what Cope and Kalantzis (1993) described as the infinite classifying of and creation of component categories. It is the fixed deterministic structure models that cement linguistically oriented realizations and structural components that have been causing issues in academic writing analysis. Linguistic variations, in particular the semantic ones that used to complicate structural analysis using previous frameworks for genre components, are unlikely to be a problem. There are infinitely possible lexicogrammatical and semantic elements and their combinations to realize academic texts. In this way, new instances of genre become analysable without complicating the model. For example, a stretch of discourse that points out issues/gaps external to epistemology, such as political or societal issues/gaps – a semantic variation, can be analysed as 'the rest' without its semantic variation complicating the model.

However, an analyst may still encounter difficult cases to classify between 'research' and 'the rest'. Semiotic Square is useful to sort out the relational functions of diverse components that are difficult to classify. The Semiotic Square for research writing is displayed in Figure 9.4.

The second level of the Semiotic Square promises a flexible analysis of atypical academic writing components. For example, an analyst may find it difficult to classify Example 2, which occurs in an introductory chapter of a PhD thesis in history, as it is not a typical element in that it is a personal narrative of the author's ethnic and gender background.

(2) My own obvious bias is that of a twenty-first-century Australian woman who remembers very well, with great admiration and affection, her Welsh-speaking great grandmother, Jane Williams. She emigrated to Australia in the early twentieth century and lived to a very great age. She and other female Welsh relatives whom I know must inform my work. (Richards 2005: 22)

It is clarified elsewhere in the introduction that the thesis explores the medieval Welsh noblewomen's contributions to history; therefore, Example 2 should not occupy the 'research' position on the Semiotic Square. The function of Example 2 becomes clearer with Example 3 which immediately precedes Example 2.

(3) Historiography – the methodology used to look at the past – is of necessity coloured by our own contemporary experience – by the times in which we live. Our value judgments determine our interpretation of the information we find. My own interpretation of my findings must be qualified by my own belief systems, by my modern (sic) or twenty-first-century view of the world, in the same way that the writings of historians living in the late nineteenth and early twentieth centuries constructed their own view of the world. (Richards 2005: 22, (sic) in the original)

Example 2 represents a postmodern turn in the humanities theses characterized by authors' awareness of subjectivity (Hall 1985; Hodge 1995). Therefore,

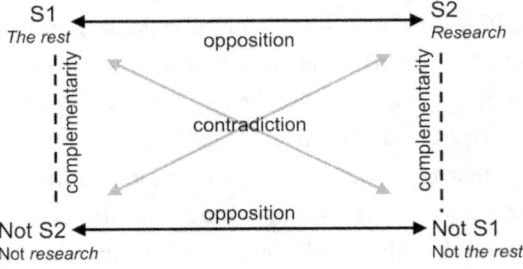

Figure 9.4 Academic writing generic structure components on the Semiotic Square. Reprinted from Sawaki (2016).

Example 2 occupies 'not research' as it provides information on what bias the author's background may influence the 'research' – the author's historical interpretation. It is in a complementary relationship to 'the rest', indicating that it should be classified as 'the rest'. Similarly, unclear components that occupy 'not the rest' (Not S1) indicates 'research'. For example, an analyst may wonder if a component that presents 'methodology' should be classified as 'research' or 'the rest'. Presenting 'methodology' is 'not the rest' (Not S1) as it does not justify or claim a gap in methodology. It is in a complementary relationship to 'research', indicating that it should be classified as 'research'. As shown, the Semiotic Square for research writing sorts out the function of atypical or newly encountered elements by clarifying similarities with and differences from typical generic structure elements.

The Role of ICMs and Conceptual Metaphors

In the present model, elements of genre are understood as prototypes that are idealized through a shared understanding of the world. The conceptualization and text construction processes are theorized in relation to ICMs and conceptual metaphors. Taking *lack*-ICMs as an instance of key conceptualizing elements in today's mainstream English research writing, I present how conceptual moulds, together with its other conceptualizing elements such as conceptual metaphors and image schemas, achieve cohesion and the construal of generic structural components.

Lack-ICM as a Dominant ICM in Introductions

Lack-ICM is arguably the most salient ICM that can be identified in the introductory portions of today's mainstream English research writing. *Lack*-ICM largely overlaps with what Swales (1990, 2004) termed Move 2 in creating a research space (CARS) model – a rhetorical organization model for research article introduction sections. The CARS model consists of three moves, establishing a territory (Move 1), establishing a niche (Move 2) and occupying the niche (Move 3). One of the major steps that constitute Move 2, namely 'indicating a gap' that typically occurs following the centrality claim in Move 1, increases the tension in discourse and anticipates the gap to be filled by new research. *Lack*-ICM also links with the concept of *exigence* in New Rhetoric, or 'an imperfection marked by urgency; it is a defect, an obstacle, something waiting to be done, a thing which is other than it should be' (Bitzer 1968: 6).

The foreground and background conditions for *lack*-ICM in academic writing are as follows:

- The background condition: The research community *should have* something (a specific knowledge/situation).
- The foreground condition: The research community does *not* have it.

Importantly, these two conditions are dependent on each other. The boundaries between these two conditions are fuzzy, being an abstraction from reality. Similarly, Move 1 and Move 2 in Swales's CARS model can be understood as a single conceptualization that has a fuzzy boundary. Move 1 provides background information and claims centrality by mainly referring to previous research. Move 2 points out issues in the prior research, which creates a gap to be filled. These moves work together to construct an image that new research is necessary. Thus, Move 1 and Move 2 are not distinct components but dependent on each other, which often results in difficulty drawing a boundary between these. On the other hand, Move 3 is fairly straightforward to identify since it is about the new research, reflecting its functional difference from Move 1 and Move 2. In the binary generic structure model, therefore, these two moves form a single conceptualized component ('the rest'), whose opposite position is occupied by Move 3 elements ('research'). Hence, the binary model reduces the CARS components into a pair of minimal functions.

Lack-ICM conceptualized with backgrounding and foregrounding conditions occupies the 'the rest' position, too, accompanied by a 'research' component. These complex conceptualizations in the binary model can be sorted out on the Semiotic Square, as shown in Figure 9.5. The background condition that the research community 'should have' something occupies the S1 position. This condition is in opposition to S2 'research' since the need for research is not research. The foreground condition that the research community does

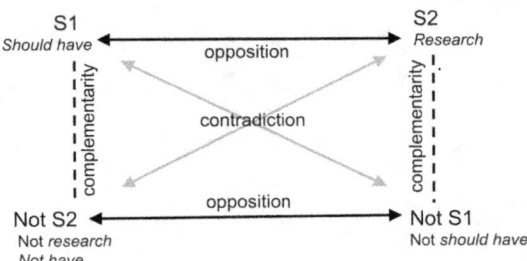

Figure 9.5 *Lack* on the Semiotic Square. Reprinted from Sawaki (2016).

'not have' it occupies the Not S2 position since the absence of research is not research. The foreground condition '*not*' is complementary to *should have*, as both of these are conditions for a *lack*-ICM. However, Not S2 position is more appropriate for *not*, since pointing out an absence or gap is known to be less salient or prototypical than claiming importance or providing background in particular in Languages Other Than English (LOTE) (Árvay and Tankó 2004; Fakhri 2004; Kanoksilapatham 2007; Loi 2010; Sawaki 2023; Taylor and Chen 1991). This complementary relation shows that the foreground and background conditions inform a single conceptualization, *lack*.

It is important to note that *lack* conceptualizations in research writing can exhibit linguistic variations such as semantic and text type variations. Semantic variations range from indicating that something lacks in the previous studies, in the real world outside of epistemology (Samraj 2002), in methodology and so on. *Lack*-ICM can also occur across sections. In other words, all these variations to justify and increase the value of the research are processed through the same conceptual mould, *lack*-ICM.

Figure 9.6 represents the location of *lack*-ICM in relation to the variations in realizing 'the rest'. 'Importance', a background condition, and 'absence', a

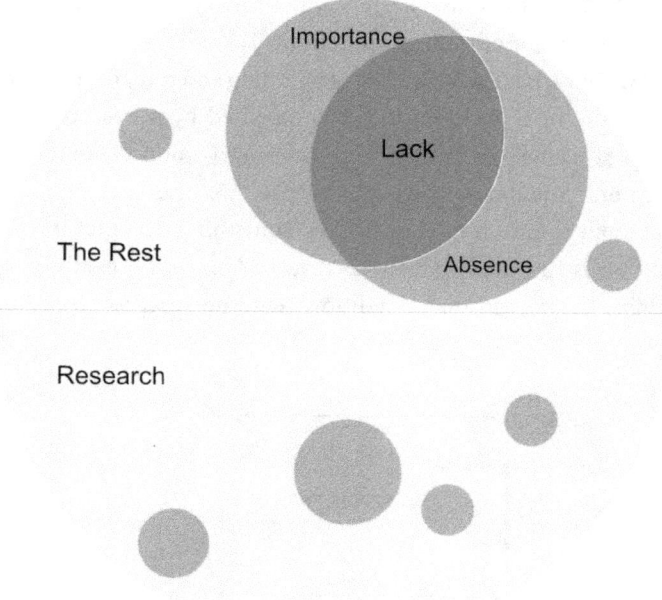

Figure 9.6 *Lack*-ICM within 'the rest'.

foreground condition, overlap to conceptualize a *lack*-ICM. The areas of 'importance' and 'absence' that do not overlap represent components that do not have a corresponding component to form *lack* (e.g. components that indicate the importance of something without having a component that indicates the absence of it, and vice versa), which can realize 'the rest' by justifying research without conceptualizing a *lack*. The *lack*-ICM is one of the possible components to realize 'the rest', serving to justify 'research'. Components outside of the *lack* or of the 'importance' and 'absence' components still have a function to justify 'research', thereby forming 'the rest'. Example 2, which is a personal narrative, does not form a *lack*-ICM but still justifies 'research'. All components within 'the rest' category have similarities and differences, some overlapping with each other, having no definite definitions to be included as a member of 'the rest'.

Conceptual Metaphors, ICMs, Image-Schemas and Cohesion

The model considers that conceptualizing elements such as conceptual metaphors, ICMs and image-schemas play a key role in the idealized realization of academic discourse and the structuring and cohering of a text. The choice of conceptual metaphor does not always end with the sentence but can become the basis for determining expressions in other parts of the text and further impact on the rhetorical structuring of the text. Some of the major source domains in research writing are displayed later in the text.

RESEARCH IS A JOURNEY

(4) As a first *step* toward this *goal* . . . (Azevedo et al. 2018: 7)
(5) to scale up the implementation, we need to *overcome* several *obstacles*: (Zhang et al. 2022: 15)
(6) It *follows* that . . . (Asongu and Odhiambo 2019: 6)

RESEARCH IS A BUILDING

(7) an approach to professional development that is *grounded* in . . . (Stewart and Jansky 2022: 7)
(8) using 80K chip data to *build* a linear genomic relationship matrix . . . (Ye et al. 2020: 1558)

RESEARCH IS A PRODUCT

(9) this work has *produced* two prevalent explanations . . . (Olofsson et al. 2022: 1)

RESEARCH IS MONEY

(10) The discovery of fossil melanosomes has resulted in *a wealth of research* ... (Vinther 2016: 220)

RESEARCH IS SEEING

(11) From a more specific *perspective*, ... (Vijayaraghavan et al. 2015: 1)
(12) These results *shed light on* a longstanding debate in the political science literature ... (Vijayaraghavan et al. 2015: 6)

RESEARCH IS A HIDDEN OBJECT

(13) We *found* that for the galaxies of the SLUGGS survey ... (Bellstedt et al. 2017: 4556)

RESEARCH IS A WAR

(14) Premise (3) can be *attacked* from a geometrical view ... (Linnemann and Visser 2018: 7)

Systematically using RESEARCH IS A BUILDING metaphors such as *an approach to professional development that is grounded in* Example 7, for example, constructs a rhetorical tension that new research needs to be conducted to make the body of research more stable.

As cognitive linguistics holds (e.g. Kövecses 2005), culture is a major factor in determining a conceptual metaphor to be systematically used in the text. The choice of metaphors can be determined not solely through shared understanding but also through the interactions of various factors. Ideational factors, including research context, may also play a part in the selection of metaphors. For example, WAR metaphors can appropriately reflect a research context where fierce conflicts between theories and approaches exist.

Systematic deployment of conceptual elements plays an important role in knowledge and text construction by entailments with multiple metaphors and conceptualization elements. For example, systematic use of JOURNEY metaphors can construct a tight, coherent text. Entailments between conceptual metaphors also occur and cohere a text. Example 15 from Richards's (2005) thesis introduction constructs a *lack*-ICM effectively with multiple metaphors.

(15) This thesis *argues* that the daughters, wives and mothers of the perpetrators of the action in the history of Wales *played a significant part* in the outcomes and it is essential they be *recognised*. ... A full

understanding of Welsh medieval history in the thirteenth century *demands recognition* of the experience of women, particularly Welsh noblewomen, in that history.... Their *absence* from the historical *narrative* is a *glaring oversight*.... In this thesis I have endeavoured to correct this anomaly in the fascinating history of Wales at this particular period. It has been my aim to *trace* some medieval Welsh noblewomen with *a view* to documenting their lives and setting down the contribution they made to the events unfolding in Wales during this often turbulent era. Through the *process* of *scanning* the footnotes of the narratives of modern historians and closely researching printed primary sources I have become acquainted with the lives of several interesting, and I believe outstanding, Welsh noblewomen and *the role they played* in the society of their day.... This thesis is certainly timely. Wales has been slow to produce this work and my project advances this *goal*. (Richards 2005: 3–6)

The main conceptual metaphors that can be identified in Example 15 include THESIS IS AN ARGUMENT, HISTORY IS A STORY, HISTORY IS SEEING and RESEARCH IS A JOURNEY. The use of SEEING metaphors as in *recognise, absence, oversight, trace, a view* and *scanning* constructs a consistent image that Welsh women in medieval history are invisible despite the important roles they played in the history, activated by the CENTRE-PERIPHERY image schema. The SEEING metaphors further map the image that the lack of female viewpoints and perspectives caused the absence of female figures in Welsh history, entailing a JOURNEY metaphor and a *lack*-ICM. A conceptual metaphor, HISTORY IS A STORY, is also prevalent in Example 15, exemplified with *played a significant part, narrative* and *the role they played*.

Example 15 shows that the conceptual metaphor RESEARCH IS A JOURNEY plays a crucial part in cohering the discourse, motivated by the SOURCE-PATH-GOAL image schema. In Example 15, the *lack*-ICM that is conceptualized through the women's *absence* from the historical discourse in turn conceptualizes a missing point in research JOURNEY. SOURCE-PATH-GOAL schema is a fundamental image schema (Johnson 1993; Katz and Taylor 2008; Ritchie 2008), which can be widely activated to construe a purpose-oriented movement or action. Research being a purposeful activity, SOURCE-PATH-GOAL schema is commonly activated. Systematic deployment of conceptual elements exemplified by Example 15 thus effectively coheres the discourse.

Systematic deployment of conceptual elements can be as powerful as cohering the entire text. For example, the *lack*-ICM on the SOURCE-PATH-GOAL schema effectively connects 'the rest' and 'research'. The past research, the *lack*-ICM and the future research, which constitute 'the rest', are mapped onto the SOURCE-PATH-GOAL schema. By filling the gap in research with new 'research', the schema completes, constructing a coherent text. It is this dependency between the conceptual elements and the structure in the construction of text that shapes the present model.

Such consistent use of a specific conceptual metaphor is idealized. Turner (1988: 29–30) pointed out that JOURNEY metaphor is prevalent in the Western academic writing tradition exemplified by the 'pursuit of knowledge', typically conceptualized as an exploratory journey. A number of previous studies reported that pointing out an absence or gap is known to be less salient in LOTE (Árvay and Tankó 2004; Fakhri 2004; Kanoksilapatham 2007; Loi 2010; Sawaki 2023; Taylor and Chen 1991), indicating that *lack*-ICM and journey metaphor are idealized in English academic writing. Academic writing conceptualizations depend on the socioculturally shared experience and understanding of genre. This is how the socio-cognitive perspective of the present model is characterized. All the elements of genre are idealized cognitive elements. Social factors of genre are contained within cognitive elements rather than social and cognitive elements being separated.

Implications, Application of the Model and Final Remarks

Approaches in cognitive linguistics and Paris School structuralism were previously little explored and so were their pedagogic applications. The flexibility of the model that has been presented in this chapter has the potential to enable flexible EAP teaching that takes into account diverse students' needs and variations in academic writing as well as genre that is constantly evolving. The linguistic theories that enabled the flexibility in the model, namely the binary structure model, idealized cognitive model, conceptual metaphors and cognitive semantics, have various pedagogical implications, integrating social, cultural, pragmatic, cognitive and linguistic aspects of academic discourse in EAP settings.

Pedagogies that are based on the proposed model include a metaphor-oriented pedagogy. This can be conducted by a pair of discourse analysis activities and writing tasks. The discourse analysis activities may include identifying discursive *lack*-ICMs and metaphors in an authentic instance of academic writing. The RESEARCH IS A JOURNEY metaphor and *lack*-ICM are a typical, mainstream conceptualization in English research writing and therefore can serve as a useful resource in writing to advance in an original academic text. Utilizing them helps the audiences smoothly process and accept a new instance of genre that orients non-mainstream values and ideologies, as exemplified in Richards's (2005) thesis introductory chapter (Examples 2, 3 and 15). Strategically utilizing shared writing conceptualization is a useful writing skill to advance original knowledge. Students can identify *lack* in the writing and metaphors used in the text (RESEARCH IS A JOURNEY, BUILDING, WAR, CONTAINERS, etc.). Making an observation how, for example, the construction of *lack* relates to JOURNEY metaphor to form a larger set of discourse on the SOURCE-PATH-GOAL image schema can develop the understanding that systematic use of specific metaphors is an effective resource to cohere a text.

Along with the identification of the presuppositions of *lack* and metaphors, their linguistic realization features in terms of semantics can also be identified. Semantic realization features students can identify and label include *lack* or a specific conceptual metaphor by epistemology, the real world outside epistemology, methodology and so on. By doing so, students can develop knowledge that diverse academic writing can be constructed successfully by utilizing crucial conceptualizing elements such as *lack* and metaphors. Having this knowledge may help students to construct a piece of successful writing in a new writing situation that involves different types of research materials (semantics) in a context where the conceptualization of *lack* is commonly shared.

Then, students can engage in writing tasks keeping in mind the potential of text structuring and the cohesive function of the useful conceptualizing elements identified in the analysis activities. Students can be encouraged to consciously utilize metaphors to construct a sense of *lack* to justify various aspects of their research. Writing can be followed by a reflection. The reflection task aims to develop students' meta-awareness of the function of metaphors and conceptualization in constructing effective discourse (Kövecses 2002) by explaining how the students strategically utilized metaphors in their writing task. In the reflection writing, students can be instructed to include the following elements:

- Explain what metaphors (RESEARCH IS A JOURNEY, BUILDING, WAR, CONTAINER, etc.) are used.
- Provide reasons why the particular metaphors were chosen (discipline, field, ideology, culture, research materials, audience expectation, etc.).

- Explain how the metaphors that were utilized help to cohere the text.
- Spell out the presuppositions of *lack*.
- Explain how the research is justified through the *lack* conceptualization.
- Explain what is original in their research.

Through completing the tasks, the deployment of conceptualizing elements can become a conscious choice the writer makes to construct a meaningful, original text that is appropriate at a specific writing context. The reflection task helps students to establish a habit of observing what metaphors are used in their target discipline, making a conscious choice within a range of metaphors available to use in the target community and utilizing systematically the chosen conceptualization patterns to organize a text. This further helps students to effectively advance in originality while producing a text that is acceptable to the target audience.

As shown, the flexible binary model with cognitively oriented components enables the integration of cognitive and pragmatic aspects of genre, which becomes an effective textual resource to structure a text. This chapter has shown that the model, grounded in structuralism and cognitive linguistics – underexplored linguistic theories in EAP – has the potential to resolve some issues in the present EAP research and practices related to genre. Diverse idealized conceptualizations of genre within a community that includes diverse members might become a site where a piece of non-mainstream academic writing has a higher risk of being misinterpreted or misjudged. However, the risk could be minimized if a new generation of researchers and academics develops an understanding of sociocultural shared aspects of academic writing conceptualizations. Future studies may further explore the application of the model to develop effective EAP pedagogies that can promote academic diversity and evolution.

References

Aristotle (1996), *Topics*, trans. R. Smith, New York: Oxford University Press.

Armstrong, S. L., L. R. Gleitman and H. Gleitman (1983), 'What Some Concepts Might Not Be', *Cognition*, 13 (3): 263–308.

Árvay, A. and G. Tankó (2004), 'A Contrastive Analysis of English and Hungarian Theoretical Research Article Introductions', *International Review of Applied Linguistics in Language Teaching*, 42 (1): 71–100.

Asongu, S. A. and N. M. Odhiambo (2019), 'Basic Formal Education Quality, Information Technology, and Inclusive Human Development in Sub-Saharan Africa', *Sustainable Development*, 27 (3): 419–28.

Azevedo, N., D. Pinheiro, S. Z. Xanthopoulos and A. N. Yannacopoulos (2018), 'Who Would Invest Only in the Risk-Free Asset?', *International Journal of Financial Engineering*, 5 (3): 1850024.

Bellstedt, S., D. A. Forbes, C. Foster, A. J. Romanowsky, J. P. Brodie, N. Pastorello, A. Alabi and A. Villaume (2017), 'The SLUGGS Survey: Using Extended Stellar Kinematics to Disentangle the Formation Histories of Low-Mass S0 Galaxies', *Monthly Notices of the Royal Astronomical Society*, 467 (4): 4540–57.

Biber, D. (1989), 'A Typology of English Texts', *Linguistics*, 27 (1): 3–44.

Bitzer, L. F. (1968), 'The Rhetorical Situation', *Philosophy & Rhetoric*, 1 (1): 1–14.

Bruce, I. (2008), 'Cognitive Genre Structures in Methods Sections of Research Articles: A Corpus Study', *Journal of English for Academic Purposes*, 7 (1): 38–54.

Bruce, I. (2009), 'Results Sections in Sociology and Organic Chemistry Articles: A Genre Analysis', *English for Specific Purposes*, 28 (2): 105–24.

Combes, A., S. Price, A. S. Slutsky and D. Brodie (2020), 'Temporary Circulatory Support for Cardiogenic Shock', *The Lancet*, 396 (10245): 199–212.

Cope, B. and M. Kalantzis (1993), 'Introduction: How a Genre Approach to Literacy Can Transform the Way Writing Is Taught', in B. Cope and M. Kalantzis (eds), *The Powers of Literacy: A Genre Approach to Teaching Writing*, 1–21, London: Falmer Press.

Fakhri, A. (2004), 'Rhetorical Properties of Arabic Research Article Introductions', *Journal of Pragmatics*, 36 (6): 1119–38.

Fauconnier, G. (1985), *Mental Spaces: Aspects of Meaning Construction in Natural Language*, Cambridge, MA: MIT Press.

Fillmore, C. J. (1975), 'An Alternative to Checklist Theories of Meaning', in C. Cogen, H. Thompson, G. Thurgood and J. Wright (eds), *Proceedings of the First Annual Meeting of the Berkeley Linguistics Society*, 123–31, Berkeley: Berkeley Linguistics Society.

Fillmore, C. J. (1982), 'Frame Semantics', in The Linguistic Society of Korea (ed.), *Linguistics in the Morning Calm*, 111–37, Seoul: Hanshin Publishing.

Fillmore, C. J. (1985a), 'Linguistics as a Tool for Discourse Analysis', in T. Van Dijk (ed.), *Handbook of Discourse Analysis*, 11–39, London: Academic Press.

Fillmore, C. J. (1985b), 'Frames and the Semantics of Understanding', *Quaderni Di Semantica*, 6 (2): 222–54.

Geeraerts, D. (2010), *Theories of Lexical Semantics*, Oxford: Oxford University Press.

Gibbs, R. W. (1994), *The Poetics of Mind: Figurative Thought, Language, and Understanding*, Cambridge: Cambridge University Press.

Givón, T. (1986), 'Prototypes: Between Plato and Wittgenstein', in C. Craig (ed.), *Noun Classes and Categorization*, 78–102, Amsterdam/Philadelphia: John Benjamins.

Greimas, A. J. (1983), *Structural Semantics: An Attempt at a Method*, trans. D. McDowell, R. Schleifer and A. Velie, Lincoln: University of Nebraska Press.

Hall, S. (1985), 'Signification, Representation, Ideology: Althusser and the Post-Structuralist Debates', *Critical Studies in Mass Communication*, 2 (2): 91–114.

Hjelmslev, L. (1961), *Prolegomena to a Theory of Language*, trans. F. Whitfield, Madison: University of Wisconsin Press.

Hodge, B. (1995), 'Monstrous Knowledge: Doing PhDs in the New Humanities', *Australian Universities' Review*, 38 (2): 35–9.

Hyon, S. (1996), 'Genre in Three Traditions: Implications for ESL', *TESOL Quarterly*, 30 (4): 693–722.

Ibarretxe-Antuñano, I. (2013), 'The Relationship between Conceptual Metaphor and Culture', *Intercultural Pragmatics*, 10 (2): 315–39.

Jackson, B. (1985), *Semiotics and Legal Theory*, London: Routledge.

Johnson, M. (1987), *The Body in the Mind*, Chicago: University of Chicago Press.

Johnson, M. (1991), 'Knowing through the Body', *Philosophical Psychology*, 4 (1): 3–18.

Johnson, M. (1993), *Moral Imagination: Implication of Cognitive Science for Ethics*, Chicago: University of Chicago Press.

Kanoksilapatham, B. (2007), 'Writing Scientific Research Articles in Thai and English: Similarities and Differences', *Silpakorn University International Journal*, 7: 172–203.

Katz, A. N. and T. E. Taylor (2008), 'The Journeys of Life: Examining a Conceptual Metaphor with Semantic and Episodic Memory Recall', *Metaphor and Symbol*, 23 (3): 148–73.

Kövecses, Z. (2002), *Metaphor: A Practical Introduction*, New York: Oxford University Press.

Kövecses, Z. (2005), *Metaphor in Culture: Universality and Variation*, Cambridge: Cambridge University Press.

Lakoff, G. (1987), *Women, Fire, and Dangerous Things: What Categories Reveal about the Mind*, Chicago: The University of Chicago Press.

Lakoff, G. (1993), 'The Contemporary Theory of Metaphor', in A. Ortony (ed.), *Metaphor and Thought*, 2nd edn, 202–51, Cambridge: Cambridge University Press.

Lakoff, G. and M. Johnson (1980), *Metaphors We Live By*, Chicago: University of Chicago Press.

Laurence, S. and E. Margolis (1999), 'Concepts and Cognitive Science', in E. Margolis and S. Laurence (eds), *Concepts: Core Readings*, 3–81, Boston: MIT Press.

Lévi-Strauss, C. ([1958] 1983), 'Structure and Form: Reflections on a Work by Vladimir Propp', in C. Lévi-Strauss (ed.), *Structural Anthropology II*, trans. M. Layton, 115–45, Chicago: University of Chicago Press.

Linnemann, N. S. and M. R. Visser (2018), 'Hints towards the Emergent Nature of Gravity', *Studies in History and Philosophy of Science Part B: Studies in History and Philosophy of Modern Physics*, 64: 1–13.

Loi, C. K. (2010), 'Research Article Introductions in Chinese and English: A Comparative Genre-Based Study', *Journal of English for Academic Purposes*, 9 (4): 267–79.

Olofsson, T., S. Mulinari, M. Hedlund, Å. Knaggård and A. Vilhelmsson (2022), 'The Making of a Swedish Strategy: How Organizational Culture Shaped the Public Health Agency's Pandemic Response', *SSM – Qualitative Research in Health*, 2: 100082.

Paltridge, B. (1995), 'Working with Genre: A Pragmatic Perspective', *Journal of Pragmatics*, 24 (4): 393–406.

Paltridge, B. (1997), *Genre, Frames and Writing in Research Settings*, Amsterdam: John Benjamins.

Propp, V. (1968), *The Morphology of the Folktale*, trans. L. Scott, Austin: University of Texas Press.

Richards, G. (2005), 'From Footnotes to Narrative: Welsh Noblewomen in the Thirteenth Century', unpublished PhD thesis, Sydney: Department of History, University of Sydney.

Ritchie, L. D. (2008), 'X IS A JOURNEY: Embodied Simulation in Metaphor Interpretation', *Metaphor and Symbol*, 23 (3): 174–99.

Rosch, E. (1975), 'Cognitive Representations of Semantic Categories', *Journal of Experimental Psychology (General)*, 104: 192–233.

Samraj, B. (2002), 'Introductions in Research Articles: Variations across Disciplines', *English for Specific Purposes*, 21 (1): 1–17.

Sawaki, T. (2014), 'The CARS Model and Binary Opposition Structure', *The Public Journal of Semiotics*, 6 (1): 73–90.

Sawaki, T. (2016), *Analysing Structure in Academic Writing*, London: Palgrave Macmillan.

Sawaki, T. (2023), 'High Use of Direct Questions and Relative Absence of Promotional Intention in Japanese Peer-Reviewed Research Article Introductions Compared to Their English Counterparts', *English for Specific Purposes*, 69: 19–32.

Stewart, T. T. and T. A. Jansky (2022), 'Novice Teachers and Embracing Struggle: Dialogue and Reflection in Professional Development', *Teaching and Teacher Education: Leadership and Professional Development*, 1: 100002.

Swales, J. (1990), *Genre Analysis: English in Academic and Research Settings*, Cambridge: Cambridge University Press.

Swales, J. (2004), *Research Genres: Explorations and Applications*, Cambridge: Cambridge University Press.

Taylor, G. and T. Chen (1991), 'Linguistic, Cultural, and Subcultural Issues in Contrastive Discourse Analysis: Anglo-American and Chinese Scientific Texts', *Applied Linguistics*, 12 (3): 319–36.

Turner, J. (1998), 'Turns of Phrase and Routes to Learning: The Journey Metaphor in Educational Culture', *Intercultural Communication Studies*, 7: 23–36.

Vijayaraghavan, V. S., P.-A. Noël, Z. Maoz and R. M. D'Souza (2015), 'Quantifying Dynamical Spillover in Co-Evolving Multiplex Networks', *Scientific Reports*, 5 (1): 15142.

Vinther, J. (2016), 'Fossil Melanosomes or Bacteria? A Wealth of Findings Favours Melanosomes: Melanin Fossilises Relatively Readily, Bacteria Rarely, Hence the

Need for Clarification in the Debate over the Identity of Microbodies in Fossil Anim', *BioEssays*, 38 (3): 220–5.

Wittgenstein, L. ([1953] 1958), *Philosophical Investigations*, 2nd edn, trans. G. Anscombe, Oxford: Basil Blackwell.

Ye, S., H. Song, X. Ding, Z. Zhang and J. Li (2020), 'Pre-Selecting Markers Based on Fixation Index Scores Improved the Power of Genomic Evaluations in a Combined Yorkshire Pig Population', *Animal*, 14 (8): 1555–64.

Yu, N. (2008), 'Metaphor from Body and Culture', in R. W. Gibbs, Jr. (ed.), *The Cambridge Handbook of Metaphor and Thought*, 247–61, Cambridge: Cambridge University Press.

Zhang, K., A. Prakash, L. Paul, D. Blum, P. Alstone, J. Zoellick, R. Brown and M. Pritoni (2022), 'Model Predictive Control for Demand Flexibility: Real-World Operation of a Commercial Building with Photovoltaic an Battery Systems', *Advances in Applied Energy*, 7: 100099.

Index

abstract   145–66, 173, 177
abstraction   34–5, 43, 45, 56–7, 201–2, 207
academic discourse   1, 3–5, 11, 27, 35–6, 41, 43–4, 57, 79–80, 209, 212
   written   3, 5, 89–90, 108
academic literacy   4, 56, 90
academic writing   3–6, 65, 71, 80, 89–91, 101, 112, 133–4, 145–6, 148–9, 151, 166, 168, 193–4, 203–5, 207, 212–14
accuracy   4–5, 38, 56, 65, 77, 113, 118, 120, 127–8, 130–1
adjective/al   39–40, 43–4, 68, 78, 80–1, 96–7, 101, 105–7, 179–80
adverb   39, 48–9, 80, 180
adverbial   39, 54, 94, 97, 99–104, 110–11
affix   4, 66–9, 71–3, 77–84, see also prefix; suffix
affixation   44, 67
argumentation   56, 149, 175, 188
Aristotelian category/ization   194, 196
article abstract, see abstract
article comments   6, 168–89
attitude markers   147, 149–50, 157
authentic language use   11–12, 22
authentic text   37–8, 42, 50–1

Basturkmen, H.   11–12
Bauer, L.   67–9, 72, 78, 81, 83–4
Belcher, D.   168–70
Biber, D.   3–4, 11, 15–16, 89–90, 94, 101, 108, 110, 197
boosters   147, 150, 158, 162
Bruce, I.   1, 36–7, 63, 183, 196–7

CARS (Create a Research Space) model   133, 200, 206–7
CASAP (Corpus of Agricultural Sciences Academic Papers)   91–4
clarity   6, 56, 77, 81, 83
clausal structures   39, 90, 101, 108

cluster   11, 14–17, 19–20, 22–4, 26, 28–9
coherence   45, 63, 151, 164, 166
cohesion   63, 164, 166, 206, 209
complement   90, 94, 97–101, 105–7, 110–11
complex dynamic system   118–19, 122–4, 134–5
complex dynamic systems theory (CDST)   5, 117–27, 132–6
complexity   3–4, 31, 56, 69–71, 73, 80–3, 90–1, 117–18, 120, 127
   clausal   89
   derivational   64–7, 69, 71, 73, 77
   lexical   4, 64–6
   morphological   4, 65–6, 73, 82–4
   phrase/al   4, 90, 108
   syntactic   4–5, 83, 120, 128–30
complex noun phrase   89, 108
comprehension   37, 50–3, 65
conceptual mould   201–2, 206, 208
congruent/ce   34–6, 40–1, 43–6, 48–54, 56
conjunction   40, 42, 45–7, 52, 54, 94, 97, 176
conventions   5–6, 89, 148, 168
cooperative principle   145–6, 148
corpus linguistics   2, 4, 15
Corpus of Agricultural Sciences Academic Papers, see CASAP (Corpus of Agricultural Sciences Academic Papers)
Corpus of English as a Lingua Franca in Academic Settings, see ELFA (English as a Lingua Franca in Academic Settings) corpus
Coxhead, A.   64, 66
Create a Research Space model, see CARS (Create a Research Space) model

de Bot, K.   118–20, 122–3, 133–4
derivational awareness   64, 66–7, 69, 77–80, 83–4
derivational bases   65–6, 68, 78

derivational knowledge   66–7, 83
Diani, G.   6, 168–9, 177, 186–7
discourse analysis   1–2, 112, 212
discourse markers   71, 78

Egbert, J.   15–16, 90
ELFA (English as a Lingua Franca in Academic Settings) corpus   13–14, 16–17, 20, 23
English as a lingua franca (ELF)   3, 12–13, 15–17, 22, 27–8, 30–1, 151, 153, 165
English for specific purposes (ESP)   154, 193
epistemology/ical   119, 121–3, 126, 204, 208, 213
evaluative acts   172–3, 182–6, 188
evaluative genres   6, 168–70, 177, 185, 187
experiential meaning   3, 41, 43
explicit instruction   50, 67, 79, 83

family resemblance   194–6
Feak, C. B.   147–9, 157
Fillmore, C. J.   197, 201
first language (L1)   2, 12, 14–15, 30–1, 66, 91, 118, 122
Flowerdew, J.   151, 163
fluency   2–3, 11, 31, 65, 83, 120, 127
Fogal, G.   117, 119, 121, 126
formulaic language   11–12, 14, 22, 30
formulaic sequences (FSs)   2–3, 11–12, 14–15, 19, 26–8, 30–1
fractal   119–20

generic structure components   193, 198–9, 204–5
generic structure model   194, 198, 207
genre
    cognitive and social   197
    cognitive aspects   193–4, 196–7
genre analysis   2, 147–8, 193, 195–7
gerund   78, 96–7
Greimas, A. J.   198–200
Greimassian   194, 197–9
Grice, H. P.   5–6, 145–53, 166

Halliday, M. A. K.   34–6, 43, 47, 57
hard sciences   117–18, *see also* natural sciences
hedge/ing   104–5, 133–4, 147, 150–1, 158, 161–2, 185

Hewings, M.   170, 172
Hjelmslev, L.   199
humanities   14, 57, 205, *see also* soft sciences/disciplines
Hyland, K.   1–3, 6, 147–8, 150–2, 158, 165, 168–70, 175, 185, 187

ideational metafunction   22, 38, 41, 43
incongruent/ce   44, 48–50, 53, 56, 201
infinitive   94, 101, 107
inflection/al   1, 66, 68, 78
interpersonal metafunction   38, 41, 48
introduction   147–8, 159, 177, 197, 205–6

Johnson, M.   193, 197–8, 202–3, 211

keyness   15–16, 19

lack-ICM   206–12
Lakoff, J.   193, 195, 197–8, 201–3
language
    acquisition   1–2, 5, 41, 65, 117–19
    learning   37, 117–21, 123, 130, 134
    proficiency   4, 63–71, 73–4, 77–8, 80, 82–4
    teaching   2, 64, 122, 135–6
Larsen-Freeman, D.   65, 118–23, 126, 133, 135–6
Leech, G.   94
Lévi-Strauss, C.   198, 203
lexical diversity   5, 64–5, 73, 79, 82, 128, 130–1
lexicogrammar/tical   35, 37, 42, 52, 56, 197–9, 203–4
Liardét, C. L.   34–5, 43, 45–6, 50–1, 55–6
linguistic realization   6, 12–13, 16, 22, 38, 197, 213
Lovejoy, K. B.   146–9, 158, 160, 163, 166
Lowie, W.   119–20, 122–3, 125, 133–4

Martin, J. R.   45–7
Mauranen, A.   13–14, 22, 30–1
maxim of manner   145, 147, 151, 155, 157, 160, 163–6
maxim of quality   145, 147, 150–1, 161–2, 166
maxim of quantity   145, 147, 149–50, 157, 159–60, 166

maxim of relation   145, 147–9, 157–61
metadiscourse   6, 147–8
metalanguage   3, 36–8, 50–1, 56–7
metaphor
  conceptual   42, 194, 198, 201–2, 209–13
  experiential   45
  grammatical   3, 34–6, 43–5, 48, 50–1, 56–7
  interpersonal   3, 36, 41, 48, 50, 54–7
  logical   3, 45–7, 52–4
modality   3, 41, 47–8, 54, 150, 161–2
modifiers, see post-modifying/ier; pre-modify/ication
mood   3, 41, 48, 56
morphologically complex words   4, 64–6, 72–80, 82
move   6, 160, 170, 172–80, 182–6, 188, 206–7

Nation, I. S. P.   4, 64, 66–9, 72, 80–1, 83–4
natural sciences   14, see also hard sciences
neoclassical compounds   82
nominal group   35, 44–6, see also noun, group
nominalization   34–6, 41, 43–7, 51, 53–4, 57, 128, 130–1
non-finite clause   4–5, 89–90, 92, 95, 97, 99
  adverbial   101
  complement   90, 105
  noun post-modifying   108, 110
non-linear development   128–31
non-linearity   118–19, 127–8, 130, 136
noun   43–5, 47, 105, 108
  group   34, 39, 45, 47, 51
  phrase   89–90, 108, 120
Nunn, R.   146–52, 158, 161, 166

occluded genre   6, 170, 172
ontology/ical   119, 121–3, 126

Paltridge, B.   168, 170, 179, 185, 189, 196–7
paraphrase/ing   49, 51, 56, 71
Paris school structuralism   194, 197–8, 203, 212

participle   68, 78, 90, 94, 97, 108–9
pedagogical implications   1, 64, 111, 136, 153, 158, 160, 162, 165–6, 189, 194, 212
peer review   6, 159, 163, 168–73, 177–89
postgraduate   2, 38, 124, 127, 130, 159, 163
post-modifying/ier   44, 47, 51, 90, 94, 97–101, 108–11
prefix   69, 72–3, see also affix
pre-modify/ication   44–5, 47, 54
prepositional phrase   39, 44
prototype theory   194–6, 198, 201, 203

rejoinder, see article comments
relational knowledge   66, 79, 83
relevance   5, 147–9, 153–60
review genres, see evaluative genres
Rosch, E.   194–5, 198
rote learning   4, 66, 79

second language   2, 22, 28, 31, 65–7, 118–22, 127–8
  development   119, 136
  learner/ing   11, 15, 66, 119–20
  speakers   12, 30–1, 69
  writers   11, 89–91, 101, 113
semantic variation   204, 208
seminar   3, 11–17, 19–20, 22–7, 29–31
seminar discussion   12–13, 15–17, 19–20, 22–3, 26, 29
Semiotic Square   199–200, 204–7
social sciences   14, 46, see also soft sciences/disciplines
soft sciences/disciplines   117, 175, see also humanities; social sciences
SOURCE-PATH-GOAL schema   202, 211–13
speech functions   12–13, 16, 18–19, 23
spelling   68, 72, 80–1
spoken genres   11, 27
stance   11, 50, 56, 161, 175, 179, 197
structuralism, see Paris School structuralism
subordinate clause   4, 91, 94
subordination/ing   4, 40, 90–1, 128, 130
suffix   68, 73, 78, 80–2, see also affix

Swales, J. 6, 147–9, 157, 170, 172, 195–6, 203, 206–7
Systemic Functional Linguistics (SFL) 3, 35–8, 43, 45, 50–1, 133, 193, 197

TESOL (Teaching English to Speakers of Other Languages) 36, 63
textbooks 2–3, 11–13, 16–19, 22, 24, 28, 30–1
text dispersion keyness, *see* keyness
textual metafunction 22, 38
turn-taking 28, 30, 38
type-token ratio (TTR) 64–5, 128

undergraduate 14, 38, 70, 146

variability 11, 31, 91, 102, 118, 120, 122–3, 127, 130, 132, 134, 136
verb/al 34–5, 38–44, 46, 48–9, 54, 56, 68, 92, 94, 96–8, 100–2, 104–11, 113, 128, 164, 175, 179–80
  group 40, 46, 48
  phrase 120
Verspoor, M. 117, 119, 122–5, 133–5
vocabulary 4, 35, 40, 42, 63–7, 69, 71, 78–9, 83–4, 120, 164

Wittgenstein, L. 194–5
word
  family 4, 66–7, 84
  formation 4, 64–6, 69
  list 63, 122

www.ingramcontent.com/pod-product-compliance
Lightning Source LLC
Chambersburg PA
CBHW071830300426
44116CB00009B/1503